Story Solutions

Story Solutions

Using Tales to Build Character and Teach Bully Prevention, Drug Prevention, and Conflict Resolution

Kevin Strauss

LIBRARIES UNLIMITED

AN IMPRINT OF ABC-CLIO, LLC
Santa Barbara, California • Denver, Colorado • Oxford, England

Library of Congress Cataloging-in-Publication Data

Strauss, Kevin, 1969-
   Story solutions : using tales to build character and teach bully prevention, drug prevention, and conflict resolution / Kevin Strauss.
     p. cm.
  Includes bibliographical references and index.
  ISBN 978-1-59158-764-4 (pbk. : alk. paper) 1. Storytelling. 2. Problem solving in children. 3. Conflict management. I. Title.
  LB1042.S87 2011
  372.67'7--dc22   2010053650

ISBN: 978-1-59158-764-4

15 14 13 12 11   1 2 3 4 5

This book is also available on the World Wide Web as an eBook.
Visit www.abc-clio.com for details.

Libraries Unlimited
An Imprint of ABC-CLIO, LLC

ABC-CLIO, LLC
130 Cremona Drive, P.O. Box 1911
Santa Barbara, California 93116-1911

This book is printed on acid-free paper ∞
Manufactured in the United States of America

Contents

Acknowledgments

Any book is a team project, and in that vein, I thank Andrea, Sarah, and Annie for their help, support, attention, and occasional silliness. I thank my editors, Barbara Ittner and Sharon DeJohn, for their technical assistance and booksmart ideas, and I thank all of the schoolchildren and teachers who gave me feedback on my school programs and helped to make the stories and activities in this book the best that they could be.

Preface: Can Stories Really Solve Problems?

Whoever tells the stories defines the culture.

—Dr. David Walsh, author and founder of the National Institute
on Media and the Family

It seems like everyone is always looking for a "silver bullet" to solve society's ills. But life is consistently more complicated than the average situation comedy or drama on television. Solving community problems like bullying, alcohol/tobacco/other drug use, and conflicts takes work. I am under no illusion that simply writing this book or telling these stories will magically make these problems disappear.

But I take comfort in the fact that humans in every culture have used stories to educate, inspire, entertain, and warn the next generation. In the twentieth and twenty-first centuries, mass media outlets like radio, movies, television, and the Internet have taken over many of the "storytelling" functions in our society. This isn't necessarily a bad thing. There are quality programs on the radio and television. The problems occur when these electronic storytellers don't have the same values as your community, school, or family.

Dr. David Walsh, founder of the National Institute on Media and the Family, says that, "Whoever tells the stories defines the culture" (Walsh 2007). He argues that in many ways, we are the sum total of all the stories that we see and hear in our lifetimes. If the sum total of the stories we see in our lives and on television and the stories we hear from our friends and family are violent, we tend to think that the world is a dangerous place and that violence is an acceptable response to problems. If, on the other hand, the stories we see and hear show characters who think before they act, talk before they fight, and are kind rather than cruel, then we are more likely to act that way toward others.

According to Walsh, all kinds of stories set cultural norms and values for a society. I wrote this book to give parents, teachers, and community leaders the narrative tools that they need to make the world a better place. When told or read at the right time and in the right way, these stories and activities can give us a roadmap to follow and the inspiration we need to solve social problems like bullying, drug use, and conflicts.

Welcome to the tales.

Introduction

The Power of Story

Truth and Story

Long, long ago, Truth walked the world as an old man. Everything about him was old: his hands, his face, even his clothes. His skin was wrinkled and his clothes were so ragged that it looked like he wore no clothes at all. When he would arrive in a town, he would walk up to the first person he found and say, "Hi, how's it going?" But the response was always the same. The person would look at the ground, turn, and walk away.

"I don't understand, wouldn't people want to hear what Truth has to say?" said Truth to himself. "When I am not around, people always talk about wanting to hear the Truth. But now that I'm here, they avoid me."

Then Truth saw a large crowd assembled in a town square. They seemed to be listening to someone. He approached the crowd, thinking that surely someone there would want to listen to him. But as he approached, the crowd parted like the Red Sea, half going one way and half going the other. Soon the only person left in the square was the speaker. Her name was Story. Story was dressed in fine, colorful robes. Her clothes had every color of the rainbow. They sparkled silver and gold in the sunshine. They even had colors that changed as she moved, going from red to blue to green as she talked.

"I don't understand what is going on," said Truth to Story. "Why don't people want to hear what I have to say? Perhaps it's because I am old."

"I don't think so," said Story. "Look at me. I am old as well, and people still listen to me."

Then looking at the state of Truth's clothing, she added. "Perhaps the problem is that you are just showing a little too much of yourself. Come home with me, and I will give you one of my beautiful robes to wear."

So Truth went home with Story and put on one of Story's bright-colored story robes. Then the two of them went walking arm in arm down the street. Truth noticed that now, rather than turning and walking away, people were coming up to talk with them. Truth and Story were invited into a house for dinner, and they talked well into the night.

And that is how it is today. When Truth walks naked in the world, people turn and look away. But when Truth walks with Story, he is invited into our houses and into our hearts.

Story from the Jewish Hassidic tradition

Definitions

The preceding story lies at the heart of why storytelling should be a part of any education program. But before we get started, let's review some terms.

- **Story:** a narrative of an actual, fictional, legendary, or mythical event
- **Storytelling:** the live act of using voice and body language to communicate a narrative directly from one person to another

Storytelling is much more than just words or gestures. In the process of telling a story, a storyteller takes mental images, translates them into words and body language, and then transmits them to the minds of listeners. Storytelling is actually an act of co-creation. The teller transmits the images, but the listeners play an even more important part. They create the story pictures in their own minds. As the audience reacts to a story, an experienced storyteller adjusts the story, making each telling of a tale a unique, living experience.

Why Tell Stories?

There once was a famous Rabbi who, rather than preaching in the temple or giving people advice on the street, would always tell them stories. One Sabbath, a young man came up to the Rabbi and said, "Teacher, I like hearing your stories, but I was wondering . . . when were you going to get around to teaching us something."

The Rabbi looked at the young man for a while and then a smile slowly crept across his face.

"That is a very good question," he said. "In fact, it reminds me of a story . . . ."

—Story from the Jewish tradition

It is clear from historical records that people have been telling stories for a long time. Aesop, one of the best-known storytellers in history, lived around 600 BCE (Zipes 1992), and a literary collection of *Aesop's Fables* is still in every library in America. But according to folklorists and anthropologists, people had been telling stories long before that (Pellowski 1990). What's more, most people use some aspects of storytelling every day of their lives. When we talk about how our day went or describe a favorite book, we are telling stories. Anything so well ingrained in our lives must be there for a reason and must come with benefits; otherwise humans would have stopped doing it long, long ago. So why should you use folktales to address problems like bullying, drug abuse, and conflicts?

I use folktales, myths, and legends in my bullying, drug, and conflict prevention programs because children and teens will listen to stories when they won't listen to lectures or "just say no" workshops. These ancient stories also give children and teens a roadmap that helps them solve problems like bullying and peer pressure to try drugs.

The Effects of Storytelling

Storytelling can be such a useful tool because of the effects that a well-told story has on our brains, our bodies, and our minds.

- **Storytelling is fun.** It is a captivating, economical, nonelectronic form of entertainment accessible to most people regardless of income or educational level. This is the primary reason that most people tell and listen to stories. We enjoy the experience.

- **Stories define cultural "norms."** The stories that we hear and the stories that we see on television and on the computer teach us how the world is. If the stories that a child hears and sees show people using violence or bullying to solve a problem, then that child is more likely to use those same techniques. If the stories that a child sees and hears show people talking respectfully and using creative and nonviolent ways to solve a problem, then that child will learn those pro-community skills as well (Walsh 2007).

- **Storytelling builds language and comprehension skills, the precursors to literacy and creative writing.** Very young children can learn new words from stories. Older children learn narrative patterns of beginnings, middles, and ends; character development; and foreshadowing. Children and adults who tell and listen to stories exercise the creative parts of their brains (Brand and Donato 2001). This "imaginative exercise" helps children and adults write literature and solve problems more effectively later in life (Haven 2000).

- **Storytelling is an effective way to teach factual information.** According to storyteller and researcher Kendall Haven, "stories match how humans naturally perceive, process, think, and learn" (Haven 2007). This means that learning through stories is like rolling a rock downhill; it is easy for most people. Several studies have shown that children and adults learn a wide range of material better as a story than through lectures or lists (Haven 2007). Human brains seem to retain material put in story form much better than a list of unrelated facts (Haven 2000; Weaver 1994).

- **Storytelling improves logical thinking skills and general learning.** After an eighteen-year study of college students, Professor Robert Coles determined that hearing and reading stories "enhanced and accelerated virtually every aspect of learning" (Haven 2007). Though it has been well-established that hearing stories improves child literacy skills, recent studies have also confirmed that it improves math and science learning skills. Because we are "hardwired" to enjoy stories, storytelling also increases student motivation for learning a wide range of subjects (Haven 2007).

- **Storytelling is a gentle and effective way to pass on lessons and values.** "One upon a time . . ." is far more powerful than "You really shouldn't . . . " When someone gives you advice, especially unsolicited advice, what's your reaction? You normally get defensive, put up barriers, and ignore it. On the other hand, if you hear a story about a foolish bear and what happened to him in a similar situation, you are much more likely to heed the warning. The same is true for children and teens. Several recent studies have demonstrated how stories are "a vehicle to teach social relationships and values" (Haven 2007).

- **Storytelling helps to build bridges among people.** While people have set up many barriers to divide humanity by race, gender, income, geography, and sexual orientation, many stories contain themes that remind us that humans are much more alike than we are different. Stories from China and Kenya that are more than 500 years old address many of the same themes and concerns that people have today. What's more, story listeners can imagine that they are living in a different place, in a different time, or in a different culture as they read or listen to a story. This "walking in another's shoes" experience can create empathy among groups of people who feel that they have nothing in common (Sima and Cordi 2003; Haven 2007).

- **Storytelling gives storytellers and story listeners control over an important part of their world.** More and more school programs are creating storytelling clubs and using storytelling in their speech competitions. For children, the ability to learn and perform a story can be a powerful confidence builder. It can also give children control over a part of their lives.

   At a time when parents and teachers have a great deal of control over a child or teen's life, storytelling gives children a way to face their fears and live out their fantasies in a safe, imaginative environment. Telling stories also gives children a chance to practice public speaking skills and develop confidence in their ability to communicate with others (Sima and Cordi 2003).

With so many positive effects, it is easy to see why storytelling and story reading should be an integral part of effective educational and prevention programs.

How to Use This Book

The stories and activities in this book can be used in several different ways:

- You can use them to supplement the prevention and character education programs you already use at home, in your library, or in your classroom.

- You could use sections of this book as your bully prevention or drug prevention unit for the year. Use one story and one activity per day (if you were planning a two-week unit), or use one story and activity per week (if you were planning a longer-term, eight-week unit).

- You could also use the stories and activities in this book on a case-by-case basis to address specific challenges that you see in your library, classroom, or community.

The Building Block Approach to Solving Social Problems

In order to prevent and stop bullying, avoid mood-altering chemicals, and resolve conflicts, we all need a series of "building block" social skills. The stories and activities in this book are organized according to the skills children (and adults) can learn from them. Because most stories can serve multiple purposes, and some of the same skills that help you deal with bullies also help you avoid mood-altering chemicals, some stories could fit in several chapters. Consult the "Story Skills Index" and "Activity Skills Index" in the back of this book for a complete list of tales and activities organized by skills.

Six Building Block Skills That Help Us Solve Problems

- **Self-Control**—People with this skill demonstrate the ability to control their thoughts, words, emotions, and actions so that they do not harm others or themselves. Children who have a positive sense of self and good control of their emotions are more likely to be able to control their bored, fearful, or aggressive impulses. They can also better use their rational minds to come up with short-term and long-term solutions to problems.

- **Kindness**—People with this skill demonstrate the interest and ability to care about others and to treat others with respect, friendship, and helpfulness. Children who care about others tend to have a lot of friends and have more family and friend support to help them resolve problems.

- **Problem Solving**—People with this skill demonstrate the ability to think carefully about a difficult situation and use a step-by-step approach to resolve that situation. They also have the ability to come up with several possible solutions for a problem and to determine and implement the best of several possible solutions to a problem.

- **Goal Setting**—People with this skill demonstrate the abilities to decide what is important to them, set priorities, plan for the future, and create a process for following those plans. Children who can set goals for the future and imagine themselves achieving their goals are usually too busy to "waste time" with mood-altering chemicals (or television and video games, for that matter).

- **Teamwork**—People with this skill demonstrate the ability to cooperate with a group of people to determine and accomplish a common goal. Children who have the ability to work together to find common goals and develop "win-win" solutions to conflicts will have a much easier time resolving problems than those who lack this skill (Drew 2004).

- **Assertive Communication**—People with this skill can verbally describe how they think and feel in a respectful manner. They can also actively listen to, understand, and respect the thoughts and feelings of others.

Story Sources

Truth and Story (Jewish)

Baltuck, Naomi. *Apples from Heaven*. North Haven, CT: Linnet Books, 1995. 143pp. ISBN 0-208-02434-4pa.

Strauss, Kevin. *Tales with Tails: Storytelling the Wonders of the Natural World*. Westport, CT: Libraries Unlimited, 2006. 231pp. $35.00pa. ISBN 1-59158-269-5pa.

Strauss, Susan. *The Passionate Fact: Storytelling in Natural History and Cultural Interpretation*. Golden, CO: North American Press, 1996. 152pp. $16.95pa. ISBN 1-55591-925-1pa.

Why Tell Stories (Jewish)

Baltuck, Naomi. *Apples from Heaven*. North Haven, CT: Linnet Books, 1995. 143pp. ISBN 0-208-02434-4pa.

Simms, Laura. *Making Peace, Heart Uprising* (CD). Chicago: Earwig Music, 1993. 4925CD.

Strauss, Kevin. *Tales with Tails: Storytelling the Wonders of the Natural World*. Westport, CT: Libraries Unlimited, 2006. 231pp. $35.00pa. ISBN 1-59158-269-5pa.

References

Brand, Susan Trostle, and Jeanne M. Donato. 2001. *Storytelling in Emergent Literacy: Fostering Multiple Intelligences*. Albany, NY: Delmar. 354pp. $33.95pa. ISBN 0-7668-1480-7pa.

Branden, Nathaniel. 1997. *The Six Pillars of Self-Esteem*. New York: Simon & Schuster. 346pp. $22. 95. ISBN 0553095293.

Chansky, Tamar E. 2008. *Freeing Your Child from Negative Thinking: Powerful, Practical Strategies to Build a Lifetime of Resilience, Flexibility, and Happiness*. Cambridge, MA: DaCapo Press. 321pp. $15.95pa. ISBN 978-0-7382-1185-5pa.

Coloroso, Barbara. 2003. *The Bully, the Bullied and the Bystander: From Preschool to High School—How Parents and Teachers Can Help Break the Cycle of Violence*. New York: HarperCollins. 218pp. $13.95pa. ISBN 0-06-001430-Xpa.

Drew, Naomi. 2004. *The Kid's Guide to Working Out Conflicts: How to Keep Cool, Stay Safe, and Get Along*. Minneapolis, MN: Free Spirit Publishing. 146pp. $13.95pa. ISBN 1-57542-150-Xpa.

Haven, Kendall. 2000. *Super Simple Storytelling*. Englewood, CO: Teacher Ideas Press. 229pp. $25.00pa. ISBN 1-56308-681-6pa.

Haven, Kendall. 2007. *Story Proof: The Science Behind the Startling Power of Story.* Westport, CT: Libraries Unlimited. 152pp. $25.00. ISBN 978-1-59158-546-6pa.

Houghton Mifflin Co. 1985. *The American Heritage Dictionary.* Boston: Houghton Mifflin Co. 1586pp. ISBN 0-395-32944-2.

Judson, Karen. 2005. *Resolving Conflicts: How to Get Along When You Don't Get Along.* Berkeley Heights, NJ: Enslow Publishers. 112pp. ISBN 0-7660-2359-1.

McKay, Matthew, and Patrick Fanning. 2000. *Self-Esteem: A Proven Program of Cognitive Techniques for Assessing, Improving, and Maintaining Your Self-esteem.* New York: MJF Books. 317pp. $17.95pa. ISBN 1-56731-499-6pa.

Pellowski, Anne, 1990. *The World of Storytelling.* New York: H. W. Wilson. 322pp. $75.00. ISBN 0-8242-0788-2.

Schwebel, Robert. 1998. *Saying No Is Not Enough: Helping Your Kids Make Wise Decisions About Alcohol, Tobacco and Other Drugs.* New York: Newmarket Press. 290pp. $14.95pa. ISBN 1-55704-318-3pa.

Sima, Judy, and Kevin Cordi. 2003. *Raising Voices: Creating Youth Storytelling Groups and Troupes.* Teacher Ideas Press. 239pp. $32.50pa. ISBN 1-56308-919-Xpa.

Walsh, David. 2007. *No: Why Kids of All Ages Need to Hear It and Ways Parents Can Say It.* New York: Free Press. 309pp. $23.00. ISBN 978-0-7432-8917-7.

Weaver, Mary, ed. 1994. *Tales as Tools.* Jonesborough, TN: National Storytelling Press. 213pp. $19.95pa. ISBN 1-879991-15-2pa.

Zipes, Jack. 1992. *Aesop's Fables.* New York: Signet Classic. 288pp. $4.95pa. ISBN 0-451-52565-5pa.

Chapter 1

A Crash Course in Storytelling
(for Librarians, Parents, and Other Educators)

Three apples fell from heaven. One for the teller, one for the listener,
and one for the person who took the story to heart.

—Armenian proverb

Kinds of Stories

As you are plunging into the world of traditional and values-based folktales, this is a good time to familiarize yourself with various kinds of stories you can use. This section acts as your map through the "Land of Storytelling."

You see, stories are "brain tools," and just as you wouldn't use a screwdriver to pound a nail, you want to make sure that you use the right kind of story for the right situation. Here's the toolbox:

- **Fables or anecdotes:** Short stories that contain a clear moral or message. Although some versions of "Aesop's Fables" end with the phrase, "The moral of the story is . . . ," modern storytellers seldom pound the moral into their listeners' ears. If a story is a good story, you don't need to say the moral for listeners to "get it." "The Tortoise and the Hare" is one example of a fable.

- **Fairy Tales:** Longer stories that involve supernatural intervention by fairies, witches, or other magical folk. Common collections include "Grimm's Fairy Tales." "Cinderella" is an example of a fairy tale.

- **Folktales:** Sometimes a catchall term for traditional stories told by "the people" (or folk), as opposed to "literary stories" created by a specific author (e.g., Jane Austen). More specifically, folktales are similar to fairy tales in that they are longer stories. But these stories don't necessarily involve supernatural intervention. "Little Red Riding Hood" and the "Three Billy Goats Gruff" are examples of folktales.

- **"Why," "Pourquoi," or Explanation Stories:** "Why" stories explain how things got to be the way they are. "How Bear Got A Short Tail" is an example of a "Why" story.

- **Myths or "World View" Stories:** Stories that demonstrate the worldview of a particular group of people during a particular period of time. Most religious stories fall into this category. "Myth" acquired its secondary meaning of "things that aren't true" when members of one religious group tried to discredit the beliefs of another religious group. Creation stories are an example of mythic tales.

    In the storytelling sense, a "myth" isn't a story that "never happened." It is more accurately an archetypal story whose themes happen again and again in our personal stories, histories, and literature. The Greek myth of Prometheus bringing fire to humans is an example of a traditional myth.

- **Legends:** Stories that may have begun as historical tales but grew and developed fictional or "legendary" aspects over time. The legends of King Arthur and the Knights of the Round Table are an example of this kind of story.

- **Tall Tales:** Stories that include unbelievable or exaggerated events. The stories of Paul Bunyan and Pecos Bill are examples. The characters are often giants or have giant-sized abilities, like the ability to cut down a forest of trees with one swing of an ax, the way Paul Bunyan does.

- **Personal Stories:** Stories of something that happened to you or your family. Though these stories are based on factual events, a storyteller might "improve upon" facts to make a narrative flow better. This doesn't make them fictional stories; they are merely "creative nonfiction." Remember that a story can be emotionally "true" even if every element isn't perfectly "factual."

- **Histories**: Personal stories that happened to someone that we don't know. While some high school history teachers will teach history as if it is an endless series of dates and rulers, my favorite history teacher just told us stories about the people who made a difference in medieval European history.

    Historians sometimes object when writers create narratives about historical events or people, because they think telling a story as history could make it less "factual." But in reality, humans have always related history through narratives. Storytellers may have to make some assumptions when telling a historical story, but by putting the "story" back in "history," a good storyteller can help listeners get excited about history and actually care about what happened in England in 1066 or why our government invented the Social Security system.

How to Become a Story Reader or Storyteller

You probably already tell stories. You may not think of the narratives you tell as "stories," but that is exactly what they are. Everyone is born with the tools to tell stories. Some people decide that they want to tell stories as a job or as part of their "day job" at a library, school, office, clinic, or consulting service.

Others only want to share stories with their families and friends. Whether you decide to pursue storytelling as a profession, choose to incorporate storytelling into your current profession, or decide to tell stories as an inspired amateur, the way to be a good storyteller is to practice and tell stories as much as possible. Like any other skill or art form, the more you do it, the better you get. The most important thing is that you give yourself license to tell stories.

Remember that though it may seem like a great leap to go from being a story listener to a story reader or storyteller, it is really only a distance of about five inches: the distance from your ear to your mouth. Once you hear a good story, all you have to do is retell it in your own way, and suddenly you are a storyteller. What's more, a good story will carry you over that short distance with ease.

Finding a Story

There are many good resources for social problem-solving stories. Start with the stories that you already know. How can those stories help you teach about dealing with bullies, avoiding drugs, or resolving conflicts? This book includes more than fifty stories for you to use, along with discussion questions and extension activities. Visit your library; section 398.2 in the Dewey Decimal system, and the children's section, J398.2, have great story resources.

Learning a Story

There are many ways to learn and tell a story. The following steps have worked well for both beginning and experienced storytellers.

1. Begin with a Short Tale That You Love

It is difficult to tell any story that doesn't appeal to you. To tell a story well, you have to be invested in it. The story should connect with you on an emotional level. That way, you will spend the time to craft the story and tell it well. If you feel that you "must" tell a particular story whether you like it or not, it will probably come out with as much energy as the Shakespearen sonnet that you had to memorize and perform in sixth grade. Although it is possible to tell a story that you don't like, I wouldn't recommend it, for you or your listeners.

When I started telling stories as a naturalist, I would flip through folktale books looking for a story about a particular species like a deer or a bear. I would read the story a couple of times and then try it out with children. It only took a couple of times for me to realize that something wasn't working right. I noticed that partway through the story, I wasn't enjoying telling it. What's more, my boredom was coming through in my performance. My listeners' eyes glazed over, and they began fidgeting or looking away. It wasn't my audience's fault that they weren't engaged in my story. It was my fault for choosing the wrong story to tell.

When you are starting out in storytelling, choose stories that are only one to three pages long and can be told or read in two to four minutes. After you have learned a few shorter tales, you will be ready to move on to longer (five- to eight-minute) stories.

2. Read the Story Four Times

Read the story once to make sure that you like it. Read it again for the plotline. Read it a third time for the dialogue, and read it once more to put it all together. Then put the book away for a while. After reading a story four times, it should be stuck in your brain.

3. Think about the Setting of the Story

All stories are related to a place, and the storyteller must bring that sense of place to life for listeners. Close your eyes and imagine the surroundings in a story. Try to describe them with all five senses. You don't want to "tell" people about the story setting; you want to "take" them to that place, using vivid sensory descriptions and strong verbs to carry the action.

4. Make Your Story Outline

Think of the story as if it were a series of pictures in your head (not just words on a page). While some storytellers do well writing out a text outline of the story, others prefer to use a "Story Scene Outline" (see box, p. 4).

The Story Scene Outline

Draw four boxes on a piece of paper. Number them 1 through 4. Draw a picture of the opening scene of the story in the first box. Draw a picture of the closing scene of the story in the last box. Then draw pictures in the second and third boxes to get listeners from the beginning to the end of the story. Now you have four pictures that carry you from the beginning to the end of the story. It is these images that you will remember when you tell the story. As you share your story, you move from describing one picture to describing the next, fleshing out the story as you go. By connecting these picture events in a narrative, you will complete the story.

When you think about a story as something that you tell "scene by scene," not "word by word," it is less likely that you'll get stuck. The idea is that tellers should not try to memorize the text of a story. Though there is nothing inherently wrong with memorizing a story, it is usually more difficult for people than learning a story "scene by scene."

As you become more familiar with the story scene outline, making story pictures in your head will become second nature. Soon you won't even need to write them down; you will just automatically make the story scenes in your head as you read or hear a story. Using "story scenes" also speeds up the process of helping you create your own unique version of a particular story.

---

5. Practice, Practice, Practice

Tell your story into a recorder, in front of a mirror, in the shower, in the car, and with your friends and family. You will notice that the more often you tell a particular story, the more it grows and changes into your own unique version of that tale. The more a story grows, the better it gets and the easier it will be for you to tell. I usually tell a story five times to a mirror or recorder before I try it out on a live audience.

6. Know How to Start a Story and How to End Your Story

Always know how you will start your story (like "Once upon a time . . ." or "Long, long ago . . . ") and how you will end it (like "They lived happily ever after." or "And that's the end of the story."). Knowing the first line and the last line of your story will give you "bookends" or "borders" to the story. Those borders help me feel more comfortable when telling a new tale. A pause before the last line of a story can add to its power and signal to listeners that the story journey is at an end.

7. Tell the Story to Strangers

You can read about storytelling and practice storytelling all you want, but until you tell a story to another person, you aren't a storyteller. This is one of the scariest parts of the process, but it is also the most rewarding. If you are a librarian, teacher, parent, or naturalist, then your job gives you a built-in audience. If you don't have an audience already, volunteer to tell stories at a school library or at an open mic performance, so you can "get your feet wet" in the world of storytelling. You'll be glad you did. Really!

Telling a Story

Storytelling and story reading are a lot like learning to ride a bike. We start on tricycles and then get a bike with training wheels. Once we have our balance, the training wheels come off, and we sail down the street on our two-wheel bikes. Soon it is second nature to balance on two skinny wheels. In my mind, learning a story is the "tricycle stage" of storytelling. Telling a story to a recorder, mirror, or pet is the "training wheel stage" of storytelling, and telling a story to another person is "riding the bike."

At some point you have to take the training wheels off and tell a story. This can be a scary thing. You are going on a quest. But the dragon you face isn't a fifty-foot, fire-breathing reptile; it is your own fear of public speaking. But that's okay. Most people are afraid of speaking in public. So if you're nervous, it's normal. And if stories teach us anything, they teach us that even ordinary people can be heroes.

Chapter 2

Blocking and Preventing Bullying Behavior

Bullying has probably been around as long as people have. But that doesn't make it okay. Children and adults in each generation have to develop ways to keep themselves, their friends, and their community safe from bullies. Luckily, folktales and personal stories give us a roadmap for dealing with bullies in ways that are effective, assertive, and nonviolent.

But before we look at how stories can help with bullying, let's review some definitions.

Definitions

- **Bully** (bull-EE). *noun.* Someone who takes part in antisocial bullying behavior.

- **Bullying** (bull-EE-ing). *verb.* 1) Repeated physical, verbal, or social abuse that a powerful person uses to scare, control, ridicule, hurt, or terrorize someone who is less powerful. 2) Behavior in which a person who is bigger, stronger, or more popular uses that unfair advantage to harm someone else or to control the "target's" behavior for no good reason. Behaviors could include hitting, kicking, shoving, taunting, calling mean names, inappropriate physical touching, heckling, excluding children from play, spreading mean rumors, theft, vandalism, threats, and other repeated abusive behavior.

- **Bystander** (BYE-stan-der). *noun.* A person who watches bullying behavior take place and does nothing to stop it. Bystanders may remain silent, they may laugh at the bullying behavior, or they may even join in with the bullying at times. Bullies usually assume that bystanders agree with them, unless a bystander asks the bully to stop.

- **Hero** (HEER-o). *noun.* 1) A person who sees bullying behavior take place and who takes actions to stop it, report it, help the target, and/or make sure it doesn't happen again in the future. 2) A person who takes action to help other people, even at the risk of his or her own safety.

- **Target** (tar-GET). *noun.* A person whom a bully chooses to physically, verbally, or socially abuse. While a bully might pick on some characteristic of a target (weight, height, speech, ethnicity, perceived disability), these are often excuses for bullying, since *anyone* can be a target.

How Serious Is the Bullying Problem?

Many bullying incidents go unreported because victims are often scared or embarrassed by the abuse (Coloroso 2003). But research indicates that bullying is having a huge impact on children and teens.

Research Results

A 2001 survey of 823 children ages eight to fifteen and 1,249 parents by the Kaiser Family Foundation found that "teasing and bullying" was the most common problem among these children. More than one out of two elementary school children ages eight to eleven (55 percent) and two out of three middle school students ages twelve to fifteen (68 percent) rated "teasing and bullying" as a big problem for their age. About three-quarters of elementary students (74 percent) report seeing bullying or teasing at school. Almost nine out of ten middle school students (86 percent) report seeing bullying at school (Kaiser Family Foundation 2001). This tracks closely with other surveys that report bullying behavior "peaking" in the middle school years (Kaiser 2001; Coloroso 2003).

Recent studies show that almost one in four U.S. students (15–25 percent) are bullied with some frequency ("sometimes or more often"). Up to one in five U.S. students (15–20 percent) report that they bully others with some frequency (Melton et al. 1998; Nansel et al. 2001). Nationally, about one in three U.S. students (almost 30 percent) are involved in bullying as either a target, a bully, or both (Pearmain 2006).

Facts About Bullying

- Bullying is the most common form of violence in our society (Wisconsin Department of Public Instruction 2009). Surveys consistently show about 30 percent of students are involved in bullying as victims and/or bullies. But over-three quarters (76 percent) have been bullied as schoolchildren, with one in seven (14 percent) of those children reporting severe problems from bullying (Maudlin 2002).

- Many children who are bullied suffer long-term psychological effects from the abuse (Coloroso 2003).

- Most targets of bullying do not tell an adult about the situation because they are too ashamed or too scared to report the bullying, so the behavior continues (Coloroso 2003).

- A majority (more than 60 percent) of people who used bullying behavior in middle school have least one criminal conviction by age twenty-four (Olweus 1993).

- Bullying can lead bullying targets to have suicidal thoughts or actions and thoughts of revenge on the bully. Bullying targets are more likely than other children to feel depressed, lonely, and anxious; have low self-esteem; feel unwell; miss school; and think about suicide (Olweus 1993). Many cases of "school violence" have been linked to bullied students who were seeking revenge against their tormentors (Coloroso 2003).

- Bystanders reinforce bullying behavior (by joining in or remaining silent) on the playground or at school in 81 percent of episodes. Those same bystanders intervene to stop bullying behavior in only 13 percent of bullying episodes at which they are present (Pearmain 2006). Motivating bystanders to intervene can have a big impact on bullying behavior (Coloroso 2003).

- Possibly because of how seldom bullying is reported and how carefully bullies avoid detection, there is a big gap between student and teacher (or child and adult) perceptions of how often teachers intervene to stop bullying incidents. A 1991 study found that while over two-thirds of teachers (71 percent) thought that they intervened "often or almost always," less than a quarter of bullied students (23 percent) felt the same way (Coloroso 2003). Clearly bullies are good at hiding their abusive behavior. Remember, just because adults don't see bullying behavior doesn't mean that it isn't happening.

Who Gets Hurt by Bullying?

Targets, bystanders, and bullies all suffer when bullying happens. As a result of bully abuse, targets often suffer from depression, low self-esteem, and anxiety. They may miss school to avoid bullies, and their grades can suffer (Olweus 1993). These effects can last for years after a student graduates from high school. Many adults can still vividly recall bullying incidents from their past. Bully targets can develop a fear of going to school, riding the bus, or even using the bathroom (National Education Association 2003).

Bystanders can also suffer from anxiety and fear because seeing bullying happen at school shows them that they aren't safe there (Banks 1997). Bullying changes the school environment by creating a schoolwide climate of fear and disrespect. Bullying even has a negative impact on overall student learning (National Education Association 2003).

Even though bullies abuse targets and frighten bystanders, they aren't immune to the negative effects of school bullying. If school bullies learn that threats and intimidation are a good way to get what they want in life, they are setting themselves up for a rude awakening when they turn eighteen. Although adults are sometimes willing to overlook childhood bullying, once a child becomes an adult, we call those activities assault, terroristic threats, and extortion. One study of school bullies found that 60 percent of children who were bullies in school had adult criminal records by the time they turned twenty-four. That is four times the national average (Olweus 1993).

There hasn't been much research on how "heroes" are affected by bullying, but there is a fair amount of anecdotal evidence that teaching children and teens how to deal with bullies in an assertive and nonviolent way develops heroes' problem-solving and confidence-building skills (Strauss 2010). These skills help them stay safe from bullies and solve future problems. This is not to say that being a hero isn't also dangerous. But given the choices of the four roles to play in a school's bullying drama, it seems that heroes receive the fewest scars.

What Skills Do Children Need to Block Bullying Behavior?

Researchers have identified several skills that help children resist and block bully abuse. By teaching bullying self-defense skills like those listed below, we are in effect armoring children against bullying attacks and making it more difficult for bullies to succeed in a school or community.

- **Self-Control:** Children who have a positive sense of self and good control of their emotions are more likely to be able to control their fearful and aggressive impulses that play right into a bully's hands. They can also better use their rational minds to come up with short- and long-term solutions to bullying attacks.

- **Problem Solving:** Children who can take a problem apart in their heads and generate several options for dealing with that problem can much more effectively learn and practice the words and behaviors that will keep a bully off balance and block bullying attacks.

- **Kindness:** Children who care about others and have a lot of friends are less likely to be targeted by bullies. Children who care about others are also much more likely to intervene to stop bullying behaviors or to report bullying to adults. Few children can resolve bullying problems on their own, so it is important to teach children how to be a hero with these kindness social skills (Coloroso 2003).

Top Five Myths about Bullying

To address the problem of bullying, you must first understand what it is and how it happens. Then you can better target ways of addressing and resolving this social problem.

1. If you "just ignore" a bully, he or she will leave you alone.

WRONG: A generation ago, parents often told their children to "just ignore" a bully, assuming that if a bully doesn't get a reaction from a target, then he or she will just go away. That approach didn't work well then, and it doesn't work any better now.

Bullies are experts at getting attention for their actions either from their target or the bystander audience. And if the audience thinks a particular bullying attack is funny, the bully will keep on doing it, even if the target doesn't respond. Besides, ignoring a bully never resolves the situation. That's why children should always remember the phrase "Always Do Something," even if it is just turning and walking away.

Just standing there and trying to ignore what a bully says or does is like just standing still while someone throws a punch at you. It isn't a good idea. Every second that a bully is standing in front of you, he or she is winning the intimidation game. So you always want to take some sort of action, even if it is just walking away and reporting the bully attack to school officials or another trusted adult.

A bully likes to intimidate and control other people through threats and violence. That bully isn't going to stop until someone makes him or her stop, and that usually requires adult help. So at the very least, children should keep a written record of bullying attacks and tell a trusted adult every time one happens. Look over the other bully defense techniques in chapter 4 for more ideas.

2. Children always tell adults when they are being bullied.

WRONG: One of the biggest problems with bullying is that most of it goes unreported. This can lead school officials to think that they "don't have a bullying problem." But not knowing that you have a bullying problem and not having a bullying problem are two different things. Many studies report that only 25–50 percent of bullying incidents are ever reported to an adult (U.S. Department of Health & Human Services 2008). On average, girls and younger children are more likely to report bullying, while boys and older children of both genders do not. Children who are targets often feel that they "deserved" the abuse for some reason, or they fear that saying something to an adult will lead to more bullying abuse. The ironic thing is that by staying silent, a target makes it even easier for a bully to abuse him or her. Keep in mind that reporting a bullying incident to a trusted adult can be the fastest and most effective way to block a bully and keep him or her from hurting others in the future.

3. Bullying is simply a normal part of "growing up."

WRONG: Bullying is a form of physical and/or emotional abuse, and just as we wouldn't say that being mugged is part of being an adult, it is time for adults and children to stop making excuses for bullying behavior. Being the target of abuse doesn't necessarily make people "tougher." In many cases, this abuse continues to hurt targets for years afterward as they struggle with the low self-esteem and anxiety that often result from bullying abuse.

4. Most bullying is physical (hitting, shoving, and kicking).

WRONG: Although physical bullying is one of the easiest kinds of bullying to identify at school, it probably isn't the most common. Verbal bullying and name calling are more common in schools, according to surveys (U.S. Department of Health & Human Services 2008). Taunts and social bullying, which are more subversive and harder to spot, are also common in schools, especially in middle school. While schools and communities are good at defining and discouraging the more obvious cases of physical abuse, it is much more difficult to rein in verbal, cyber, or social bullying through school disciplinary procedures.

5. "Bullying" is the same thing as "conflict" between two people.

WRONG: "Bullying" behavior is repeated action intended to harm a "weaker" or "less popular" person physically or emotionally. Bullying happens between people with an imbalance of power. It is far different from two people having a disagreement. If two people with equal power (age, size, strength, number of friends) were just having a disagreement, then a teacher or other mediator could help them resolve the conflict or argument. But bullies don't want to change their behavior. They like having control over other people through threats and violence. When someone who is bigger, older, stronger, or more popular uses that power repeatedly to pick on or abuse someone else, mediation or trying to "work things out" will be ineffective because bullies don't want to cooperate. What's more, forcing a target to sit down and talk with a bully gives the bully yet another chance to intimidate the target through words, threats, and body language.

Just as we wouldn't expect a mugging victim to sit down and "talk things out" with a mugger, we shouldn't expect standard conflict mediation processes to resolve a bullying problem.

Addressing Bullying in Libraries, Schools, and Communities

Since bullying is a learned set of behaviors, they can be unlearned. Bullies are made, not born (Coloroso 2003; Maudlin 2002). Bullies, or more accurately, people who engage in bullying behavior, act that way because somehow they have learned that abusing others is a way to get what they want in life. As long as bullying behavior has a "payoff" for the bully (increased social status, money, fun), he or she will keep acting like a bully. So if we want to block bullying behavior in our schools and communities, we need to find ways to make abusive behavior costly and difficult for the perpetrator.

Bullying is an active verb. Though many children might feel angry or afraid, it is only those who channel those feelings into repeatedly abusing others who receive the label "bully." Internally, bullies often tell themselves that their targets "deserve" the bullying, possibly because they are "weak," "crybabies," "fat," or some other category. Ironically, some bullies even tell themselves that they are heroes who use their abusive behavior to protect their friends from other school bullies. Most children know who the bullies are in their classroom. Fewer teachers know who the bullies are, because bullies often act when no adults are around.

The best way to stop bullying in the long run is to create a system of procedures at school that identify bullying behavior and penalize bullies for their abusive behavior (Olweus 1993). The best way to protect children from bullying in the short term is to give them the stories and skills they need to block bullying attacks and keep themselves safe while they report the bullying behavior to a responsible adult (Coloroso 2003). Chapters 2–4 provide the resources to do both of these things.

According to researchers like Dr. Dan Olweus, Dr. Ken Rigby, and the U.S. Department of Heath and Human Services, the most effective approach to dealing with bullying in the long term is to take a "community" approach to changing the organizational climate so that children, school or library staff, and parents all understand and agree to a set of bullying prevention standards. Researchers and educators have developed several comprehensive school curriculums. Search "bullying prevention curriculum" online for an up-to-date list. Be sure that any curriculum that your school uses is both research-based and has a track record of actually reducing bullying in schools.

Although it can take time to change the bullying prevention climate in a school, stopping bullying is worth the effort. Some schools combine a comprehensive bullying prevention program with targeted efforts to give students the skills they need to report on and block bullying behavior in the short term on their own.

Cool Rules to Block Bullies

In his 1993 book *Bullying at School*, researcher Dr. Dan Olweus describes three class rules that teachers have used effectively in Norway to stop bullying in their schools:

1. We shall not bully other students.

2. We shall try to help students who are bullied.

3. We shall make a point to include students who become easily left out.

When children, librarians, teachers, administrators, and parents all use the same bullying prevention principles, Olweus contends, it is much easier to create a safe "antibullying" climate at schools (Olweus 1993). Building on Olweus's rules and recommendations by Coloroso (2003) and the U.S. Department of Health and Human Services (2008), I developed the following of "Safe School Rules" to address bullying and other antisocial behavior in schools.

Safe School Rules

To create a safe and healthy learning community, the children, library or school staff, and parents agree on the following:

1. **We will tell adults at home, in the library, and at school when we see bullies trying to hurt others** (problem solving, kindness). One of the reasons that bullies continue to cause problems is that no one reports their behavior to adults (Coloroso 2003). Teach *children* to report bullying behavior using the four Ws (Who was involved? What happened? When did it happen? Where did it happen?). See Activity 4-10 in chapter 4 for more on bully prevention reporting techniques.

2. **We will not hurt other people with our words or our actions** (self-control, kindness). In some cases, children who bully others simply have difficulty controlling their anger. In other cases, children have learned that abusive behavior is one way to get what they want in the world (Olweus 1993). In either case, it is critical that school and community officials create systems that identify and address bullying behaviors quickly and effectively. The sooner children learn that bullying behavior is unacceptable, the sooner they can develop more pro-social ways of solving their problems.

3. **It is our job to help and protect all of our classmates when bullies try to hurt them** (problem solving, kindness). Some bullies are smart enough to not abuse other children in front of adults. Unfortunately a school or library often has places (bathrooms, locker rooms, hallways, playgrounds) that allow a bully to abuse children out of sight of adults. That is why it is so important that any bullying prevention program enlist children to act as heroes who report bullying behavior and help targets (Coloroso 2003).

4. **We will always include everyone in our games, conversations, lunch tables, and activities, especially those who are new to school or who don't have very many friends** (kindness). Say it with me: "BULLIES ARE COWARDS" (Strauss 2010). They always pick on people who are younger, smaller, or less popular that they are. They want to pick on only one person at a time. That's why making new friends can be a great bullying defense. Having lots of friends gives students more people to talk to and hang out with when a bully is prowling around. Since bullies love to find people sitting alone at lunch or walking alone down the hall, spending time with a friend can help protect a student from a bully. While some kids might worry that if they make friends with a target the bully will pick on them as well, this simply isn't true. Once a bully can't isolate a person to pick on, he or she usually moves on to easier targets. In addition, by making a new friend, students gain an ally who can stick up for them if a bully tries to give them a hard time in the future.

   Of course, friends also provide people who can give children support and advice about dealing with a bully. They can be a kind voice in their heads when a bully calls them "stupid" or "ugly." In general, the more friends a child has, the less likely it is that a bully will choose him or her as a target. The more friends a child has, the more that student will be "armored" against any mean things that a bully might say or do. So making friends is a win-win for bystanders, targets, and heroes.

5. **It is our job to remind our classmates about our Safe School Rules if they seem to forget them.** If children, school and library staff, and parents all talk from the same bullying and violence prevention "playbook," they can start to change the climate in any organization, making it harder and harder for any bully to hurt others and to remain hidden (Coloroso 2003; Olweus 1993).

Safe Schools Shorthand

Here's another way to list the Safe School Rules:

1. **Report All Bullying**
2. **Don't Hurt Others**
3. **Help Others**
4. **Include Everyone**
5. **Remind Others for A Safer School**

Long-Term Commitment

Researchers recommend that schools offer in-depth antibullying programs, not just a single day or week of programs. Schools should also use staff in-service training, parents meetings, assembly programs, and regular classroom lessons (twenty to thirty minutes per week in classrooms) to help create a culture in which no one tolerates bullying behavior and all children will report the bullying that they observe (Olweus 1993; U.S. Department of Health & Human Services 2009).

The stories and activities in chapters 3 and 4 provide a rich resource for teachers to use during those weekly bullying prevention sessions.

Sample Bullying Prevention Curriculum

Educators can use the stories and activities in this book to enrich a schoolwide antibullying program or an extended library program, as a stand-alone bullying prevention unit or program, or as a way to help children develop specific skills like self-control or kindness. Following are examples of a week-long bullying prevention program for children in grades 4–5 and grades 6–8. The stories are in chapter 3 and the activities in chapter 4.

Grades 4–5 Bullying Prevention Unit

Day 1: What Is a Hero? What Is a Bully?

Story: "Three Goats and a Troll" (adapted from Norway)

Activity 4-5: Four Roles in the Bullying "Drama"

Day 2: Staying Safe from Physical Bullies

Story: "The Three Clever Pigs" (England)

Activity 4-1: Deep Breath, Smile, Walk Away

Day 3: Responding to Verbal Bullies

Story: "The Monster in the Cave" (Masi, Kenya) or "Three Butterfly Friends" (Germany)

Activity 4-2: Verbal Safe Schools

Day 4: How to Be a Hero, Part 1

Story: "The Samurai and the Island" (Japan)

Activity 4-3: How to Be a Hero, Part 1

Day 5: How to Be a Hero, Part 2

Story: "How Beetle Won a Colorful Coat" (Brazil)

Activity 4-4: How to Be a Hero, Part 2

Grades 6–8 Bullying Prevention Unit

Day 1: What Is a Hero? What Is a Bully?

Story: "The Doorways of Success and Failure" (Japan)

Activity 4-7: You Make the Call—Bullying or Something Else

Day 2: Staying Safe from Verbal Bullies

Story: "The Samurai and the Island" (Japan) or "The Monster in the Cave" (Masi, Kenya)

Activity 4-2: Verbal Safe Schools

Day 3: Making Friends

Story: "The Lion and the Mouse" (Aesop)

Activity 4-6: School Safety Survey

Day 4: Responding to Social Bullies

Story: "Three Butterfly Friends" (Germany)

Activity 4-12: Safe School Role-Plays

Day 5: How to Be a Hero

Story: "The Moon Goddess" (China)

Activity 4-3: How to Be a Hero, Part 1

References

Banks, R. 1997. *Bullying in Schools*. ERIC Report No. EDO-PS-97-170. Champaign-Urbana: University of Illinois Press.

Coloroso, Barbara. 2003. *The Bully, the Bullied and the Bystander: From Preschool to High School—How Parents and Teachers Can Help Break the Cycle of Violence*. New York: HarperCollins. 218pp. $13.95pa. ISBN 0-06-001430-Xpa.

Kaiser Family Foundation. 2001. *Talking with Kids About Tough Issues: A National Survey of Parents and Kids.* Menlo Park, CA. Available at http://www.kff.org (search for "bullying" on the site).

Lee, Chris. 2004. *Preventing Bullying in Schools: A Guide for Teachers and Other Professionals.* Thousand Oaks, CA: Sage Publishing. 102pp. $70.95pa. ISBN 0-7619-4472-9pa.

Maudlin, Karen. 2002. *Sticks and Stones: Parent and Teacher Guide to Preventing Bullying.* Nashville, TN: W Publishing Group, 139pp. $10.99pa. ISBN 08499-4356-6pa.

Melton, G. B., S. Limber, V. Flerx, P. Cunningham, D. W. Osgood, J. Chambers, S. Henggler, and M. Nation. 1998. *Violence among Rural Youth.* Final Report to the Office of Juvenile Justice and Delinquency Prevention.

Nansel, T., M. Overpeck, R. S. Pilla, W. J. Ruan, B. Simmons-Morton, P. Schmidt. 2001. "Bullying Behaviors among US Youth." *Journal of American Medical Association* 285: 2094–2100.

National Education Association. 2003. *National Bullying Awareness Campaign.* Available at www.neaorg/schoolsafety/bullying.html. Accessed August 12, 2005.

Olweus, Dan. 1993. *Bullying at School.* Malden, MA: Blackwell Publishing. 140pp. $28.95pa. ISBN 0-631-19241-7pa.

Pearmain, Elisa Davy. 2006. *Once Upon a Time . . . Storytelling to Teach Character and Prevent Bullying.* Greensboro, NC: Character Development Group. 377pp. $32.95pa. ISBN 1-892056-44-5pa.

Strauss, Kevin. 2010. *Building Heroes/Blocking Bullies: The Teacher and Parent Guide to Simple, Repeatable, Assertive Techniques That Anyone Can Use to Stay Safe and Stop Bullies.* Eden Prairie, MN: Trumpeter Press. 204pp. $25.00pa. ISBN 978-0-9814667-4-3pa.

U.S. Department of Health & Human Services. 2008. *Myths About Bullying.* Washington, DC: GPO. Available at http://stopbullyingnow.hrsa.gov/HHS_PSA/pdfs/Fact_sheet_Myths_32.pdf.

U.S. Department of Health & Human Services. 2009. *Steps to Address Bullying at Your School: Tips for School Administrators.* Washington, DC: GPO. Available at http://stopbullyingnow.hrsa.gov/adults/tip-sheets/tip-sheet-15.aspx.

Wisconsin Department of Public Instruction. 2009. *Bullying Prevention Curriculum: Classroom Instructional Units Grades 3-5.* Madison: Wisconsin Department of Public Instruction. 171pp. ISBN 978-1-57337-140-7.

Chapter 3

Bully Prevention Stories

This section includes stories about trolls, lions, and monsters that try to bully humans and other smaller creatures. One of the great things about stories is how they often show that bullies almost always fail in the end. The bullying characters in these stories also help students see models of what makes a bully and what makes a hero, so children can emulate the heroes and avoid bullying behavior.

One challenge that educators have when dealing with bullying issues is that some aggressive bullies feel that they are really acting as "heroes," and the person they are picking on "deserved it" for some reason (Strauss 2010). That is why it is important to present assertive and nonviolent ways to be a hero. That is also why it is important to emphasize the building block skills that children need to prepare them for encounters with life's bullies.

Reference

Strauss, Kevin. 2010. *Building Heroes/Blocking Bullies: The Teacher and Parent Guide to Simple, Repeatable, Assertive Techniques That Anyone Can Use to Stay Safe and Stop Bullies*. Eden Prairie, MN: Trumpeter Press. 204pp. $25.00pa. ISBN 978-0-9814667-4-3pa.

Three Goats and a Troll (Adapted from Norway)

Skills: Self-Control, Problem Solving

Safe School Rule: 3.) It is our job to help and protect all of our classmates when bullies try to hurt them.

Once upon a time, three goats lived on a grassy hill next to a river. There was a Big Billy Goat, a Medium Billy Goat, and a Little Billy Boat. But as the summer went on, the sun beat down and the grass turned brown on the hill. One night, the Little Billy went in search of fresh green grass. He could smell fresh grass across the river, so he walked across a bridge, "trip, trap, trip, trap."

But under that bridge lived a huge, ugly, young Troll. And since it was night, the Troll climbed out and roared, "Who's walking on **MY** bridge?"

"It's me, the Little Billy Goat," squeaked the goat.

The ugly green Troll climbed up onto the bridge railing. In the moonlight, the Little Billy Goat could see that the Troll's big head was covered with greasy black hair and he had a mouth full of black, broken teeth.

"Well, if you're a goat, then I'm going to beat you up and eat you for dinner!"

The Little Billy Goat remembered what his parents had told him about running into Trolls. They always said, "If you meet a Troll, take a deep breath and smile." So that's what he did.

The Troll was surprised. No one had ever smiled at him before. He wasn't sure what to do, so he talked.

"Hey, what are you smiling for, kid? I'm going to eat you up!"

And as the Troll hesitated, the Little Billy Goat remembered something else about Trolls. They are afraid of sunlight. You see, it turns them to stone.

Looking over the Troll's shoulder, the little goat said, "Hey, is that the sun rising over there?"

"Where?" said the Troll, looking all around. The moment the Troll turned around, the Little Billy Goat ran across the bridge, safe and sound.

Later that night, the Middle Billy Goat noticed that his younger brother was gone. So he went looking for him. He saw the bridge and remembered that his brother wanted to find more grass. So he started across the bridge.

He went, "Trip, Trap, Trip, Trap."

But the Troll was still there. He roared, "Who's walking on **MY** bridge?"

"It's me, the Middle Billy Goat," squeaked the goat.

The Troll climbed up onto the bridge railing and reached for the goat with his large, muscular green arms.

"Then I'm going to beat you up and eat you for dinner!"

The Middle Billy Goat also remembered what his parents had told him about running into trolls. So he took a deep breath and smiled. Then he remembered that his parents always said, "Make a plan for how to escape." So he started to plan.

The Troll was surprised again.

"Hey, what are you smiling about? I'm going to gobble you up!"

When the Troll hesitated, the Middle Billy Goat put his plan into action. He knew that same thing about trolls that his younger brother did.

"Hey, isn't that the sun rising over there?"

"Where?" said the Troll, looking all around. The moment the Troll turned around, the Middle Billy Goat ran across the bridge, safe and sound.

Early in the morning, before the sun rose, the Big Billy Goat noticed that his two younger brothers were gone. So he went looking for them. He saw the bridge and remembered that his youngest brother wanted to find more green grass. So he started across the bridge.

He went, "TRIP, TRAP, TRIP, TRAP."

The now very hungry Troll roared, "Who's walking on **MY** bridge?"

"It's me, the Big Billy Goat," growled the goat.

After letting two billy goats sneak past him, the Troll leaped onto the bridge to block the way.

"Good. Then I'm going to beat you up and eat you for dinner!" roared the Troll as he spread his arms, blocking the bridge completely.

The Big Billy Goat, remembering what his parents had said, took a deep breath and smiled. Then he made a plan **AND** made a backup plan.

"Hey, is that the sun rising over there?"

"Hah, I've heard that one before," laughed the Troll. "Now it's dinner time!"

Since his first plan didn't work, the Big Billy Goat switched to his backup plan.

"What about 'fast food'?" he said as he turned and ran for the woods.

The Troll took off after him.

After running for a while, the Big Billy Goat saw the eastern sky was turning pink. That gave him an idea. He climbed a hill and stopped at the top.

The Troll licked his lips. "Tired, goat?"

"No," said the Big Billy Goat.

As the Troll climbed the hill, the clouds parted and the sun blazed across the hilltop.

"I'm just stopping to watch the beautiful sunrise," said the Big Billy Goat.

"AHHHH!" screamed the Troll as he hardened into stone. And that was the end of that mean young Troll.

The Big Billy Goat crossed the bridge and ate the fresh green grass with his brothers. And after that, the Big Billy Goat and all his brothers made sure that everyone could cross that bridge whenever they wanted, day or night. And that's the end of the story.

Discuss

1. Describe who was the hero and who was the bully in this story, based on their behaviors.

2. What effect did the goats' smiles have on the Troll?

3. At the end of this story, the Big Billy Goat was the strongest creature in the valley. He could have taken over the bridge and decided who could cross and who couldn't. Why do you think he didn't do that?

Sources

Arbuthnot, May Hill. *The Arbuthnot Anthology of Children's Literature.* Chicago: Scott, Foresman, 1961. 1088pp. ISBN 0688417256.

Asbjornsen and Moe. *A Time for Trolls: Fairy Tales from Norway.* Oslo, Norway: Johan Grundt Tanus Forlag, 1962. 82pp. ISBN 820518-0081-1pa.

Booss, Claire, ed. *Scandinavian Folk & Fairy Tales.* New York: Avenel Books, 1984. 666pp. $29.00. ISBN 0517436205.

The Three Clever Pigs (England)

Skills: Problem Solving, Kindness

Safe School Rule: 3.) It is our job to help and protect all of our classmates when bullies try to hurt them.

Once upon a time in a village not far from here, there lived a family of pigs. And when the three pig children were old enough, the Mother Pig said to them, "Children, it is time for you to make your way in the world. Go off and seek your fortunes!"

So the three little pig children set off. Percy Pig, being the oldest, was used to telling the others what they should do.

"I think the first thing we should do is build houses for ourselves. Then we can plant gardens and look for jobs."

Peter and Patty Pig agreed.

When the pigs came to a crossroad, Percy decided to go north, toward the farms. Peter decided to go east toward the forest, and that left Patty with the road that went south, to the village. They agreed that they'd meet at the crossroads one month later.

It wasn't long until Percy met a farmer who was harvesting hay in his field.

"Kind sir," said Percy, because his mother always taught him to be polite. "That seems like a lot of work for one person. I would be happy to work for you for the week if you would give me as payment some straw so I could build a house."

The farmer agreed, and at the end of one week, Percy had a pile of straw. At the end of two weeks, he had a snug straw house with a wood stove and everything.

Meanwhile, Peter walked into the woods and met a woodcutter. The man had a huge pile of sticks on the ground, but he had no wagon or donkey to help haul them away.

"Kind sir," said Peter, because his mother always taught him to be polite. "That seems like a lot of work for one person. I would be happy to work for you for the week if you would give me as payment some sticks so I could build a house."

The woodcutter agreed, happy for the help. At the end of one week, Peter had a pile of sticks. At the end of three weeks, he had a snug stick house with a wood stove and everything.

At about that same time, Patty walked into the village and saw a brick maker toiling to carry clay from the riverbank so he could bake it into bricks.

"Kind sir," said Patty, because her mother always taught her to be polite. "That seems like a lot of work for one person. I would be happy to work for you for the week if you would give me as payment some bricks so I could build myself a house."

The brick maker agreed. At the end of one week, Patty had a pile of bricks, but they weren't enough for a house. So she worked another week, and another week, and another week.

When a month went by and Patty didn't meet her brothers at the crossroads, they walked south to the village to look for her. They found her toiling away on the foundation of her brick house.

"Why are you working so hard, sis?" asked Percy. "I built a house out of straw. It took me just a week."

"My stick house only took two weeks," chirped Peter.

From *Story Solutions: Using Tales to Build Character and Teach Bully Prevention, Drug Prevention, and Conflict Resolution* by Kevin Strauss. Santa Barbara, CA: Libraries Unlimited. Copyright © 2011.

"Well, this house will take longer to build," said Patty. "But once it's up, it'll stay up."

"While you're working on your house, we're planting our gardens and looking for work," laughed Percy.

"You do it your way, I'll do it mine," said Patty as she turned back to her task.

Her brothers just laughed and walked away.

Now it just so happened that in the fall, a new creature came to that part of the countryside. It had a red plaid jacket, thick gray fur, sharp teeth, and very, very bad breath. Early one morning, the shadowy creature sneaked up on a house made of straw and sniffed the air.

"Mmmm, I love pig for breakfast. And it seems that this little piggy stayed home."

The Big Plaid Wolf walked up to the door and shouted in his loudest voice, "Little pig, little pig, let me come in!"

Percy dove under his bed and squeaked out in his highest voice, "Not by the hair of my chinny chin chin!"

"Then I'll snarl and I'll growl and I'll knock your house in!"

Wolf backed up and took a running start, and he ran right through the straw wall. But he was going so fast that he ran right out the other side. Then he tripped and fell "plop" right into a well that Percy had been digging in his back yard. Percy took that opportunity to run out the front door and down the road to Peter's house. By the time Wolf had crawled out of that well, Percy was long gone. But if there's one thing that wolves are good at, it's tracking. Wolf followed his nose right to Peter's stick house in the woods.

Wolf sniffed the air. "Mmm, two little piggies. Breakfast and lunch!"

He walked up to the door and shouted in his loudest voice, "Little pigs, little pigs, let me come in!"

Percy and Peter both dove under the bed and squeaked out in their highest voices, "Not by the hairs of our chinny chin chins!"

"Then I'll snarl and I'll growl and I'll knock your house in!"

Wolf backed up and ran right at Peter's stick wall. He broke through the wall, but he was running so fast that he broke through the back wall and he slammed "Bam!" right into an old oak tree, knocking himself out cold.

While the wolf was unconscious, Percy and Peter ran out the front door and down the road to Patty's brick house. When they got there, they told her all about the Big Plaid Wolf.

Patty closed all her shutters and locked and barred her strong oak front door. But it wasn't long before Wolf followed his nose to her house, too.

Wolf sniffed the air. "Mmm, three little piggies. Breakfast, lunch, and dinner!"

He walked up to the door and shouted in his loudest voice, "Little pigs, little pigs, let me come in!"

Percy and Peter both dove under the bed. But Patty picked up her cast iron frying pan, stood tall, and called out in a firm voice. "Not by the hair of **MY** chinny chin chin!"

"Then I'll snarl and I'll growl and I'll knock your house in!"

"You can try and try, but you won't get in!" called Patty.

Wolf noticed that those brick walls might be a little hard. So he backed up and ran right at the oak front door. But when he hit it, "Bam!" it was as hard as that oak tree. Wolf knocked himself right out. When he woke up, he walked around the house, looking for another way in. Then he noticed the chimney.

Soon Patty heard the unmistakable sound of someone climbing on the roof.

"Quick, bring me more wood!"

The brothers brought Patty armfuls of wood, and she started a fire and put a pot on to boil.

Wolf smelled the wood smoke.

"Hah, they think a little smoke will scare me off. No such luck."

Wolf climbed off the roof and ran to the river to soak his fur. Then the dripping wet wolf climbed back onto the roof.

When wolf came sliding down the chimney, he landed with a splash, right in the scalding hot water.

"Yow!" yelled Wolf.

Patty slammed the lid onto the pot, trapping the wolf inside. And that was the end of that Big Plaid Wolf.

Discuss

1. Bullies usually try to get targets alone on the playground or in the school hallway to do their bullying. What are some "safe places" you could go if you see a bully coming toward you? Describe a safe place.

2. What are the "most dangerous" places to run into a bully at your school? How do you deal with having to go through those places? (Travel with friends? Take another route? Avoid them altogether?)

Sources

Gruenberg, Sidonie. *Favorite Stories Old and New.* Garden City, NY: Doubleday, 1955. 512pp.

Lang, Andrew. *The Green Fairy Book.* New York: Longmans, Green, 1948. 248pp. $12.99pa. ISBN 1604595493pa.

Steel, Flora Annie. *Goldilocks and the Three Bears and Other Classic English Fairy Tales.* New York: Random House, 1994. 203pp.

The Monster in the Cave (Masi, Kenya)

Skills: Self-Control, Problem Solving

Safe School Rules: 1.) We will tell adults at home and at school when we see bullies trying to hurt others. 3.) It is our job to help and protect all of our classmates when bullies try to hurt them.

One day, Caterpillar was walking through the forest when he came to a cave. Feeling nervous, he crawled into the empty cave.

"Is anybody here?" said Caterpillar. But his voice echoed and sounded louder in the cave. "Cool," thought Caterpillar.

Later that day, Rabbit came home to his cave. But before he could walk inside, he heard a voice bellow out. "I'm I giant worm and I'll make you squirm. I eat hippos for lunch and elephants for dinner. If we fight, I'll be the winner!"

Rabbit ran down the path, crying, "Help, help, there's a monster in my house!"

Rabbit met Fox and asked her for help. So Fox walked up to the cave and shouted, "Who's in there?"

A deep voice bellowed out. "I'm I giant worm and I'll make you squirm. I eat hippos for lunch and elephants for dinner. If we fight, I'll be the winner!"

Fox was so scared that he ran down the trail to where Rabbit was waiting, and the two of them began crying, "Help, help, there's a monster in Rabbit's house!"

It wasn't long before they met Leopard on the trail.

"What's wrong?" asked Leopard.

"There's a big mean worm living in my cave," cried Rabbit.

"A worm?" said Leopard. "I'll take care of this."

Leopard walked up to the cave and shouted, "Who's in there?"

A deep voice bellowed out, "I'm I giant worm and I'll make you squirm. I eat hippos for lunch and elephants for dinner. If we fight, I'll be the winner!"

Leopard was so scared that he ran down the trail to where Rabbit and Fox were waiting, and the three of them began crying, "Help, help, there's a monster in Rabbit's house!"

It wasn't long before Frog came hopping by. "What's wrong?" asked Frog.

"There's a big mean worm living in my cave," cried Rabbit.

"A worm?" said Frog. "Let me see what I can do."

Frog walked up to the cave and shouted, "Who's in there?"

A deep voice bellowed out, "I'm I giant worm and I'll make you squirm. I eat hippos for lunch and elephants for dinner. If we fight, I'll be the winner!"

But Frog wasn't scared. He called back, "My friend Rabbit lives in this cave. It's not very nice of you to steal his home."

"I'll steal whatever I want, you slimy, green-skinned, bug-eyed freak!" said the voice.

At first the voice made Frog feel a little embarrassed. But then he took a deep breath and smiled, and he felt better.

"What do you mean by that?" asked Frog.

"I mean you're ugly and no one wants you around anyway," said the voice.

Frog took another deep breath and took another step toward the cave.

"What do you mean by that?" he asked.

"I mean you must be dumb because everyone else was smart enough to run away," said the voice.

Frog took another deep breath and took another step toward the cave. He noticed that the closer he got to the cave, the more scared that voice in the cave sounded.

"What do you mean by that?" he asked.

"Uh, I-I mean that, um . . . . I don't know," said the voice.

Frog was now close enough to see that the voice came from Caterpillar.

"Come back everybody," called Frog. "It's not a monster; it's just a caterpillar who likes to scare animals."

When Rabbit, Fox, and Leopard saw the "monster," they burst out laughing.

"I'm sorry," said Caterpillar. "I just wanted a good place to hide. I thought if I scared you, you'd leave me alone."

"There's plenty of space in the cave; why don't we share it?" said Rabbit.

So that's what they did.

Discuss

1. Who was the bully, who was the target, and who was the hero in this story? Describe the behaviors that define these roles. What behavior makes someone a bully, a target, or a hero?

2. Caterpillar used threats to scare and control Rabbit, Fox, and Leopard. Can you think of a time when someone threatened you? What happened?

3. Caterpillar acted like a bully because he felt scared. Fear can often lead to aggressive or bullying behavior. How did Rabbit address the issue of Caterpillar's fear? Could this work in the human world as well?

Sources

Arbuthnot, May Hill. *The Arbuthnot Anthology of Children's Literature.* Chicago: Scott, Foresman, 1961. 1088pp. ISBN 0688417256.

Heady, Eleanor B. *Jambo Sungura: Tales from East Africa.* New York: Norton, 1965. 93pp.

Ragan, Kathleen, ed. *Outfoxing Fear.* New York: W.W. Norton & Co., 2006. 259pp. $27.95. ISBN 0-393-06036-5.

The Danger of Fear (Iran)

Skills: Self-Control

Safe School Rule: 2.) We will not hurt other people with our words or our actions.

Glossary:

Dervish (DER-vish). *noun.* A Muslim holy man.

Mulla Nasrudin (moo-LA NAZ-roo-deen). *noun.* The "wise and foolish" religious teacher in stories from the Muslim communities in Turkey, Egypt, Iraq, and other Middle Eastern nations.

One dark night, the wise and foolish teacher Mulla Nasrudin was walking down the road when he heard a strange noise. It sounded a bit like a snore and a bit like a growl. Nasrudin walked faster, thinking about all of the scary creatures that could make such a noise.

"It could be a lion, or an evil genie," thought Nasrudin. He worried himself so much that he started running down the dark road until he tripped and fell, "Bam!," flat on his face. He had tripped over a dervish (a holy man) who had dug a small cave in the hillside next to the road.

"Who are you?" stammered Nasrudin.

"I am a dervish, and this is where I am contemplating my existence," said the dervish.

"Well, you'll have to contemplate existence with company tonight. I heard a strange sound, and I'm so frightened that I can't go any further."

"Then come inside," said the dervish. "But please keep quiet. I need silence for my contemplation."

An hour later, Nasrudin called out, "Do you have any water? I am thirsty."

"Go down the road to the stream," said the dervish.

"I can't. I'm too afraid."

"Then I'll go. Since you are my guest, I should serve your needs."

"NO! Don't leave me here all alone!" begged Nasrudin.

"Here," said the Dervish. "Take my knife to defend yourself. I'll only be gone for a few moments."

While the dervish was gone, Nasrudin's imagination got the best of him. By the time he heard footsteps on the road, he was even more terrified.

"That evil genie could still be out there, or maybe a ghost!" thought Nasrudin.

"Stop where you are!" shouted Nasrudin.

"But it's just me, your friend the dervish. I brought you some water," said a voice.

"How do I know that? You might be some monster disguised as my friend!"

"Don't be a fool. Why would a monster bring you a drink of water to quench your thirst?"

"It's the perfect ploy to let you sneak into my cave."

"YOUR cave?"

"Yes, my cave. You can sleep somewhere else."

From *Story Solutions: Using Tales to Build Character and Teach Bully Prevention, Drug Prevention, and Conflict Resolution* by Kevin Strauss. Santa Barbara, CA: Libraries Unlimited. Copyright © 2011.

"It seems, my friend, that your fear is stronger than thirst, friendship, or common sense," said the dervish, shaking his head as he walked down the road. "And you don't have to have fear to suffer from it."

Discuss

1. Fear can make us do strange things sometimes. Think of a time when fear made you do something you wouldn't normally do. What happened?

2. We have two kinds of fear: "reasonable fear" and "imaginary fear." Reasonable fears are fears of things that really are dangerous, like rattlesnakes, busy highways, and high cliffs. This kind of fear makes us be careful so we don't get hurt. Imaginary fears are fears of things that aren't all that dangerous, like being afraid of the dark, water, garter snakes, or beetles. These fears often go away once we learn that these things aren't really all that dangerous.

   Generally speaking, bullies try to play on your imaginary fears to control your behavior. They know that they would get in big trouble if they really beat you up. So they threaten you and get you to imagine what they might do to you if you disobey.

   Think of something that you used to be afraid of but are no longer afraid of. What has changed?

3. How can you figure out whether a bully is a real danger or an imaginary danger? (In many cases, it might be safest to assume that a bully is a real danger and to get away from the bully right away. Then go tell a responsible adult about the threat. The adult can help you decide whether a bully is a real danger or not. He or she can also let the school know about the bullying threats so the principal can get involved to stop the bullying.)

Sources

MacDonald, Margaret Read. *Peace Tales.* Hamden, CT: Linnet Books, 1992. 116pp. $14.95pa. ISBN 0-208-02329-1pa.

Shah, Indries. *The Exploits of the Incomparable Mulla Nasrudin.* New York: E. P. Dutton & Co., 1972. 160pp. ISBN 0-525-47339-4pa.

Strauss, Kevin. *Building Heroes/Blocking Bullies: The Teacher and Parent Guide to Simple, Repeatable, Assertive Techniques That Anyone Can Use to Stay Safe and Stop Bullies.* Eden Prairie, MN: Trumpeter Press, 2010. 204pp. $25.00pa. ISBN 978-0-9814667-4-3pa.

The King and His Falcon (Wales, Great Britain)

Skills: Self-Control

Safe School Rule: 2.) We will not hurt other people with our words or our actions.

Long ago a king went hunting with his falcon. He rode his horse out into the field with his falcon riding on his arm. When he released the bird, she flew high into the sky and searched the ground for a rabbit or duck. Once she found prey, the falcon would dive to kill the prey for her master. The king was a generous man and always shared the prey with his falcon.

The sun shone bright on this day, and soon the king's throat was dry. He began looking for a stream or spring where he could drink. Finally he found a place where a spring trickled out of a cliff. The king unpacked his golden cup to catch the water as it fell from the rock. Meanwhile the king's falcon flew into the air to search for prey. But as the king raised the cup to his lips, suddenly he saw a flash of brown feathers as the falcon knocked the cup from his hand, spilling the water.

"Aaaah!" yelled the king, swatting the bird away. The falcon flew to a nearby branch and landed, watching her king carefully.

The king picked up his cup and held it under the dripping water again. When it was half full, he once again raised it to his lips. But once again, the falcon knocked the cup from his hand.

"Foolish bird!" yelled the king.

Once more the king began filling his cup, and when it was just a quarter full, the falcon swooped down and tried to grab the cup and fly off. But the falcon wasn't fast enough and only succeeded in spilling the water once again.

"Idiot bird! Try that again and I'll cut you in two," roared the red-faced king.

The falcon flew into the air and circled the king. As he filled his cup the falcon swooped down, and this time, the king was ready. He slashed at the bird with his dagger. The bird crumpled to the ground, but not before knocking the king's cup into a deep crevice in the rocks. The king tried to reach his cup, but it was beyond his reach.

Still hot and thirsty, the king cursed and began climbing up the cliff, hoping to find a pool where he could drink. Part way up the cliff he found a pool and lying in the pool was a dead and very venomous snake. The snake's deadly venom was mixing with the water. Suddenly the king realized why his loyal falcon had knocked the cup from his hands. The king climbed down the cliff and carefully picked up the falcon and placed her in his hunting bag. He buried her with honors in the royal cemetery. He also buried his dagger there, promising to never again act in anger.

From *Story Solutions: Using Tales to Build Character and Teach Bully Prevention, Drug Prevention, and Conflict Resolution* by Kevin Strauss. Santa Barbara, CA: Libraries Unlimited. Copyright © 2011.

Discuss

1. Have you ever been so angry with a friend that you said or did something that you later regretted? What happened?

2. How could the king in this story have acted differently? Why didn't he?

Sources

Bennett, William J., ed. *The Book of Virtues.* New York: Simon & Schuster, 1993. 832pp. ISBN 0-671-68306-3.

Cullen, Lynne. *The Mightiest Heart.* New York: Dial Books for Young Readers, 1998. 32pp. $29.99. ISBN 0803722923.

Tolstoy, Leo. *Fable and Fairy Tales.* New York: Simon & Schuster, 1962. 141pp.

The Doorways of Success and Failure (Japan)

Skills: Self-Control

Safe School Rule: 2.) We will not hurt other people with our words or our actions.

Once there was a samurai who had won many battles. No one and nothing had ever stood in his way. One day, he thought of a question that it seemed no one could answer in his village. So he traveled far into the mountains to a monastery. He threw open the door and walked right in, shoving monks out of his way. He walked right up to the abbot's quarters and shoved open the door. The abbot had his back to the door and was pouring himself some tea.

"Abbot!" bellowed the samurai. "I want you to teach me something. Where is the door to success, and where is the door to failure?"

The abbot didn't turn around.

"Didn't you hear me? Are you deaf?" growled the samurai. He was a man who was used to getting what he wanted.

Still facing the wall, the abbot responded, "Teach you something? I'm not sure that is possible these days."

"You insolent worm!" yelled the samurai, drawing his sword and charging toward the abbot. "I'll teach you how to treat a samurai!"

The abbot turned around.

"Behold the door to failure," he said in a steady voice.

The samurai stopped with his sword just inches from the abbot's nose. He took a deep breath, sheathed his sword, and bowed to the wise abbot.

The abbot smiled and bowed.

"Behold the door to success."

Discuss

1. What did the abbot mean by the "doorways to success and failure"?

2. Anger often leads us to do or say things that we regret later. Can you think of a time when this happened to you? Describe what happened.

Sources

Pearmain, Elisa, ed. *Doorways to the Soul: 52 Wisdom Tales from Around the World.* Cleveland, OH: Pilgrim Press, 1998. 138pp. $13.00pa. ISBN 1556357400pa.

Porcina, John. *Spinning Tales, Weaving Hope: Stories, Storytelling, and Activities for Peace, Justice and the Environment.* Philadelphia: New Society Publishers, 1992. 296pp. $24.95pa. ISBN 0865714479pa.

Strauss, Kevin. *Building Heroes/Blocking Bullies: The Teacher and Parent Guide to Simple, Repeatable, Assertive Techniques That Anyone Can Use to Stay Safe and Stop Bullies.* Eden Prairie, MN: Trumpeter Press, 2010. 204pp. $25.00pa. ISBN 978-0-9814667-4-3pa.

How Beetle Won a Colorful Coat (Brazil)

Skills: Problem Solving, Kindness

Safe School Rule: 2.) We will not hurt other people with our words or our actions. 4.) We will always include everyone in our games, conversations, lunch tables, and activities, especially those who are new to school or who don't have very many friends.

Long ago in the Amazonian rain forest there was a rat who loved to pick on other animals. She would taunt the turtles and frighten the frogs.

"Outta my way, flipper-feet!" yelled Rat, and she pushed a frog off the path and into the bushes.

"Gimme that seed!" she yelled at a mouse as she grabbed the food from his mouth. "It's mine now. Go get your own!"

Some mice, wanting to feel important, hung around with Rat, mimicking rat's mean behavior. One day, Rat and her gang saw a black beetle walking down the path.

"Hey, look at that, it's a rock with legs!" laughed Rat.

She tossed Beetle off the path and kept on laughing. "Have a nice trip. See you next fall, har, har-har."

It so happened that in that part of the rain forest there lived a magical green parrot. Parrot flew down and helped turn the beetle right side up.

"Someone should teach that rat a lesson," thought Parrot, as she looked at Beetle. "Hmmm . . . ."

The next day, Parrot called all the animals together for a meeting.

"I have heard that you walking and crawling animals would like a different color for your fur or scales or skin. So we will hold a contest, a race from this tree to the great kapok tree at the far side of the forest. Whichever animal reaches the tree first can choose a brand new magical coat. Now who wants to race?"

Rat could hardly believe it. She had always wanted a bright blue coat instead of her dull brown fur.

"I'll race, and I dare anyone else to try to beat me," roared Rat.

Most of the smaller animals looked at the ground and shook their heads. They were afraid to challenge Rat.

But Beetle stepped forward. "I'll try."

"Good," said Parrot.

Rat looked over at the small beetle.

"You call those legs? Hah, you'll never make it all the way to the kapok tree," said Rat as she stretched her strong rat legs.

Beetle didn't say a thing. She just looked toward the kapok tree. Then Parrot said, "On your marks, get set, go!"

The two animals ran off through the forest. Rat trampled over flowers and dove through bushes while beetle ran under the flower leaves. After running halfway there, Rat slowed down.

"Hey bug! Where are you?" said Rat, looking around.

From *Story Solutions: Using Tales to Build Character and Teach Bully Prevention, Drug Prevention, and Conflict Resolution* by Kevin Strauss. Santa Barbara, CA: Libraries Unlimited. Copyright © 2011.

Rat didn't see the beetle anywhere.

"Why bother running so hard?" thought Rat. "I'll just walk to the finish."

As she walked, she thought about what color she would like to be.

"Blue would be nice, but what about green? Maybe some spots . . . ."

Then Rat heard some cheering in the distance. When she ran into the clearing, she saw Beetle standing on the roots of the kapok tree. Rat ran up to her.

"H-how did you get here so fast? I never saw you pass me."

"I flew," said Beetle softly.

"You can't fly!" said Rat.

Beetle turned and looked Rat in the eye.

"Just because you didn't know I could fly, doesn't mean that I can't," she said.

Rat was speechless.

"There is a lot that you don't know about the creatures you tease," said Parrot. "All creatures have special gifts. You just never noticed. So, Beetle, what color coat would like?"

Beetle looked at the world around her, then turned to Parrot and said, "I'd like a coat that's blue like the sky and green like the leaves and shiny like the water in the river."

And that is why to this day, all of beetle's children have shells that are blue and green and shiny. As for rats, they are still brown, but they don't seem to bother other animals so much.

Discuss

1. Why do you think Rat was so surprised by Beetle's flying ability?

2. Have you ever judged people by how they looked, only to be wrong about them? What happened?

Sources

Carpenter, Frances. *South American Wonder Tales.* Chicago: Follett, 1969. 191pp.

Hamilton, Mary, and Mitch Weiss. *How & Why Stories: World Tales Students Can Read and Tell.* Little Rock, AR: August House, 1999. 96pp. $14.95pa. ISBN 0874835615pa.

Neuman, Shirlee. *Folk Tales from Latin America.* New York: Bobbs-Merrill, 1962. 123pp.

The Fox with Hundreds of Tricks, Cat with One (Aesop)

Skills: Problem Solving, Self-Control

Safe School Rule: 3.) It is our job to help and protect all of our classmates when bullies try to hurt them.

One day, Fox and Cat were walking down the road, and Fox was boasting.

"You know, Cat, I have hundreds of tricks for getting away from hunting dogs!"

"Really?" said Cat. "I only have one."

"How can that be?" said Fox. "Dogs are dangerous. If your one trick doesn't work, then what will you do?"

"I'll tell you when that happens," said Cat.

Just then, the two animals heard the unmistakable barks and growls of hunting dogs as they ran through the woods.

"I've got hundreds of tricks, hundreds of tricks," said the nervous Fox. "Which one should I choose, which one should I use? Should I play dead? Should I hide in a cave? Should I run and jump into a river? Should I run in a circle to throw them off the trail?"

Cat, using her one trick, leapt up into a tree and sat there.

"Hurry up, Fox, the dogs are almost here. Just do something!"

"Which one should I choose? Which one should I choose?" said Fox.

But a moment later, the dogs rushed out of the forest, grabbed the indecisive Fox, and ate him right up.

Discuss

1. How many solutions do you need to a particular problem?

2. What was a problem with Fox's approach to learning tricks?

3. This could be read as a story of "quality over quantity." Cat knew her one trick very well, while Fox probably knew several tricks, but he hadn't practiced any of them very much. Discuss the advantages and disadvantages of each strategy.

Sources

Artzybasheff, Boris, ed. *Aesop's Fables.* New York: Viking, 1933. ISBN 0670106356.

Strauss, Kevin. *Building Heroes/Blocking Bullies: The Teacher and Parent Guide to Simple, Repeatable, Assertive Techniques That Anyone Can Use to Stay Safe and Stop Bullies.* Eden Prairie, MN: Trumpeter Press, 2010. 204pp. $25.00pa. ISBN 978-0-9814667-4-3pa.

White, Anne Terry. *Aesop's Fables.* New York: Random House, 1964.

The Samurai and the Island (Japan)

Skills: Problem Solving, Self-Control

Safe School Rules: 2.) We will not hurt other people with our words or our actions. 3.) It is our job to help and protect all of our classmates when bullies try to hurt them.

Once there was a famous samurai warrior named Bokuden, who had won many battles. But when peace came to his land, he took off his armor and began traveling from temple to temple on a pilgrimage. It so happened that while traveling on a ferryboat on Lake Biwa, the samurai met another warrior. But this man was nothing like Bokuden. While Bokuden was calm, this man was loud. While Bokuden moved slowly and deliberately, this ruffian moved like an angry bird.

This ruffian pushed people out of the way and threatened them with his sword. He pushed his way onto the boat, and as the boatman prepared to leave, the ruffian saw Bokuden sitting calmly in the back of the boat and looking right at him. The ruffian couldn't stand having anyone look him in the face. He stomped up to Bokuden with a scowl on his face.

"Hey, warrior," said the ruffian. "You must think you're pretty tough. I challenge you to a duel, right here and right now."

Bokuden slowly rose to his feet, looked the ruffian right in the eye, and spoke calmly.

"I am sorry, but I cannot fight you here. My kind of fighting might hurt too many innocent people on this ferry. Perhaps we can fight another day."

"Ha! You're afraid. You carry swords, yet you are afraid to use them," scoffed the ruffian.

"I do not carry swords to cut my enemies," said Bokuden. "I carry swords to cut my own arrogance, to remind me not to get too full of myself."

"Pah! That is the talk of a coward. Will you fight now or surrender?"

"Very well," said Bokuden. "Since you are so certain that you want to fight today, I accept your challenge on one condition. We will fight on that small island out there in the lake."

"Agreed," said the ruffian.

"Then I shall defeat you without even touching you," said Bokuden.

"Ha! That's impossible, old man. I look forward to taking your swords as a trophy."

Bokuden asked the boatman to steer the boat to the island. Before the boat even reached the island, the ruffian leaped into the water and swam to shore. He pulled out his sword with a grin.

Bokuden turned to the boatman and said, "We are done here, boatman. Turn the boat and go." The boatman turned the boat and sailed it away from the island.

"Wh-what's going on? You're running away, you coward. Why don't you face me like a man?" shouted the ruffian.

"I did face you like a man," said Bokuden. "And I defeated you like one. I told you that I would defeat you without even touching you, and that is what I have done. You are trapped and we are free, and I didn't even have to touch you."

 From *Story Solutions: Using Tales to Build Character and Teach Bully Prevention, Drug Prevention, and Conflict Resolution* by Kevin Strauss. Santa Barbara, CA: Libraries Unlimited. Copyright © 2011.

Discuss

1. Sometimes people think they need to fight a bully to beat him or her. Is that always true? What other ways can you defeat a bully?

2. Some people read this story and think that Bokuden is a coward for not fighting the ruffian. What do you think?

Sources

Fauliot, Paul. *Martial Arts Teaching Tales of Power and Paradox.* Rochester, VT: Inner Traditions, 2000. 128pp. $12.95pa. ISBN 0892818824pa.

Krensky, Stephen. *Bokuden and the Bully: A Japanese Folktale.* Minneapolis: Milbrook Press, 2008. 48pp. $6.95pa. ISBN 1580138470pa.

Turnbull, Stephen. *The Samurai Swordsman.* North Clarendon, VT: Tuttle Publishing, 2008. 208pp. $44.95. ISBN 978-4-8053-0956-8.

It's Not Our Problem (Burma)

Skills: Problem Solving

Safe School Rules: 1.) We will tell adults at home and at school when we see bullies trying to hurt others. 3.) It is our job to help and protect all of our classmates when bullies try to hurt them.

Long ago in the warm and green land of Burma, there was a capital city. And in that capital there was a palace, and on the balcony of the palace sat the king and his chief advisor. As they sat and talked, looking over the city, they ate honey on their rice cakes. That day the king was feeling happy, and he laughed loud and long at his advisor's joke. But as he laughed, a drop of honey fell from his rice cake onto the railing.

"My king," said the advisor. "You have spilled some honey on the rail. Let me call a servant to clean it up."

"What's the hurry?" said the king. "I don't want to be disturbed. This drop of honey is not our problem. I'll have my servants clean it up later."

As the morning wore on, the sun warmed the drop of honey, and it slowly dripped down to the road below. Soon flies began to gather to lick up the sweet treat.

"My king," said the advisor. "The drip has fallen to the road and it is attracting flies. Let me call a servant to clean it up."

"I have told you, we are important people. This drop of honey is not our problem. See, let me prove it to you."

The king took another rice cake, covered it with gooey honey, and dropped it over the rail. Soon even more flies gathered on the road. Before long a green lizard darted from a crack in the palace wall and began catching flies on his tongue. It wasn't long before the baker's cat saw the lizard across the street and began stalking the scaly green meal. Just as the cat was about to pounce, the butcher's dog barked and lunged for the cat. The cat hissed. The dog barked, and the standoff erupted into a fight.

"My king," said the advisor. "Animals are fighting in the street. We should send a servant to break that up."

"My good man," said the king. "We are important men. We can't be bothered with such trivial matters. Let someone else deal with it."

And the king was right. Before long, the baker ran out of his shop with his rolling pin and began beating the dog. Then the butcher grabbed a club and began beating the baker. Then the baker's and the butcher's friends and neighbors got into the fight.

"My king," said the advisor. "Now people are fighting in the street. We should send some guards to break that up."

"My good man," said the king. "We are important men. We can't be bothered with such trivial matters. Let someone else deal with it."

Soon some soldiers came running to the fight. But some of the soldiers were friends with the baker and some were friends with the butcher. So rather than ending the fight, the soldiers chose sides and joined the fight. The fight grew into a riot, and soon people were breaking windows and burning the shops in town.

"My king," said the increasingly nervous advisor. "Now people are setting the buildings on fire. We should send some servants to put out the flames."

"My good man," said the king. "We are important men. We can't be bothered with such trivial matters. Let someone else deal with it."

But the flames soon spread to surrounding buildings. Then they spread to the palace. The king and his advisor had to flee the city.

A day later, when the army had ended the riots and the fires had all burned out, the king and his advisor returned to the hot, dry city to survey the charred ruins.

There, in front of the burned palace, the king saw a small brown puddle. He dipped his finger into it and smelled the substance.

"It's honey," said the king.

Then, turning to his advisor, he said, "You know, you were right. Perhaps we should have had a servant clean up that first drop of honey."

Discuss

1. Often people don't want to "get involved" to help solve a problem. What are some excuses that people give for not getting involved?

2. What is one way that you can get involved to help people in your school or community?

Sources

MacDonald, Margaret Read. *Peace Tales.* Little Rock, AR: August House, 2005. 116pp. $14.95pa. ISBN 0874837839pa.

Pearmain, Elisa Davy. *Once Upon a Time: Storytelling to Teach Character and Prevent Bullying.* Greensboro, NC: Character Development Group, 2006. 377pp. $32.95pa. ISBN 1-892056-44-5pa.

Strauss, Kevin. *Building Heroes/Blocking Bullies: The Teacher and Parent Guide to Simple, Repeatable, Assertive Techniques That Anyone Can Use to Stay Safe and Stop Bullies.* Eden Prairie, MN: Trumpeter Press, 2010. 204pp. $25.00pa. ISBN 978-0-9814667-4-3pa.

The Moon Goddess (China)

Skills: Problem Solving, Self-Control

Safe School Rules: 2.) We will not hurt other people with our words or our actions. 3.) It is our job to help and protect all of our classmates when bullies try to hurt them.

Glossary:

> **Herb** (ERB). *noun.* A green, flowering plant, sometimes used in medicines or cooking.

Long ago, there lived in China an evil king who would beat his servants and tax his people to the edge of starvation. If a family couldn't pay the taxes, the king would have his soldiers beat the parents, and his tax collectors would sell their children as slaves. When the king had roads or palaces to build, his soldiers would take the father or oldest son from every family and force them to work as slaves for years on end. As time when on, the people got poorer and poorer, while the cruel king and his generals got richer and richer.

From time to time the king's advisors suggested that the people couldn't pay such punishing taxes. But the king would throw those advisors into prison and have them executed the next day. After that, the advisors kept their mouths shut.

While the king was often cruel and angry, his wife, Chang Her, was just the opposite. She would send her servants to sell her jewels in the marketplace and use the money to feed the poor. She tried to soften her husband's heart, but he only laughed at her.

"I am a king, and a king has the right to tax his people," he roared. "It is their job to find a way to pay. If they can't pay, then that is no fault of mine. They will get what they deserve."

But as time went on, the king accumulated so much wealth that there was no way he could spend it all on fine clothes, sparkling jewelry, beautiful palaces, and powerful armies. It was then that he wished for something more.

"I want to be immortal," he said one day while sitting in his throne room surrounded by his generals and advisors. "I want to live forever as king of this land."

The king looked at his generals.

"I will give half of my wealth to any man who can bring me the secret of immortality."

The generals and their armies traveled far and wide in search of this secret. And in a far-off land, one general found a doctor who held the secret of immortality. The man had already lived for a thousand years after drinking a special mixture of magical herbs. The general brought the doctor to the king's palace, and the king paid him 100 bags of gold for the magical medicine. But after the doctor provided the mixture, the king stabbed him with a jeweled dagger and left him bleeding on the palace floor.

"I shall be the only one who lives forever! No one else will learn your secret."

Then the king took the medicine to his bedroom and showed it to his wife.

"See wife, let this be a lesson to you. I always get what I want. Tomorrow, in front of all my generals and nobles, I alone will drink this medicine, and then I shall live forever!"

The king and his wife went to bed, but Chang Her couldn't sleep.

"If the medicine really works, then my husband could abuse his people forever," she thought. "I've got to do something."

At midnight, she sneaked out of her bed and grabbed the medicine. Disguising herself as a servant, she sneaked out of the palace. When the king awoke the next morning and saw that both his wife and the medicine were missing, he knew what had happened.

"Guards! Guards! We must find my wife! Search the shops and search the farms! Search the forests and the barns! The man who finds my missing wife gets a bag of gold for every year of his life!"

The guards and soldiers scoured the countryside. As the sun set in the west, the king and his soldiers cornered Chang Her on a cliff in the forest. Knowing she could not escape, Chang Her raised the glass medicine bottle to her lips and drank the medicine.

"No!" roared the king.

"Now you will die like everyone else, cruel king!" said Chang Her.

She turned and ran for the cliffs as the furious king and his soldiers charged after her. Chang Her was ready to jump, when a strange thing happened. When she ran off into the open air, she didn't fall. The king, right behind her, wasn't watching and fell down and down and "Splat!" right on the rocks below. But Chang Her rose up and up, all the way to the moon, where she lives today. And if you look up at a full moon, some people say you can still see her there. In China, they call her the "Moon Goddess," a woman who saved her people and watches over them still.

Discuss

1. Chang Her took a big risk to help her people. Why do you think she did that?

2. Can you think of a time when you or someone you know took a risk to help someone? What happened?

Sources

Kendall, Carol, and Yao-wen Li. *Sweet and Sour: Tales from China.* New York: Seabury, 1979. 112pp. $6.95pa. ISBN 0618752455pa.

Ragan, Kathleen. *Outfoxing Fear.* New York: W. W. Norton & Co., 2006. 259pp. $27.95. ISBN 0393060365.

Strauss, Kevin. *Building Heroes/Blocking Bullies: The Teacher and Parent Guide to Simple, Repeatable, Assertive Techniques That Anyone Can Use to Stay Safe and Stop Bullies.* Eden Prairie, MN: Trumpeter Press, 2010. 204pp. $25.00pa. ISBN 978-0-9814667-4-3pa.

How Guinea Fowl Got Spots on Her Wings
(African American)

Skills: Problem Solving, Self-Control

Safe School Rules: 3.) It is our job to help and protect all of our classmates when bullies try to hurt them. 4.) We will always include everyone in our games, conversations, lunch tables, and activities, especially those who are new to school or who don't have very many friends.

Glossary:

> **Guinea** (GIN-ee) **Fowl** (FOUL). *noun.* A chickenlike bird native to Senegal and other areas of sub-Saharan Africa.

One day a flock of blue-feathered guinea fowl was walking through a field pecking at seeds and bugs when they encountered Sister Cow.

"Howdy, Sister Cow! What's new with you?" asked one of the birds.

"The grass is new and the warm sun is new, what more could I need?" said Sister Cow.

The guinea hens kept pecking for food while the cow kept eating grass and chewing her cud, when suddenly they heard a "Roar!"

The birds scattered in all directions, and when the dust settled, they saw a huge lion facing Sister Cow. The cow stood her ground and lowered her horns at the lion. The lion started circling around Sister Cow, trying to get past those horns. But as Lion circled, the cow turned, always keeping her horns pointed at Lion. As the guinea fowl gathered together a short way off, they started talking.

"We've got to help Sister Cow," one said.

"I've got an idea," said another of the birds.

That bird ran between the cow and the lion and started scratching and kicking up dust with her feet and fanning it into the air with her wings. Then another hen joined and another and another, until they raised such a cloud of dust that Lion couldn't see.

"Out of the way," roared Lion as he lunged at the birds. But the guinea fowl were too fast, and they scattered once again. In the confusion, Lion forgot about Sister Cow, but she didn't forget about him. Sister Cow was ready. She dipped her head and caught Lion on her horns. She lifted him into the air and threw him across the field. He landed in a heap and didn't move.

When the dust cleared again, Sister Cow looked at the guinea hens.

"I want to thank you for your help," said Sister Cow. "What can I give you as a gift?"

"Oh, don't worry about us," said one of the birds. "What we want, you can't give us."

"Don't be so sure," said Sister Cow. "You never know what animals can do until they try. Before today, I would have never guessed that a guinea hen could blind a lion. What is it that you wish for?"

One of the hens looked at her sisters and then back at Sister Cow.

"We'd like it fixed so that it would be harder for our enemies to see us."

"Really?" said Sister Cow. "Go get me a bucket."

"What do you need a bucket for?" said the hen.

"Just get the bucket and you'll see," said the cow.

Later that day, Sister Cow took the guinea hens to an old campfire. She sprinkled the birds with gray ashes and began singing a magical song. Then she filled the bucket with her milk, and using her tail, she splattered the white milk on their wings. When the guinea hen's wings dried, the color stayed. And that's why to this day, guinea hens are gray with white spots, and they are much harder to see in the tall grass and brush.

Discuss

1. Why do you think that the guinea hens decided to help the cow? Would you have done the same thing?

2. Describe a time when you did something helpful for someone else. How did it make you feel? How do you think it made the person that you helped feel?

Sources

Chase, Richard, and Joel Chandler Harris. *The Complete Tales of Uncle Remus*. Boston: Houghton Mifflin, 2002. 848pp. $35.00. ISBN 0618154299.

Harris, Joel Chandler. *Nights with Uncle Remus: Myths and Legends of the Old Plantation*. New York: Penguin Classics, 2003. 384pp. $16.00pa. ISBN 0142437662pa.

Lester, Julius. *The Last Tales of Uncle Remus*. New York: Dial Books, 1994. 176pp. $12.95. ISBN 0803713037.

The Man on the Moon (China)

Skills: Kindness

Safe School Rule: 1.) We will not hurt other people with our words or our actions.

One day a poor boy named Lin was walking down the road when he saw a swallow lying in the ditch. The boy was a farmer, so he knew a lot about animals. He picked the bird up carefully and saw that it had a broken wing.

"Poor bird," he said as he carefully wrapped the bird in a piece of cloth and carried it home.

Lin fed the bird and gave it water to drink. He splinted and bandaged the bird's wing, and after weeks of rest, the bird started to move. A few weeks later, the sparrow began to flap the bandaged wing. Lin took off the bandages, and soon the bird was fluttering around the room. The swallow seemed to bow to show how grateful it was, and then it flew out the open window.

Lin smiled and thought, "Well, that was my good deed for today."

He thought that would be the last he saw of the bird. But an hour later, the sparrow came flying back through the window. It dropped a yellow pumpkin seed on the table. Lin planted the seed in his garden. Day by day, the seed grew into a giant pumpkin vine. At the end of the vine grew a huge yellow pumpkin. When the pumpkin stopped growing, it was as big as an ox cart. Lin rolled the pumpkin to his house and got his ax so he could split it open. But when he split it open, shining silver and glittering gold poured out onto the ground.

"We're rich, we're rich," called Lin's father and mother.

The family used the money to buy a fertile farm and cows and oxen. But even though they were rich, they never forgot their neighbors. They shared their wealth and it never seemed to run out.

News of the family's luck spread. A neighbor boy named Chen heard the story and thought, "If I could find an injured bird, then I could grow a treasure pumpkin just like Lin."

But injured birds aren't as easy to find as one might think. After looking for a day, Chen thought of a new idea.

"If I can't find an injured bird, maybe I can make one."

He took a stone and threw it at a sparrow, breaking its wing. Then he ran up and grabbed the bird. He took it home and threw it in a box. He threw seeds into its box every few days, and gave it a bowl of dirty water to drink.

"Hurry up and heal so I can get rich," Chen told the bird.

Despite the poor care, a month later, the bird's wing healed and it flew out the open window.

The next day, the swallow flew back into the house and dropped a pumpkin seed on the table. Chen smiled. He planted the seed and watered it carefully. Day by day the seed grew into a giant pumpkin vine. At the end of the vine grew a huge yellow pumpkin. But when Chen broke the pumpkin open, it wasn't full of gold or silver, or even copper. Instead, a well-dressed old man climbed out of the pumpkin.

"Where's the gold, old man?" sneered Chen.

"Gold? Oh, I know where that is. Follow me," said the old man.

The old man raised his arms and the pumpkin vine twisted and rose straight up into the sky. The old man climbed up the vine, and Chen followed, all the way up to the moon.

Chen noticed that as they climbed onto the moon, the pumpkin vine withered and fell away.

"So where's the gold?" said Chen.

The old man pointed to a strange-looking cinnamon tree. It had a golden trunk and leaves made of jewels. The old man handed Chen a silver ax. Chen walked up to the tree, lifted the ax over his head, and chopped into the tree trunk. Suddenly he felt a sharp pain on his shoulder. He turned to see a white rooster standing behind him. That bird had pecked him on the shoulder. Chen chased the rooster off. But when he returned to the tree, there was no sign of the cut he had made in the trunk. Angry, Chen took another swing at the tree and cut a gash into the trunk.

"Ow!" he yelled as the rooster pecked him on his shoulder once again.

Chen chased the rooster off again. But once again, when he returned to the tree, the cut he had made was gone.

After hours chopping and chasing off the rooster, Chen was exhausted. He dropped the ax next to the tree and went looking for the old man. He found the old man sitting under another tree drinking tea.

"This is too hard," said Chen. "I want to go home."

"I can't help you there," said the old man.

"What!"

"I can't help you until you cut down that golden cinnamon tree," said the old man.

Chen sighed and slowly walked back to the tree. That is why to this day, if you look at the full moon, you may see a boy trying to chop down a cinnamon tree.

Discuss

1. How was Lin's behavior different from Chen's?

2. Which do you think would make a better friend? Why?

Sources

Eberhard, Wolfram. *Folktales of China*. Chicago: University of Chicago Press, 1965. 267pp. ISBN 0226181936pa.

Jablow, Alta, and Carl Withers. *The Man in the Moon: Sky Tales from Many Lands*. New York: Holt, Rinehart & Winston, 1969. 131pp.

Wyndham, Lee. *Folk Tales of China*. Indianapolis, IN: Bobbs-Merrill, 1963. 129pp.

The Cat Monk (Russia)

Skills: Problem Solving, Self-Control

Safe School Rules: 1.) We will tell adults at home and at school when we see bullies trying to hurt others. 2.) We will not hurt other people with our words or our actions. 4.) We will always include everyone in our games, conversations, lunch tables, and activities, especially those who are new to school or who don't have very many friends.

Long ago, a cat who had grown old and slow found a piece of brown fabric and made it into a robe for himself. Then he sat down next to a barn where he knew a lot of mice lived. But instead of hunting the mice, the cat just sat, folded his paws, and seemed to pray. The mice peeked out of their holes at the strange cat. After a day, one of the mice sneaked out to look at the cat. Then another mouse came out, and another, until a small mouse crowd had gathered.

The cat opened his eyes.

"My friends," said the cat with a smile. "I beg your pardon. I have been living my life by eating your kind, and now I see that was wrong. So to make up for my bad behavior, I have become a monk, and I promise not to eat mice any more. From now on, I will protect you from other cats and spend my day praying. All I ask of you is that you help me to sing a special song every evening."

The mice thought about this offer, talked it over, and finally agreed. That night, the mice gathered around the cat monk.

"Now to sing this song, you must line up, close your eyes, and sing 'La, la, la-la, la,'" said the cat.

The mice closed their eyes and sang the song. But while the mice sang, the cat sneaked up, grabbed a mouse from the end of the line, and popped it into his mouth. Then he sat down, closed his eyes, and pretended to pray. Day after day the mice gathered, and the cat got an easy meal. But one day a sharp-eyed mouse named Gray Patch noticed that there were fewer mice in the clearing.

"Hey, what happened to White Nose, Gray Ear, and Black Tail?" said Gray Patch. "They were all here a few days ago."

The cat glared at that mouse. "Close your mouth, mouse! Or I'll open mine."

But Gray Patch kept talking. "Why do we have to close our eyes when we sing? I think this cat is eating mice while we're singing!"

The mice began nodding their heads. "Yeah, what's going on, cat?"

Finally the cat couldn't take it any more. He leapt into the air and tried to grab Gray Patch, but he came up empty. The mice scattered in all directions, and they never came back to sing songs with the cat monk.

Discuss

1. What would have happened to the mice if Gray Patch hadn't reported what he was seeing to the other mice?

2. Can you think of a time when you had to speak up to solve a problem? What happened?

Sources

Carpenter, Frances. *Wonder Tales of Cat and Dogs.* Garden City, NY: Doubleday, 1955. 255pp.

Cary, Bonnie. *Baba Yaga's Geese and Other Russian Stories.* Bloomington, IN: Indiana University Press, 1973. 128pp.

Hardendorff, Jeanne B. *Tricky Peik and Other Picture Tales.* Philadelphia: Lippioncott, 1967. 122pp.

Three Butterfly Friends (Germany)

Skills: Problem Solving, Kindness

Safe School Rules: 3.) It is our job to help and protect all of our classmates when bullies try to hurt them. 4.) We will always include everyone in our games, conversations, lunch tables, and activities, especially those who are new to school or who don't have very many friends.

Long ago, in a field far from here at the edge of a big woods, there lived three butterfly friends. One of the butterflies had red wings, one had yellow wings, and one had wings as white as a cloud on a warm summer's day. And even though they looked different, they could still be friends because they knew that real friendship is about how you act, not how you look.

These butterflies liked nothing better than flying from flower to flower in the wide green field and smelling the flowers (with their antennae) and tasting the sweet flower nectar (with their feet), and drinking the nectar with their strawlike mouths. One day they were having so much fun that they forgot to watch the weather; and when they were in the middle of the field, they looked up to see angry gray storm clouds hanging overhead. Heavy raindrops began dropping from the sky.

"Hurry, we have to find shelter," said Red.

"Let's ask the flowers for help," said Yellow.

So they flew over to a red tulip and sang to her, "Oh please, oh please beautiful flower, give us shelter from this shower."

The tulip looked at the butterflies and frowned.

"Red, you can shelter under my leaves, but you other two, you look too strange. I only like things that look like me. You go hide under some tree."

Red looked at her friends and then turned to the tulip.

"Thank you for your offer, but I don't want to go where my friends aren't welcome."

The butterflies flew to a yellow sunflower and sang, "Oh please, oh please beautiful flower, give us shelter from this shower."

The sunflower looked at the butterflies and frowned.

"Yellow, you can shelter under my leaves, but you other two, you look too strange. I only like things that look like me. You go hide under some tree."

Yellow looked at her friends and then turned to the sunflower.

"Thank you for your offer, but I don't want to go where my friends aren't welcome."

The butterflies flew to a white daisy and sang, "Oh please, oh please beautiful flower, give us shelter from this shower."

The daisy looked at the butterflies and frowned.

"White, you can shelter under my leaves, but you other two, you look too strange. I only like things that look like me. You go hide under some tree."

White looked at her friends and then turned to the sunflower.

"Thank you for your offer, but I don't want to go where my friends aren't welcome."

Now the butterflies' wings were so wet, they couldn't fly. So they began walking in the field. And as they walked under the proud, tall flowers, they heard a small voice.

From *Story Solutions: Using Tales to Build Character and Teach Bully Prevention, Drug Prevention, and Conflict Resolution* by Kevin Strauss. Santa Barbara, CA: Libraries Unlimited. Copyright © 2011.

"Butterflies, come over here, we'll shelter you and your friends so dear."

It was the little pink clovers. "We're not as big as the other flowers, but we'll protect you from the showers."

The three butterfly friends took shelter under the clover leaves and flowers as the rain soaked the grass. And soon the winds blew the clouds away and the sun came out and dried up all the rain.

The butterflies thanked the clovers and traveled home. But ever since that day, though the butterflies still love nothing better than flying from flower to flower in the wide green field, they always remember their pink clover friends and fly down to visit them in the grass. And even though they looked different from each other and from the clover, they could still be friends.

You see, they knew that friendship isn't in a book. It is how you act, not how you look.

Discuss

1. Loyalty (sticking with your friend) is an important part of friendship. How would this story have been different if each butterfly had abandoned her friends to stay in a dry place? Do you think they would have remained friends? Why or why not?

2. Being loyal to a friend doesn't mean that you always agree with that friend or always do what a friend says you should do. Can you think of a time when you had to disagree with a friend about some activity? What happened?

Sources

Harrison, Annette. *Easy to Tell Stories for Young Children.* Jonesborough, TN: National Storytelling Press, 1992. 86pp. $8.95pa. ISBN 1-879991-14-4pa.

Pearmain, Elisa Davy. *Once Upon a Time: Storytelling to Teach Character and Prevent Bullying.* Greensboro, NC: Character Development Group, 2006. 377pp. $32.95pa. ISBN 1-892056-44-5pa.

Strauss, Kevin. *Building Heroes/Blocking Bullies: The Teacher and Parent Guide to Simple, Repeatable, Assertive Techniques That Anyone Can Use to Stay Safe and Stop Bullies.* Eden Prairie, MN: Trumpeter Press, 2010. 204pp. $20.00pa. ISBN 978-0-9814667-4-3pa.

The Strength of a Bundle of Sticks (Aesop)

Skills: Problem Solving, Kindness, Self-Control

Safe School Rules: 2.) We will not hurt other people with our words or our actions. 3.) It is our job to help and protect all of our classmates when bullies try to hurt them. 4.) We will always include everyone in our games, conversations, lunch tables, and activities, especially those who are new to school or who don't have very many friends.

Once there was a farmer who had seven sons. From the time they were young, the seven brothers were always arguing and fighting, always trying to prove that they were the best at running or riding or planting or shooting or wrestling, always trying to prove that they knew more than any of their brothers. It broke their mother's heart to see her boys fighting so much. Finally, the farmer had had enough.

"My sons, tomorrow I will decide who will inherit my farm. I want each of you to gather two stout sticks from the forest."

The next morning, after breakfast and after the chores were done, the brothers met in the farmyard with their father. They were all ready to tell him why they should inherit the farm.

"I'm the oldest," said one.

"I'm the strongest," said another.

"I am the most clever," said a third, and before long they were shoving and punching and rolling in the dirt.

"Silence!" yelled the farmer.

The boys got up and brushed off the dirt.

"I'll settle this once and for all. Take one of your sticks and show me if you can break it," said the red-faced farmer.

Each boy easily broke his first stick.

"Now give me your second stick."

The farmer bundled them together.

"The one who can break these sticks gets to own the farm," said the farmer.

Each of the brothers tried, but each failed.

"You see, on your own, you are like the single sticks, easy to break. But if you work together, you become like this bundle of sticks. If you work together, no one can defeat you."

The brothers listened, and it was like they were seeing each other for the first time. And if I told you that after that, the brothers never quarreled, I'd be telling you a story. But I do know that for the rest of their lives, each brother kept a bundle of sticks hanging above his fireplace. And if anyone ever asked about the bundle, the brother would tell this story.

Discuss

1. What bully prevention lesson did you hear in this story?

2. Can you think of a time when you helped a friend with a problem? Can you think of a time when a friend helped you with a problem?

3. Who do you think is more likely to be picked on by a bully, a person with a lot of friends or a person with few friends? Why?

Sources

Handford, S. A. *Aesop's Fables.* New York: Puffin, 1994. 212pp. $4.99pa. ISBN 0-14-130929-6pa.

Jacobs, Joseph, ed. *The Fables of Aesop.* Mineola, NY: Dover Publications, 2002. 196pp. $2.50pa. ISBN 0-486-41859-6pa.

Zipes, Jack, ed. *Aesop's Fables.* New York: Signet Classic, 1992. 288pp. ISBN 0-451-52565-5pa.

The Lion and the Mouse (Aesop)

Skills: Problem Solving, Kindness

Safe School Rules: 2.) We will not hurt other people with our words or our actions. 3.) It is our job to help and protect all of our classmates when bullies try to hurt them.

Once there was a curious mouse that wanted to see what a lion looked like. Mouse crawled up onto a sleeping lion and scurried up to its face. Lion woke up and grabbed Mouse with his paw.

"Please don't eat me! Please don't eat me!" squeaked Mouse.

"Why not?" roared the Lion.

"Because some day you may need my help," said Mouse.

"Ha, ha, ha. I am the king of the forest. Why would I ever need help from a puny creature like you?"

"You never know," squeaked Mouse. "Little help is better than no help at all, sometimes."

Lion just laughed, but he let the mouse go anyway.

A few weeks later, Lion was walking through the forest when he tripped over a rope and a heavy net fell from the trees, trapping him.

"Let me out of here, let me out of here," roared Lion.

But when most animals hear Lion roar, they run the other way. So no one came to help. No one, that is, except for Mouse.

Mouse walked up to Lion.

"Remember me? I said I'd help you some day. Do you need some help now?"

"No," lied Lion, hoping Mouse would leave. "I happen to be very comfortable in this net."

"Oh good, I wouldn't want you to be uncomfortable when the hunters come to get you," said Mouse.

"Hunters! Hunters are coming?"

"Of course, this is a hunter trap for lions. If you don't get out right away, you won't last the day."

"Well, in that case, Mouse, could you **please** chew through this net and let me out?"

Mouse set to work chewing on the net, and in no time at all, Mouse had set Lion free. And people say, in that part of the forest, lions and mice are still the best of friends, all because of a mouse who kept her promise.

From *Story Solutions: Using Tales to Build Character and Teach Bully Prevention, Drug Prevention, and Conflict Resolution* by Kevin Strauss. Santa Barbara, CA: Libraries Unlimited. Copyright © 2011.

Discuss

1. What bully prevention lesson did you hear in this story?

2. Can you think of a time when you helped a friend with a problem? How did it feel to help someone else?

3. Can you think of a time when a friend helped you with a problem? How did it feel to receive help with a problem?

Sources

Handford, S. A. *Aesop's Fables.* New York: Puffin, 1994. 212pp. $4.99pa. ISBN 0-14-130929-6pa.

Jacobs, Joseph, ed. *The Fables of Aesop.* Mineola, NY: Dover Publications, 2002. 196pp. $2.50pa. ISBN 0-486-41859-6pa.

Zipes, Jack, ed. *Aesop's Fables.* New York: Signet Classic, 1992. 288pp. ISBN 0-451-52565-5pa.

The Grasshoppers and the Monkeys
(Hmong People, Southeast Asia)

Skills: Problem Solving, Self-Control

Safe School Rules: 2.) We will not hurt other people with our words or our actions. 3.) It is our job to help and protect all of our classmates when bullies try to hurt them. 4.) We will always include everyone in our games, conversations, lunch tables, and activities, especially those who are new to school or who don't have very many friends.

Long ago the people say that the grasshoppers were the first creatures to live on the earth. But the sky spirit wasn't satisfied with just having grasshoppers in the world, so he made all the other creatures, including the monkeys. The monkeys were a strong and pushy family. They usually got what they wanted in the forest because none of the other animals would stand up to them.

But one day a group of grasshoppers came across the body of a dead monkey on the trail.

"It must have fallen from a tree," said one of the grasshoppers.

Suddenly, two monkeys came up the trail. "Hey, what did you do to that monkey?"

"Nothing," said one of the grasshoppers. "He was dead when we found him."

"A likely story," said the monkey. "I think that you killed him!"

The monkeys ran back to their family trees. "Grasshoppers our killing our cousins! Grasshoppers our killing our cousins!"

All of the monkeys came down to the village clearing. Soon they were talking about how the terrible grasshoppers had killed their cousin.

"We should teach those grasshoppers a lesson," said one monkey.

"We should hurt them the same way that they hurt us," said another.

The grasshopper people sent messengers to the monkey village to tell them that they hadn't hurt that monkey. But by that time, the monkeys didn't want to listen.

"This means war!" roared the chief of the monkeys.

"We don't want war, but if that's what you want, then we'll meet you at the clearing on the hill when the sun is high in the sky tomorrow," said the grasshopper messenger.

The next day, the monkeys grabbed big sticks and ran up the hill looking for grasshoppers. When they reached the clearing, they couldn't find any grasshoppers. The insects were all hiding in the tall grass. Then, all at once, the grasshoppers buzzed, "Now!"

The grasshoppers hopped onto the heads of the monkeys. Seeing grasshoppers, the angry monkeys started swinging their sticks. But instead of hitting the fast-hopping grasshoppers, they hit other monkeys.

"Bam, bam!" Two monkeys fell.

"Bam, bam." Two more fell. The grasshoppers were so fast that by the time a monkey swung his stick, the grasshopper was gone and another monkey lay on the ground. Finally there was only one monkey left. The grasshoppers came out of the grass and danced on the bodies of their enemies. The last monkey screamed and ran into the woods, never to return.

From *Story Solutions: Using Tales to Build Character and Teach Bully Prevention, Drug Prevention, and Conflict Resolution* by Kevin Strauss. Santa Barbara, CA: Libraries Unlimited. Copyright © 2011.

That was the last time that any monkey tried to bully the grasshoppers.
And that's the end of the story.

Discuss

1. Why did the monkeys think it was OK to hurt the grasshoppers? Do you think the monkeys were right?

2. What other things could the grasshoppers have done to deal with the bullying monkeys?

Sources

Johnson, Charles, ed. *The Monkeys and the Grasshoppers.* St. Paul, MN: Macalester College, 1981.

Johnson, Charles, ed. *Six Hmong Folk Tales Retold in English.* St. Paul, MN: Free People Publications, 1992. 172pp.

Livo, Norma, and Dia Cha. *Folk Stories of the Hmong.* Englewood, CO: Libraries Unlimited, 1991. 135pp. $40.00. ISBN 0-87287-854-6.

Strauss, Kevin. *Building Heroes/Blocking Bullies: The Teacher and Parent Guide to Simple, Repeatable, Assertive Techniques That Anyone Can Use to Stay Safe and Stop Bullies.* Eden Prairie, MN: Trumpeter Press, 2010. 204pp. $25.00pa. ISBN 978-0-9814667-4-3pa.

Three Bulls and the Lion (Aesop)

Skills: Problem Solving, Self-Control

Safe Schools Goals: 3.) It is our job to help and protect all of our classmates when bullies try to hurt them. 4.) We will always include everyone in our games, conversations, lunch tables, and activities, especially those who are new to school or who don't have very many friends.

Once there were three bulls who all lived in a grassy field. They would spend their days eating grass, chewing their cud, and talking. After all, they had a lot in common. They were all bulls. And because there were three of them living in that field, they were always safe. If a lion or bear ever tried to sneak up on one of them, one of the other bulls would yell, "Look out!" and run to his friend's defense. The three bulls would charge the invader with their sharp horns and send the creature scuttling into the woods.

Soon the bulls grew big and healthy, having plenty of food and never fearing for their safety.

But one day a new lion came to that part of the forest. He would sit in the woods and watch the bulls, looking for a chance to attack.

"This requires some planning," thought Lion.

The next day, he hid behind a bush at the edge of the field. He whispered to the brown bull, "Hey, buddy, come on over here."

Brown Bull slowly walked toward the sound. He couldn't see the lion, but he could hear him.

"Hey, you know what I heard?" said the voice.

"What?"

"I heard that white bull saying that he was a lot stronger than you were. He even said that you are afraid of the dark."

"Why that dirty cow! That's not true," yelled Brown Bull, and he stomped off to the west end of the field.

A little while later, the white bull came close to the bush.

"Hey buddy, you know what I heard?"

The white bull looked up. "What?"

"I heard that gray bull laughing at you. He was telling the mice that you are afraid of cows and that you burp all night long in the field."

"That rude bug! How dare he spread rumors about me?"

White Bull stomped up to Gray Bull and kicked him. "How dare you say those things about me?" Then White Bull stomped off to the east end of the field. Gray Bull tried to follow White Bull, but White Bull refused to talk. So Gray Bull returned to the middle of the field.

The next day, Lion smiled, "Mission accomplished." Lion pounced on Gray Bull and ate him for dinner. The next week, he ate White Bull, and the next he ate Brown Bull. As he stretched out on the grass that evening, his muzzle red from the dinner, Lion thought to himself, "What a beast can't do with muscle, he can do with words. United they stand; divided they fall."

From *Story Solutions: Using Tales to Build Character and Teach Bully Prevention, Drug Prevention, and Conflict Resolution* by Kevin Strauss. Santa Barbara, CA: Libraries Unlimited. Copyright © 2011.

Discuss

1. How could the bulls have stayed friends even after Lion began spreading rumors about them?

2. Can you think of a situation in which someone spread rumors about a person just to break up a friendship? What happened?

Sources

Handford, S. A. *Aesop's Fables.* New York: Puffin, 1994. 212pp. $4.99pa. ISBN 0-14-130929-6pa.

Jacobs, Joseph, ed. *The Fables of Aesop.* Mineola, NY: Dover Publications, 2002. 196pp. $2.50pa. ISBN 0-486-41859-6pa.

Zipes, Jack, ed. *Aesop's Fables.* New York: Signet Classic, 1992. 288pp. ISBN 0-451-52565-5pa.

A Trumpeter Taken Prisoner (Aesop)

Skills: Self-Control

Safe School Rule: 2.) We will not hurt other people with our words or our actions.

Amid the chaos of a battle, a trumpeter found himself surrounded by enemy soldiers. He dropped his trumpet and begged for mercy.

"Please don't hurt me. After all, I'm just a humble musician. I carry no weapons. I have killed no soldiers. All I carry is this trumpet."

"Ha!" said the enemy captain. "You are more responsible for this battle than anyone else. If you hadn't blown your trumpet, your army would never have charged into battle. You deserve worse than all the other soldiers put together, because you sounded the attack. They just carried out orders."

Discuss

1. In some cases, one bully gets his friends to pick on a particular target. Do you think that this "trumpeter" bully is responsible for the bullying as well? Why or why not?

2. Do you think the captain is right in this story? Is the trumpeter really more responsible for the battle than the individual soldiers? Would your answer change if the captured man were a general, who gave the orders, rather than just a trumpeter who sends messages to the troops?

Sources

Handford, S. A. *Aesop's Fables.* New York: Puffin, 1994. 212pp. $4.99pa. ISBN 0-14-130929-6pa.

Jacobs, Joseph, ed. *The Fables of Aesop.* Mineola, NY: Dover Publications, 2002. 196pp. $2.50pa. ISBN 0-486-41859-6pa.

Zipes, Jack, ed. *Aesop's Fables.* New York: Signet Classic, 1992. 288pp. ISBN 0-451-52565-5pa.

The Company You Keep (Aesop)

Skills: Self-Control

Safe School Rule: 2.) We will not hurt other people with our words or our actions.

One day, after eating a meal of fish, a stork was resting in a field when a flock of cranes flew by.

"Come with us," said the cranes. "We know where we can find lots of food."

Stork opened his wings and joined the flock. But when the cranes landed, it was in a farmer's field. The cranes set to work feeding on the grain. Stork began looking for worms. But the birds where so busy eating that they didn't notice the farmer hiding behind a bush. The farmer threw a net and caught two cranes and the stork. The remaining cranes flew off across the field.

"Hah! I've finally caught you, you thieves!"

"Wait, this is all some kind of mistake," protested Stork. "I didn't eat any of your grain. I only eat fish and worms."

The farmer looked at the stork.

"Perhaps you're right, and perhaps you're wrong. But if you keep company with troublemakers, you get to share their fate."

And that was the end of that stork.

Discuss

1. Do you think Stork makes a good case for why the farmer should let him go?

2. Can you think of a time when you got in trouble because of the company you kept, rather than because of your individual behavior? What happened?

Sources

Handford, S. A. *Aesop's Fables.* New York: Puffin, 1994. 212pp. $4.99pa. ISBN 0-14-130929-6pa.

Jacobs, Joseph, ed. *The Fables of Aesop.* Mineola, NY: Dover Publications, 2002. 196pp. $2.50pa. ISBN 0-486-41859-6pa.

Zipes, Jack, ed. *Aesop's Fables.* New York: Signet Classic, 1992. 288pp. ISBN 0-451-52565-5pa.

Putting Feathers Back in the Pillow (Jewish)

Skills: Self-Control, Problem Solving

Safe School Rule: 2.) We will not hurt other people with our words or our actions.

Long ago in a village, there was a tailor named Hershel who loved to gossip. From morning to night, as Hershel sewed, he would leave his window open and listen to the conversations of the people outside. If he heard something particularly interesting, he would write it down and save that bit of gossip for later. Day after day Hershel would collect and share gossip with his friends.

Hershel liked gossip. It let him feel like he knew more than other people, and that made him feel important. He didn't have big muscles, he figured, so at least he could have a big brain. At least that is what he thought.

One day the old rabbi in the village died, and a young rabbi came from a neighboring village to work with the community. The rabbi's name was Jacob. Now Jacob spent a lot of time listening to the people in town. He listened to their problems. He listened to their fears. And rather than telling people things like "do this . . ." or "the Talmud says . . . ," he always asked them, "What do you think?"

Now Hershel never came to Rabbi Jacob. Hershel figured that he knew so much about the world that he didn't need to talk with a rabbi. So one day, Jacob made a visit to Hershel's tailor shop.

"Hershel, I hear that you are a person who knows what is happening in this village," said Jacob.

"Yes, I know a thing or two," said Hershel, trying to hide his pride. "If you have questions about anyone, I could help you with them."

"No, I don't need that kind of help, but I do have one thing I would like you to do," said Jacob.

He picked up one of the feather pillows waiting to be patched and tore it open.

"Rabbi, what are you doing?" yelled a surprised Hershel.

"When the sun sets, take this pillow and run to my house just as fast as you can."

Hershel thought that the request was strange, but Jacob was a rabbi, so Hershel agreed to do it.

As the sun set later that day, Hershel quickly grabbed the pillow and ran to Jacob's house. When he got there, the feather pillow was almost empty. When he knocked on the door, Jacob smiled at him.

"Now I want you to put all of the feathers back into the pillow."

Hershel's face fell. This was an impossible task. Hershel tried to find a few feathers on the way home in the dark. But many feathers had already blown away in the wind. The next day he searched far and wide, but could only find a handful of feathers. Finally he went back to Jacob's house.

"Rabbi, it's impossible; I can't put feathers back into a feather pillow once they have blown into the world," said Hershel.

From *Story Solutions: Using Tales to Build Character and Teach Bully Prevention, Drug Prevention, and Conflict Resolution* by Kevin Strauss. Santa Barbara, CA: Libraries Unlimited. Copyright © 2011.

"It is the same way with gossip, Hershel," said Jacob. "Gossip is like poison. Once you release it into the world, it is almost impossible to clean it back up. The most important thing is to not to let those 'feathers' into the world in the first place. A little prevention is worth a mountain of cure."

Hershel thought about that as he walked home, picking up feathers as he went.

Discuss

1. Sometimes we hear the phrase, "Sticks and stones will break my bones but names will never hurt me." Is that phrase correct? Why or why not?

2. Think of a time when someone said something that hurt your feelings. What did they say? How did you respond? Does your memory of that incident still cause pain?

Sources

Brody, Ed, et al. *Spinning Tales, Weaving Hope: Stories, Storytelling and Activities for Peace, Justice and the Environment.* Gabriola Island, BC: New Society Publishers, 2002. 281pp. $24.95pa. ISBN 0-86571-447-9pa.

Stavish, Corinne, ed. *Seeds from Our Past: Planting for the Future.* Washington, DC: B'nai B'rith Center for Jewish Identity, 1997. 96pp. $10pa. ISBN 0-910250-31-6pa.

Strauss, Kevin. *Tales with Tails: Storytelling the Wonders of the Natural World.* Westport, CT: Libraries Unlimited, 2006. 231pp. $35.00pa. ISBN 1-59158-269-5pa.

Chapter 4

Bully-Stopper Self-Defense Techniques

Although it is important that schools, libraries, and communities create a safe environment for students, it is also true that some students will still have to deal with bullying from classmates. The activities in this section will give students the skills they need to keep themselves safe, keep their friends safe, and stop bullies cold.

These activities extend the learning that started with the stories in chapter 3. They are based on activities that I have conducted with students in my Bully Blocker™ Prevention Programs over the past ten years. They have been proven to be effective in the many schools in which I have used them, as well as when teachers have used them as follow-up activities after a Bully Blocker™ school presentation. They are most effective when used with the stories in chapter 3 and as part of a week-long or month-long bullying prevention unit.

Activity 4-1: Deep Breath, Smile, Walk Away

Objective: Students will learn how to calm themselves in the face of a bullying threat and then how to walk away from that threat safely.

Skills: Self-Control

Safe School Rule: 3.) It is our job to help and protect all of our classmates when bullies try to hurt them.

Grade Level: 4–8

Materials: none

Background

1. Take a deep breath and smile.

Whenever you face a stressful situation, whether it is a test, sports, or a bully, one of the best things you can do is to take a deep breath and smile. Taking a deep breath relaxes your body and sends more oxygen to your brain. This is important because when we feel stress, we often slow down or stop our breathing as we get ready to fight or run away. Holding your breath means that less oxygen gets to your brain, and your brain can't work as well to help you think of a way to get out of a difficult situation. Also, since bullies want to make you feel MAD, SAD, or BAD, relaxing your body with a deep breath helps protect you from the stressful emotional effects of a bully attack.

The smile is also important. When you smile at a bully, it confuses that person and throws him or her off. He or she won't be used to people smiling back. Once a bully is confused, it might be easier to make your escape. More important, forcing your mouth into a smile has been scientifically proven to help you feel better. Neurologists (brain researchers) discovered that activating the twelve facial muscles that you use to make a smile sends a signal to your brain. It tells your brain that "this person is happy, release those 'feel-good' endorphins" (Ross 2002). Your brain can't tell whether you're smiling because you really feel good or because you are faking it. So it automatically releases chemicals that actually make you feel good naturally. These chemicals are natural chemical antidotes to the "MAD, SAD, or BAD" effects of a bully attack.

2. Turn and walk away from the bully.

Bullies usually want to stand right in front of you and get in your face. That action usually intimidates a target and makes it easier for the bully to make a target feel MAD, SAD, or BAD. But if you turn your back on a bully, it is easier for that person to shove you from behind and knock you down. To protect yourself physically, try to turn sideways to a bully, so your shoulder is facing him or her. When you turn sideways, it is much harder for a bully to push you over. You can also hold your school books on the side away from the bully, so he or she can't knock them out of your hand. If the bully doesn't give up at this point, he or she will probably try to get back in front of you. If that happens, just turn again so your shoulder is facing the bully. Eventually the bully will start feeling foolish and leave you alone. If he or she doesn't, being sideways to a bully makes it even easier to walk away. You can watch the bully out of the corner of your eye as you walk away (see below).

Remember: Every second a bully is in front of you, he or she is winning. The most important thing you can do to keep a bully from trying to make you feel MAD, SAD, or BAD is to walk away and report what happened to a responsible adult.

3. Report bullying to a responsible adult (teacher, principal, or parent) right away.

Bullying is one of the most underreported problems in schools. That is because targets of bullying often feel ashamed. In some cases, they feel as if somehow they are somehow "responsible" for the bullying abuse that they received. In other cases, they fear retribution from the bully and his or her friends if they report the incident.

One study reported that only one in four bully targets ever reports the incident to an adult. Overall, older children and males were less likely to report a bullying incident, while younger children and girls were more likely to report it (U.S. Department of Health & Human Services 2008).

Role-playing Activity

1. Working with a partner. Choose one student to be the bully and one to be the target. The bully uses verbal taunts and threats (no physical contact) to intimidate the target. (Example: "Hey dork! Where's your money? Are those your books? What are you, some kind of nerd? I'm going to pound you!")

   Meanwhile, the target practices the process of taking a deep breath and smiling at the bully and looking him or her straight in the eye. Then the target turns sideways to the bully. If the bully tries to get back in front of the target, she or he turns sideways again. When possible, the target walks away. The target walks to the teacher's desk (or a blackboard or other designated spot) to "report" the incident. Don't skip the reporting part. One of the reasons that bullies can continue their abusive behavior is that no one reports them to teachers, parents, or other authority figures.

2. Switch roles and do the role-play again.

Evaluation

Have children write one-page papers or talk about what it felt like to be the target. Did the "Deep Breath, Smile, Walk Away" seem to work? Did it help them feel more in control? Do they think they could use this technique when facing problems in their own lives? How?

Activity 4-2: Verbal Safe Schools

Objective: Students will learn how to deflect and disarm the verbal bully.

Skills: Problem Solving

Safe School Rule: 3.) It is our job to help and protect all of our classmates when bullies try to hurt them.

Grade Level: 4–8

Materials: None

Background

When facing a verbal bully, you want to confuse him or her and throw him or her off the "bullying script" or plan. You do this by not responding the way a bully expects you to respond. In general, you don't want to argue with a verbal bully. That's what he or she expects you to do, so don't play that game.

Verbal Bullying Example

Verbal Bully: You're such a girly little wus.
Target: No, I'm not.

Verbal Bully: Yes, you are! You even dress like a girl.
Target: No, I don't.

Verbal Bully: Everyone knows it's true. I bet you even hit like a girl.
Target (close to tears, voice getting higher as he gets more and more agitated): No, I don't!

Verbal Bully: He even sounds like a girl. Ha ha-ha!

Techniques to Try

Ask a Question

When you ask a bully a question, it forces him or her to think quickly and come up with an answer. This can confuse many bullies. It's a good idea to keep asking the same question (as in the "broken record" technique described below). That way the bully has to think of new things to say, while you just repeat the same thing over and over. Eventually the bully starts to feel foolish and gives up.

Try these:

What do you mean by that?

I don't understand.

What do you mean?

Broken Record

The broken record technique can be combined with other verbal defenses. It works by having you repeat the same verbal response to a verbal bully attack over and over again. Since you aren't arguing with the bully and following his or her script, the bully becomes confused and eventually leaves you alone.

Example:

Verbal Bully: You're such a girly little wus.
Target: I guess that's what you think.

Verbal Bully: I mean you're wimpy. You even dress like a girl.
Target: I guess that's what you think.

Verbal Bully: I mean that your clothes are, um all colorful like girl clothes and you, uh, walk like a girl, too.
Target (still calm and confident): I guess that's what you think.

Verbal Bully: Forget it. (Turns and walks away.)

The Emotional Shrug/Fogging

This technique uses both verbal and body language bully defenses. The verbal part is stating a word or phrase that is noncommittal (doesn't agree or disagree with the bully attacker). This noncommittal answer can put a bully in a "fog," where he or she isn't sure how to react, hence the term "fogging" for this defense. The target pairs this verbal statement with an actual physical shrug, and then turns and walks away. Shrugging and turning away from the attacker (remember to turn your shoulder, not your back, to the attacker if he or she is close to you) gives him or her the message that you don't care about him or her or what he or she says. Bullies hate it when you don't seem to care about them and what they say. They want you to be afraid of them. They want you to react to them. If you don't play this game, they will often go away.

Try these:

Maybe (shrug).

Maybe not (shrug).

Whatever (shrug).

That's what you think (shrug).

You might be right (shrug).

Could be (shrug).

I can see how you might think that (shrug).

I'm sorry you feel that way (shrug).

That's too bad (shrug).

Example:

Verbal Bully: You're such a girly little wus.
Target: Whatever (shrug).

Verbal Bully: I mean you're wimpy. You even dress like a girl.
Target: Whatever (shrug).

Verbal Bully: I mean that your clothes are, um all colorful like girl clothes and you, uh, walk like a girl, too.
Target (still calm and confident): Whatever (shrug, turn and walk away).

Laugh It Off

When a bully says something rude or mean, look him or her straight in the eye and say, "Ha, that's funny." Then turn and walk away.

This technique works on a couple of different levels. It gives you a chance to look the bully in the eyes and show that she or he can't intimidate you. It gives you a chance to turn the comment into a joke, sort of. It also lets the bully know through verbal and nonverbal language that you don't care what she or he thinks and you aren't going to be intimidated.

Example:

Verbal Bully: You're such a girly little wus.
Target: Ha, that's funny.

Verbal Bully: I said you're a girly wimp! What are you going to do about it?
Target: Boy, you are funny.

Verbal Bully: What are you, retarded?
Target (still calm and confident): This is so much fun that I'd love to stay around, but I've got to go. See ya later. (Target turns and walks away.)

Role-playing Activity

1. With the class, create a list of "bullying words," those words that students call each other to hurt someone's feelings. Write the list on the board. Point out that most of those words, like "fag," "ugly," "retard," "fatso," etc., have no positive uses. Almost by definition, if a person is using these words, then he or she is acting like a bully.

2. Pair up the students. One student will be the bully and the other will be the target. The bully starts by using one of the "bullying words" that the class came up with. The target defends herself or himself by using the "What do you mean by that?"/broken record technique. After a few rounds, students switch roles. The new bully chooses a different bullying word, and the target chooses a different defense.

3. After having each student practice three or four target defenses, gather the students and discuss how things went. Which defenses were the easiest to use? Which defenses seemed to have the strongest impact on the "bullies"? How did it feel to be a bully? How did it feel to be a target?

Evaluation

Have children write a one-page reflection paper or talk further about their experience with verbal self-defense. Which techniques will they use when faced with a verbal bully in the future?

Activity 4-3: How to Be a Hero, Part I

Objective: Students will learn how they need to look, sound, think, and act to be a hero.

Skills: Problem Solving, Kindness, Self-Control

Safe School Rule: 3.) It is our job to help and protect all of our classmates when bullies try to hurt them.

Grade Level: 6–8

Materials: none

Background

Heroes come in all shapes and sizes. Parents and teachers can be heroes when they go out of their way to help other people with a problem. But in the case of bullying, it is very important that we train children to be heroes as well. The sad fact is that bullies often choose to attack other children when there are no adults around. Either consciously or unconsciously, bullies know that adults may stop bullying behavior and report it to authorities. Children often won't. To reduce bullying in our communities, we need to change that equation.

When I am working with students at school, many of my Bully Blocker™ presentations take place in the school gymnasium. So I ask the students, "How many players are there on a basketball team?" They say, "five." Then I ask them what would happen if three of those players just sat down on the court during the game.

"Then that team would lose," say the students.

The same thing is true with bullying prevention. It's a team sport. Teachers and administrators usually have a bullying prevention policy and disciplinary procedure in place. But if no adult sees bullying happening (because bullies are clever), and no students report when bullying is happening (because they're scared or "don't want to get involved"), it is difficult for the adults at school to do their job and keep students safe.

Role-playing Activity

1. How a Hero Looks

Read or tell one of the hero stories from chapter 3. That story will give students clues about how a hero looks to the outside world. Keep in mind, we aren't talking about whether a person is attractive or plain looking. We are talking about how a person carries himself or herself. A hero stands up tall. A hero looks people in the eyes when talking to them. A hero appears calm on the outside.

Pair up the students. Have them face each other. Ask them the following questions:

In your normal stance, are you standing up straight? (Most people aren't.)

Do you look people straight in the eye when you talk with them?

Do you appear calm and confident?

Imagine for a moment that you are a comic book superhero. How would you stand? How would you look at people? The great thing about using hero body language is that it not only makes you feel more confident, it also tells potential bullies that you aren't going to be an easy target. Since many bullies are lazy, they are always looking for easy targets and will be more likely to leave you alone.

2. How a Hero Sounds

A hero uses a "serious" voice when talking. A hero talks in a low tone (not a high, squeaky voice) and speaks slowly and deliberately. A hero maintains eye contact while talking.

Working with a partner, practice standing up tall and looking your partner in the eye. Then say, "Stop that right now. I don't like it," in your regular voice. Then say the same thing in a high voice. Then say the same thing in a voice that is a little lower than your regular voice. Which version of the phrase seemed more convincing?

Practice saying "Stop that right now. I don't like it," in a slightly lower voice. This "slightly lower voice" is also the voice that many dog owners use to get their dogs to follow a command. A lower tone naturally feels more authoritative. By comparison, a higher tone seems more "childlike" and less authoritative.

3. How a Hero Thinks and Acts

Heroes think that everyone is important, everyone deserves respect, and it is important to be kind, generous, and helpful to others, even people who aren't your friends.

A hero acts to help other people. A hero is polite and uses words like "please" and "thank-you." A hero speaks up and finds a way to help when someone is in trouble. A Hero helps others because it's "the right thing to do," not for any kind of reward.

Read, tell, or have students read a story that includes a hero from chapter 3. Describe how this "story hero" compares to the list of hero thoughts and actions in this section.

Evaluation

Now that students have practiced hero body language and speech, have each of them write a two-page story that starts with: "If I had one superpower, I would want it to be _____. I would use that power to help other people by _____."

Activity 4-4: How to Be a Hero, Part 2

Objective: Students will learn three effective ways to stop bullying behavior in their school or community.

Skills: Problem Solving, Kindness, Self-Control

Safe School Rules: 1.) We will tell adults at home and at school when we see bullies trying to hurt others. 3.) It is our job to help and protect all of our classmates when bullies try to hurt them.

Grade Level: 6–8

Materials: none

Background

There are many ways to be a safe school hero in your school or community. Here are three examples. Choose the technique that works best for you.

A. Report bullying to a responsible adult (librarian, teacher, principal, or parent).

One of the reasons that bullies continue to cause problems in our schools is because no one reports their behavior to adults. In some cases, bullies threaten targets and bystanders with more abuse if they report the abuse. In other cases, children worry that they'll be labeled "tattletales" if they report abusive bullying behavior. Remind your students that there is a huge difference between reporting dangerous behavior and "being a tattletale."

Here's one way to explain it: "Reporting" is telling an adult when someone is in danger and needs help. "Tattling" is telling an adult about something for the express purpose of getting someone else in trouble (Coloroso 2003). When I work with younger elementary students, I tell them that if you see Tommy spill his milk, a "tattling" response would be, "Teacher, Tommy was messing around and he just spilled his milk." A "reporting" response would be, "Teacher, Tommy just spilled his milk and we don't have any napkins. Could you get some napkins for us?"

There are at least two different ways to report bullying behavior, and one is far more effective than the other:

Reporting Method 1—Interpret What You See

Example: "Teacher, I just saw Sally being really mean to Jessica and being a bully."

Reporting Method 2—Describe What You See

Example: "Teacher, I just saw Sally hit Jessica and call her a mean name and knock her books out of her hands."

Which way do you think is more effective? Why?

As you might have guessed, method 2 is far more effective than method 1. That is because if you just tell a teacher or other adult that someone "is being mean," then when that teacher asks Sally if she was being "mean," she might say, "No, I was just kidding," or "No, I wasn't doing anything." In some cases, a target student may not want to say what happened because he or she fears retribution from the bully. Since the teacher doesn't have any more facts to go on, it is more difficult to deal with Sally's bullying behavior.

But if the teacher has a description of what happened, then the teacher can ask the children involved what happened. If the bully's description of what happened is different from everyone else's description, that is a clue that the bully might be lying. (I know it's surprising, but it happens.)

B. Stand next to the target.

Remember, BULLIES ARE COWARDS. They just want to pick on one person at a time. So if you stand next to a target, the bully is much more likely to leave that person alone. It is almost as if we each have our own personal "force fields." When you stand next to a person, you can help to protect him or her from bullying with your personal force field. After the bully leaves, be sure to remind the target that he or she didn't deserve that bullying. Remind the target that bullies often feel angry or sad inside and want to make other people feel that way, too. Then ask the target to report the bullying to a responsible adult. Remind the target that the bullying won't stop until an adult gets involved to help stop it.

C. Look the bully in the eye and say "Stop that right now, I don't like it."

If you feel comfortable doing it, you can also confront the bully and ask him or her to stop. This can be one of the most effective ways for a student to stop a bully from hurting someone else. Be sure to stand up tall, look the bully in the eye, and use your low, serious voice. Be sure to use "I" statements. A bully can argue with you about whether he or she is "being mean" or "being a bully," but not about your feelings. Only you know if you like or dislike seeing a particular behavior.

Role-playing Activity

A. Report bullying to a responsible adult (teacher, principal, or parent).

Choose a student to act as a target and role-play a bullying incident in which you are the bully. Call the student a mean name, shove him or her, and then laugh at him or her (for instance). Then ask students to write down what they saw using the four Ws (Who was involved? What happened? When did it happen? Where did it happen?). Collect the reports and read them out loud to the class. Discuss which reports did the best job of answering all of the WWWW questions.

B. Stand next to the target.

Role-play another scene in which you are the bully. Choose one student to be the target and one to be the hero. The hero just stands next to the target and looks at the bully. Then the hero invites the target to go do something fun (play a game, go to lunch, etc.).

Then divide the class into groups of three. Have students choose to be a bully, a target, or a hero. In the first round of this activity, have the bully taunt and threaten the target. In the second round, have the bully taunt and threaten the target, but have the hero walk up and stand next to the target. Change roles and repeat until everyone has had a chance to play the hero, the bully, and the target.

Discuss with the class: Did anything feel different when the hero stood next to the target? How? Was it as easy to taunt the target with the hero standing there?

C. Look the bully in the eye and say, "Stop that right now, I don't like it."

Again working in groups of three, have students choose to be a bully, target, or hero. This time the hero looks the bully straight in the eyes and in a low (hero) voice says, "Stop that right now, *I* don't like it!" Then switch roles and give each student a chance to be the hero at least once.

Discuss with the class: How did it feel to tell the bully, "Stop that right now, *I* don't like it!"? Do you think this would work with a real bully? Why or why not? When you were acting like a hero, did you feel more confident when you knew what words to say?

Evaluation

Have students write a one-page reflection paper on or talk further about which of the above hero techniques they are most likely to use in their lives and why. Remember to remind them that each of these techniques stops a bully cold. There are many ways to be a hero.

Activity 4-5: Four Roles in the Bullying "Drama"

Objective: Students will learn how to identify bullies, bullying behavior, targets, bystanders, and heroes by reviewing stories that demonstrate bullying.

Skills: Self-Control, Problem Solving

Safe School Rules: 2.) We will not hurt other people with our words or our actions. 3.) It is our job to help and protect all of our classmates when bullies try to hurt them.

Grade Level: 4–8

Materials: paper, pencils, marker board or overhead projector

Activity

1. Define the terms "bully," "bullying," "bystander," "hero," and "target," writing the definitions on the board so everyone can see them.

   Bully (bull-EE). *noun.* Someone who takes part in antisocial bullying behavior.

   Bullying. (bull-EE-ing). *verb.* 1) Engaging in repeated physical, verbal, or social abuse techniques that a powerful person uses to scare, control, ridicule, or hurt someone who is less powerful. 2) Making use of the unfair advantage of being bigger, stronger, or more popular to harm and to control the behavior of others for no good reason.

   Bystander (BYE-stander). *noun.* A person who watches bullying behavior take place and does nothing to stop it. Bystanders may remain silent, they may laugh at the bullying behavior, or they may even join in with the bullying at times.

   Hero (HEER-o). *noun.* 1) A person who sees bullying behavior take place and takes action to stop it, help the target, and/or make sure it doesn't happen again in the future. 2) A person who takes action to help other people, even at the risk of his or her own safety.

   Target (tar-GET). *noun.* A person whom a bully chooses to physically, verbally, or socially abuse.

2. Either read, tell, or have students read two to three stories from chapter 3. Have the students decide who is the bully, who are the bystanders, who is the hero, and who is the target in each story. (For older children, you can hand out copies of the stories and have students work on their own or in small groups.)

3. Create a list of the behaviors that make someone a bully, a bystander, a hero, or a target.

Evaluation

Were students able to create a list of "bullying" behaviors and a list of "heroic" behaviors? Have students write a half-page essay on which they see more often at your school: bullying behaviors or heroic behaviors.

Activity 4-6: School Safety Survey

Objective: Students will describe where they feel safe and unsafe at school and provide teachers with a sense of the size of the bullying problem at school.

Skills: Problem Solving

Safe School Rule: 1.) We will tell adults at home and at school when we see bullies trying to hurt others.

Grade Level: 4–8

Materials: "School Safety Survey" forms for each student, pencils, Scantron® forms if needed

Activity

Keeping in mind that bullying is one of the most underreported problems in many schools, this short survey can give educators, librarians, parents, and administrators a sense of the size of the problem and the bullying "hotspots" at their school. You can either hand-tabulate the results or use a Scantron® or other automatic grading system to tabulate the results.

1. Ask children to complete the "School Safety Survey" form on page 72. Tell children that this form will help teachers and administrators improve student safety at school. Remind them not to put their names on these anonymous surveys.

2. Collect and review the surveys. Look for patterns of where bullying is occurring.

3. Discuss the results with your students and ask them to come up with ways to make school safer for everyone. For example, "I see that according to our surveys, some children don't feel as safe on the playground. Can anyone think of a way we could work together to make the playground safer?"

Evaluation

Have students complete a one-page reflection paper or create an 8½-by-11-inch poster that completes the statement: "If I ran the school, I would make it safer by . . . ." Did each student think of two or three ways to make school safer?

School Safety Survey

Answer the following questions on a scale of 1–5, where 1 = never (0–10% of the time), 2 = seldom (10–40% of the time), 3 = sometimes (40–60% of the time), 4 = often (60–90% of the time), 5 = always (90–100% of the time), and NA = Does Not Apply to Me.

1. I feel safe at school.

    1   2   3   4   5   NA

2. I feel safe on the playground.

    1   2   3   4   5   NA

3. I get "picked on" or "bullied" at school.

    1   2   3   4   5   NA

4. I see other children get "picked on" or "bullied" at school.

    1   2   3   4   5   NA

5. I feel safe in the school hallways.

    1   2   3   4   5   NA

6. I feel safe in the bathrooms at school.

    1   2   3   4   5   NA

7. I feel safest at school in the _____.

8. I feel least safe at school in the _____.

9. When I get "picked on" or "bullied" at school, I report it to the teacher or principal.

    1   2   3   4   5   NA

10. When I see other children getting "picked on" or "bullied" at school, I report it to the teacher or principal.

    1   2   3   4   5   NA

11. I feel safe on the school bus.

    1   2   3   4   5   NA

12. I see physical bullying (hitting, shoving, kicking) every week at school.

    1   2   3   4   5   NA

13. I see verbal bullying (name calling, taunting, making fun of, insulting) every week at school.

    1   2   3   4   5   NA

14. I see social bullying (excluding a child from play, spreading rumors) every week at school.

    1   2   3   4   5   NA

15. To help me to feel safer, I would like to learn about (circle all that apply):

responding to physical bullies	responding to verbal bullies
responding to social bullies	how to report bullying to a teacher or parent
how to walk away from a bully	how to say "no" to a bad idea
how to feel good about myself	how to help someone who is being bullied

Activity 4-7: You Make the Call—Bullying or Something Else

Objective: Students will learn how to determine if a conflict is bullying or some other kind of interaction.

Skills: Problem Solving, Kindness

Safe School Rules: 1.) We will tell adults at home and at school when we see bullies trying to hurt others. 2.) We will not hurt other people with our words or our actions.

Grade Level: 6–8

Materials: paper, pencils, marker board or overhead projector, worksheets for small group or individual work

Activity

1. Post the definitions for bullying and bully on the marker board. Ask students to use these definitions to determine what activities constitute bullying and what are "something else."

    Bully (bull-EE). *noun.* Someone who takes part in antisocial bullying behavior.

    Bullying. (bull-EE-ing). *verb.* 1) Engaging in repeated physical, verbal, or social abuse techniques that a powerful person uses to scare, control, ridicule, or hurt someone who is less powerful. 2) Making use of the unfair advantage of being bigger, stronger, or more popular to harm and to control the behavior of others for no good reason.

2. Have students work in small groups or on their own to determine if the scenarios on the worksheet (p. 74) are "bullying" or "something else." Have students write the reasons for their answers.

3. Review the answers and answer any questions that students have.

Evaluation

Have students in small groups (or individually) create a list of three conflict events they have seen at school in the past year that would qualify as bullying, and three conflict events that wouldn't qualify as bullying. Students shouldn't use names, just terms like "Student 1" and "Student 2." Have students describe why the events qualify or don't qualify as "bullying."

"You Make The Call" Worksheet

Bullying. (bull-EE-ing). *verb.* 1) Engaging in repeated physical, verbal, or social abuse techniques that a powerful person uses to scare, control, ridicule, or hurt someone who is less powerful. 2) Making use of the unfair advantage of being bigger, stronger, or more popular to harm and to control the behavior of others for no good reason.

Scenario 1: Roger and Tony are classmates who get into an argument because Roger thinks that Tony tripped him on purpose. Tony claims that it was an accident, and if Roger "just looked where he was going," there wouldn't have been a problem.

Scenario 2: Jessica and Jamaica used to be friends. But now Jessica makes "oinking" noises whenever Jamaica is talking. They are usually so quiet that the teacher doesn't hear, but they make Jessica's friends giggle. Jessica has been doing this for a couple of weeks, and Jamaica is trying to ignore it, but that isn't working.

Scenario 3: Principal Jackson gives Isaac detention for swearing at a teacher and throwing a book across the room. Isaac complains that the principal is picking on him (this is his fourth detention this month) and that other kids do the same things and they don't get that many detentions.

Scenario 4: Samantha tells all of her friends not to talk with Nadia anymore because Nadia is so "stuck up." If Samantha sees people talking with Nadia or being nice to her, she scowls at them and then starts ignoring them as well.

Scenario 5: Eric convinces Steven to trip "that geek Andy" when he comes walking down the hall. When Steven trips Andy, Eric laughs, "Have a nice trip? See ya next fall. Ha, Ha, Ha."

Scenario 6: Sean is so angry that his ex-girlfriend Tammy is going out with Roger that he shoves Roger when he sees him in the hall. A scuffle ensues and fists fly. They both end up in detention.

Scenario 7: Popular boy Alex yells down the hall, "Hey Jenny, where'd you get those clothes, a garage sale? Ha, Ha, Ha." Jenny looks at the floor. Later Alex claims he was "just kidding," and didn't mean to hurt her feelings.

"You Make The Call" Answers

Scenario 1: SOMETHING ELSE. This seems like a garden-variety disagreement. Since the students seem to have equal power, and this isn't a repeated event, this is not an example of bullying.

Scenario 2: BULLYING. Since Jessica is trying to ridicule Jamaica by making animal noises, and because of the repeated and abusive nature of this action, it is bullying.

Scenario 3: SOMETHING ELSE. Since Principal Jackson is simply enforcing school rules, this isn't bullying. Remember, bullies try to control other people's behavior "for no good reason." It is reasonable for a school to have rules against disrespectful language and throwing books. Though Isaac may feel "picked on" by the principal, Isaac's behavior seems to warrant such action. If, on the other hand, Principal Jackson was using his authority to punish Isaac when Isaac hadn't broken any school rules, that might qualify as bullying, because the principal has more power in school than a student does.

Scenario 4: BULLYING. This is a classic case of social bullying. Samantha is trying to control Nadia by depriving her of friends. She's also trying to control the other girls in her clique.

Scenario 5: BULLYING. Eric and Steven are both being bullies. The act was premeditated and intended to scare and ridicule Andy. A conspiracy to bully someone usually isn't an isolated event, further qualifying this as bullying.

Scenario 6: SOMETHING ELSE. Sean is angry and expresses his anger through violence, but this is the first incident, and the participants seem to be equally matched. While this is aggressive behavior, it isn't bullying.

Scenario 7: BULLYING. It is clear that Alex has more social power than Jenny. He is also probably richer than she is and can afford nicer clothes. While Alex claims he didn't mean to hurt her feelings, he is either lying or lacks basic social skills. Saying you're "just kidding" doesn't take away the hurt of taunts and jeers.

From *Story Solutions: Using Tales to Build Character and Teach Bully Prevention, Drug Prevention, and Conflict Resolution*
by Kevin Strauss. Santa Barbara, CA: Libraries Unlimited. Copyright © 2011.

Activity 4-8: Bullying Prevention Values Barometer

Objective: Students will decide if they agree, disagree, or are uncertain about statements relating to bullying at school.

Skills: Kindness, Problem Solving

Safe School Rules: 1.) We will tell adults at home and at school when we see bullies trying to hurt others. 3.) It is our job to help and protect all of our classmates when bullies try to hurt them.

Grade Level: 6–8

Materials: lesson plan, "Strongly Agree" and "Strongly Disagree" signs

Activity

1. Put a large sign that says "Strongly Agree" on one side of the room and one that says "Strongly Disagree" on the other side. Ask children to stand on the line between the signs in response to statements that you will read. Explain that there are no "right" or "wrong" answers, but students should think about the reasons for their answers and may be asked to explain their answers.

2. Discuss student responses. Ask students to defend their positions on the "values barometer." Emphasize that there were no "right" or "wrong" answers in this activity; you are just exploring people's opinions and values. If students aren't sure why they think or believe a certain thing, ask them to do research, using information in either this book or books listed in the "Additional Readings" section on pages 89–91, to gather factual information about bullying.

Evaluation

Ask students to write a half-page reflection paper in which they describe something that surprised them about their answers in this activity.

From *Story Solutions: Using Tales to Build Character and Teach Bully Prevention, Drug Prevention, and Conflict Resolution* by Kevin Strauss. Santa Barbara, CA: Libraries Unlimited. Copyright © 2011.

The Bully Prevention Values Barometer Questions

Begin each statement with "I think that . . . "

1. Some students deserve to be bullied because of how they act or dress.

2. It is okay for you to "bully" a "bully" to protect other students from his or her behavior.

3. I have never seen or heard bullying in my school.

4. It is okay to pick on someone if you say, "just kidding" at the very end.

5. It's not "bullying" if you don't hit or physically harm someone.

6. Words can't really hurt people.

7. Excluding someone or not talking to him or her is a social choice, not bullying.

8. Rumors are just words; they don't really hurt anyone.

9. Bullying is a normal part of growing up.

10. The best way to stop a bully is to beat him or her up.

11. If you can't protect yourself from a bully, then you deserve what happens to you.

12. Bullying isn't a problem in our school.

13. I see bullying every day at our school.

14. Bullies are mostly loners who have low self-esteem and don't have many friends.

15. If you "ignore a bully," he or she will leave you alone.

16. Bystanders have a moral obligation to tell a person to stop bullying behavior.

17. Bystanders have a moral obligation to report any bullying behavior that they see to a teacher, principal, their parents, or another responsible adult.

18. Reporting bullying behavior to an adult is a form of "tattling."

19. If someone is being bullied and that person doesn't want to report the bullying, it is okay for him or her to keep it a secret.

20. Some people deserve to be picked on because of how they look or act at school.

From Story Solutions: Using Tales to Build Character and Teach Bully Prevention, Drug Prevention, and Conflict Resolution by Kevin Strauss. Santa Barbara, CA: Libraries Unlimited. Copyright © 2011.

Activity 4-9: Putdown Stoppers

Objective: Students will be able to identify harmful "bully speech" and develop assertive ways to respond to people who use that language.

Skills: Problem Solving, Self-Control

Safe School Rule: 3.) It is our job to help and protect all of our classmates when bullies try to hurt them.

Grade Level: 4–8

Materials: none

Role-playing Activity

1. As a class, brainstorm a list of putdowns and verbal abuse that students hear (or say) at your school. Write them on the board. Common putdowns include "you're fat," "you're ugly," "you're dumb," "you're so gay" (especially used against boys), "nobody likes you," "what a loser," "what a geek." Also list the four "Putdown Blockers" from no. 2 on the board.

2. Pair up the students. Have them stand and face each other with one student facing the front of the room (Student A) and one facing the back of the room (Student B). Student A uses a putdown from the class list. Student B takes a deep breath, smiles, and uses one of four responses to block the putdown:

    1. "What do you mean by that?"

    2. "Ha! That's funny."

    3. "*I* don't think so."

    4. "Maybe" (with a shoulder shrug).

    Student A stays on the attack with more putdowns, and Student B uses the "broken record" technique to keep repeating the same response until Student A runs out of putdowns. Switch places and jobs.

Discussion

1. Which defensive techniques were the easiest for you?

2. When you were playing the "target," did you get the sense that these techniques would protect you from a verbal bully attack? Why or why not?

3. When you were playing the "bully," could you figure out a way to get around the defensive technique? If so, what was it?

4. Do you get the sense that these techniques would work in real life? Why or why not?

From *Story Solutions: Using Tales to Build Character and Teach Bully Prevention, Drug Prevention, and Conflict Resolution* by Kevin Strauss. Santa Barbara, CA: Libraries Unlimited. Copyright © 2011.

Evaluation

1. Have participants write a one-page essay describing a time when someone used verbal bulling against them. What happened? Now that you know about verbal defenses, what would you do differently next time? (In the unlikely event that a child can't think of a time when someone called him or her a mean name, that child may describe an incident he or she saw happen to someone else.)

2. Draw a four-box poster comic strip that shows someone using verbal bullying in the first box. In the second box, the target uses an assertive verbal response. In the third box, show the bully walking away. In the fourth box, show the student reporting the bullying behavior to the principal.

Activity 4-10: Just the Facts, Ma'am

Objective: Students will learn how to record and report bullying behavior to a responsible adult by watching a series of role-plays and writing a report of what they saw.

Skills: Problem Solving

Safe School Rule: 2.) We will tell adults at home and at school when we see bullies trying to hurt others.

Grade Level: 4–8

Materials: paper and pencil for each child, "Just the Facts, Ma'am" scenario worksheet (p. 82) for each group

Activity

Reporting bulling behavior is a skill, and like any other skill (driving a car, serving a volleyball, hitting a baseball pitch, or painting a picture), children need to practice before they can become proficient at it.

1. Ask two volunteers to role-play one of the situations on the scenario worksheet. Ask participants to first determine if the incident is a case of bullying (repeated physical, verbal, or social abuse intended to scare, control, or ridicule someone who is smaller, younger, or less popular than the bully), or it is just a "conflict" between two people with equal power. If you have the option, have the children role-play the situation at various locations (in the hall, on the playground, in the lunchroom) and have the rest watch as the audience. (If you have the technology available, videorecord the role-plays.) Then have participants return to the classroom to write their reports.

2. Demonstrate how to use the four Ws format that journalists use to write a news story:
Who: Who was involved in the event? (bully, target, and bystanders)

What: What happened? (e.g., Jane shoved Brianne into the lockers and hit her.)

When: When (time of day) did it happen? (e.g., after lunch, at recess yesterday)

Where: Where did it happen? (e.g., in the hallway by the art room; by the swing set)

3. As a group, compile a list of what happened in each scenario. Then watch the videorecording (if you made one) to see if there are any details that you missed.

4. Discuss why it is important for students to use descriptive language (I saw . . . , I heard . . .) rather than evaluative language (Jane was being mean . . .) in their reports. Educators can use descriptive language to determine the facts in a case. They can't use evaluative language, because two people might evaluate the same situation in different ways. Let children know that when investigating an incident, teachers talk with several children. A story is more believable if several people report it the same way. A bully and his or her friends might claim that one thing happened. But if eight bystanders tell a different story, then the adult is more likely to believe the bystanders. The problem is that bystanders don't always want to report what they saw (out of fear of bullying retribution or being seen as a "tattletale").

It is also possible that a group of "bully friends" might conspire to lie to a teacher. So teachers need to look at the "big picture" when evaluating a situation.

Evaluation

Have participants turn in their scenario reports. Did they follow the format? Did students use descriptive language rather than evaluative language?

Bullying Reporting Forms

Bullying Reporting Form

Describe what you saw using the "Who, What, When, Where" reporter technique. Do not "interpret" what you saw by labeling it as "being mean" or "being a bully." That's for someone in authority to determine. Use the back of the form if needed.

Written by (You may leave this blank.): _____

Who was involved? _____

What happened? _____

When did it happen? _____

Where did it happen? _____

Bullying Reporting Form

Describe what you saw using the "Who, What, When, Where" reporter technique. Do not "interpret" what you saw by labeling it as "being mean" or "being a bully." That's for someone in authority to determine. Use the back of the form if needed.

Written by (You may leave this blank.): _____

Who was involved? _____

What happened? _____

When did it happen? _____

Where did it happen? _____

Just the Facts Ma'am Role-play Scenarios Worksheet

Scenario 1: Roger and Tony are schoolmates who get into an argument because Roger thinks that Tony tripped him on purpose. Tony claims that it was an accident, and if Roger looker where he was going, there wouldn't be a problem. The boys start shoving and a fight breaks out. Jessica, Tim, and Amy are in the hallway at the time. None of them intervenes.

Scenario 2: Jessica and Jamaica used to be friends. But now Jessica makes "oinking" noises whenever Jamaica is talking. They are usually so quiet that the teacher doesn't hear, but they make Jessica's friends (Amelia, Jane, and Samantha) giggle. Other classmates (Sylvia, Erin) don't laugh at the animal noises. They just look at their desks. Jessica has been doing this for a couple of weeks, and Jamaica is trying to ignore it, but that isn't working.

Scenario 3: Samantha tells all of her friends not to talk with Nadia anymore because Nadia is so "stuck up." Jessica talks with Nadia. Samantha scowls at Jessica, and then Samantha and her friend Tracy don't respond when Jessica tries to talk with them.

Scenario 4: Eric convinces Steven to trip "that geek Andy" when he comes walking down the hall. When Steven trips Andy, Eric laughs, "Have a nice trip? See ya next fall. Ha, Ha, Ha." Eric's friends, Tom and Jerry, laugh at Andy as well. Jessica and Tammy scowl at the bullying, but don't say anything to Eric or Steven. Jessica helps Andy up and helps him pick up his books.

Scenario 5: Sean is so angry that his ex-girlfriend Tammy is going out with Roger that he shoves Roger when he sees him in the hall. A scuffle ensues and fists fly. They both end up in detention. Dave and Bill see the fight. Dave tells the boys to "chill out, dude," but it does no good.

Scenario 6: Popular boy Alex yells down the hall, "Hey Jenny, where'd you get those clothes, a garage sale? Ha, Ha, Ha." Jenny looks at the floor. When Andrea tells Alex to "cut it out," Alex claims he was "just kidding." "It's no big deal, she knows I'm just kidding, right Jenny?" says Alex. Jenny just puts her head down and walks away. Andrea follows Jenny and tells her that Alex is a jerk, and she doesn't deserve to be picked on like that.

Activity 4-11: Getting Advice

Objective: Students will learn how find people who can give them good advice.

Skills: Problem Solving

Safe School Rule: 2.) We will tell adults at home and at school when we see bullies trying to hurt others.

Grade Level: 4–6

Materials: paper and pencil for each student

> Don't be afraid to ask questions. Don't be afraid to ask for help when you need it. I do that every day. Asking for help isn't a sign of weakness; it's a sign of strength. It shows that you have the courage to admit when you don't know something, and to learn something new. So find an adult you trust—a parent, grandparent or teacher; a coach or counselor—and ask them to help you stay on track to meet your goals.—President Barack Obama in an address to Wakefield High School in Arlington, Virginia, on the first day of school, September 8, 2009 (Obama 2009)

Activity

1. Children often don't know whom to turn to when they need help. Children who are the targets of bullying behavior often feel embarrassed, making them even less likely to ask for help or advice. As a class, brainstorm what makes an adult "safe" to talk to. Parents and other close relatives are often good people to talk to because they love their children and want them to succeed. Other adults who have jobs that include helping children, like teachers, clergy, medical staff, and police officers, can be a good choice as well. Who else could provide a youngster with good advice?

2. Have children make a list of adults in their own lives that they could ask for advice. Are there some things you would talk about with a parent, but not with a teacher? Are there some questions that you would rather ask a doctor or religious leader?

3. Have children make an anonymous (no names on it) list of questions that they might want to ask their teacher on topics like "bullying," "setting goals," or "making friends."

Evaluation

Review the papers that students turn in. Collect the question pages and use them to plan future classroom life skills lessons.

Activity 4-12: Safe School Role-plays

Objective: Students will practice defensive techniques to protect themselves and their classmates from physical, verbal, or social bullying attacks.
Skills: Problem Solving, Kindness
Safe School Rules: 1.) We will tell adults at home and at school when we see bullies trying to hurt others. 3.) It is our job to help and protect all of our classmates when bullies try to hurt them.
Grade Level: 4–8
Materials: copies of "Safe School" role-play sheets for each pair of participants

Roleplaying Activity

1. Though it may seem silly to "play a role" in this activity, give it a try. Practicing how to deal with a bully makes it easier to handle a bully in real life. Practice with a friend, not with a bully. Find a partner. Decide who will be Person A (the bully) and who will be Person B (the target).

2. After two minutes, switch roles.

Discussion

1. Which defensive techniques were the easiest for you?

2. When you were playing the "target," did you get the sense that these techniques would protect you from a bully attack? Why or why not?

3. When you were playing the "bully," could you figure out a way to get around the defensive technique? If so, what was it?

4. Do you get the sense that these techniques would work in real life? Why or why not?

5. Why do you think we had you role-play the process of reporting bullying to the principal? (Because that is one of the most important ways you can get help stopping bullying at your school. It is also the one step that most students don't take.)

Evaluation

Have students write a one-page paper on one of the questions above.

Role-play 1: Physical Bullying (Breath, Smile, Shoulder Turn, Broken Record)

Note: An educator or volunteer plays the principal for the whole class.

Person A: (Bully walks up to target and gets right in his face.) Hey, little wimp, what are you doing on my sidewalk?

Person B: (Takes a deep breath, smiles, turns sideways to bully.) What do you mean by that?

Person A: This is my sidewalk, and I get to say who walks on it. (May try to get back in front of the target.)

Person B: What do you mean by that? (Turns sideways to the bully again.)

Person A: I mean that I'm going to punch your lights out you little wimp. (Tries to shove target and knock his books out of his hands.)

Person B: (Has a choice, either continue asking the question, or just turn and walk away and tell an adult.)

(Later, in the school office.)

Person B: Ms. Johnson [principal or school counselor], I ran into Billy outside of the school building, and he threatened to beat me up for walking on "his" sidewalk. Then he shoved me and knocked my books out of my hands. Is there something you could do to get him to stop picking on me? Here's a written report of what happened for your files.

Principal: Thank you.

Role-play 2: Verbal Bullying (Breath, Smile, Shoulder Turn, Broken Record, Walk Away)

Note: A teacher or volunteer plays the principal for the whole class.

Student A: (Bully walks up to target and gets right in her face.) Hey jerk, where do you get your clothes, the garbage dump? Ha, Ha, Ha!

Student B: (Takes a deep breath, smiles, turns sideways to bully, shrugs shoulders.) Maybe.

Student A: You've got the crappiest clothes in school. (May try to get back in front of the target.)

Student B: Maybe. (Shrugs shoulders. Turns sideways to the bully again.)

Student A: I mean that no one has clothes as ugly as yours.

Student B: Maybe. (Turns sideways to the bully again.)

(Action continues until the bully runs out of things to say or the target walks away.)

(Later, in the school office.)

Student B: Ms. Johnson [principal or school counselor], I ran into Roger in the hall, and he was making fun of me about the clothes I wear. I realize that I don't have the most expensive clothes, but I don't like it when he makes fun of me all the time. Is there something you could do to get him to stop? Here's a written report of what happened for your files.

Principal: Thank you.

Role-play 3: Group Bullying (Breath, Smile, Shoulder Turn, Broken Record, Walk Away)

Note: Students A, B, and C are bullies; Student D is the target. A teacher or volunteer plays the principal for the whole class.

Student A: (Bully walks up to target and gets right in his face.)
              Hey, look, it's Billy the *Fairy*! (Shoves Billy.)

Students B and C: Ha, Ha, Ha!

Student D: (Takes a deep breath, smiles, turns sideways to the main
              bully, shrugs shoulders.) *I* don't think so.

Student A: (Knocks Billy's books out of his hands.) Take that, ya homo!

Student D: (Takes a deep breath, smiles, turns sideways to the main
              bully, picks up books.) *I* don't think so.

Student A: You're probably such a homo mamma's boy that you're going to
              run home crying and tell your mamma that we were picking on
              you, aren't you?

Student D: I don't think so. (Turns and walks away.)

Student A: Gayboy is running away!

Student D: I don't think so. (Keeps walking.)

(Later, in the school office.)

Student D: Ms. Johnson [principal or school counselor], I ran into
              Roger, Bill, and Tony in the hall, and they called me "a
              homo" and knocked my books out of my hands. I don't like it
              when Roger makes fun of me all the time. Is there something
              you could do to get him to stop? Here's a written report of what
              happened for your files.

Principal: Thank you.

Role-play 4: Social Bullying (Breath, Smile, Asking Questions, Fogging)

Student A: (Bully walks up to target and gets right in her face.) If you want to be our friend, I don't want to see you to talking to Jane anymore.

Student B: (Takes a deep breath, smiles.) What do you mean by that?

Student A: I mean that you've got to choose between us (the cool kids) and Jane. We don't like her, and you can't be her friend and our friend.

Student B: Really? That's too bad. I like you and I like Jane, but I really don't like when someone tries to tell me who I can be friends with. Are you trying to tell me who I can be friends with?

Student A: Yeah. You can't be friends with just *anyone* if you want to be part of our group.

Student B: That's too bad. (Fogging.)

Student A: So who are you going to choose, us or Jane?

Student B: (Takes a deep breath, smiles.) I don't think I have to choose.

Student A: (Agitated.) Of course you have to choose, or we'll choose for you!

Student B: That's too bad. (Smiles, takes a deep breath, and walks away.)

(Later, in the school office.)

Student B: Ms. Johnson [principal or school counselor], I was just talking with Martha, and she tried to tell me that I couldn't be friends with her and her friends if I was also friends with Jane. I just thought you should know. Here's a written report for your files.

Principal: Thank you.

Summary

Just as you can't learn to swim or ride a bike by reading about it, you can't learn how to deal with bullies by just hearing a lecture or watching a video. The activities in this chapter give adults the opportunity to help children and teens develop the social, emotional, and verbal skills that they will need to keep themselves and their classmates safe from bullies. They will also help a school and community to create a climate that supports students and stops bullies at every turn. For more information about dealing with bullying, check out the "Additional Readings" section below.

Additional Readings

Fiction Books (Grades 4–8)

Blume, Judy. *Blubber.* Waterville, ME: Thorndike Press, 2005. 160pp. $6.50pa. ISBN 0440407079pa.

It's easy to go along with the crowd at school, and that's exactly what Jill does when her fifth-grade classmates start bullying an overweight girl named Linda. But Jill doesn't realize how much teasing hurts until she is the bully's next target.

Bosch, Carl W. *Bully on the Bus.* Seattle, WA: Parenting Press, 1988. 58pp. $7.95pa. ISBN 0943990424pa.

This interactive "choose your path" book gives readers a chance to help Jack decide how to deal with a bully on his bus. Should Jack ignore the bully? Should he ask for help from an adult, or should he fight back? Each option comes with its own advantages and disadvantages, and readers get to see the results of Jack's actions and learn from those results.

Casanova, Mary. *Chrissa.* Middleton, WI: American Girl Publishing, 2009. 132pp. $6.95 pa. ISBN 1593695667pa.

Being the new kid in school is never easy. But when Chrissa arrives in fourth grade in the middle of the school year, some of the other girls give her a very cold reception. But they don't stop there. Teasing turns to bullying, and Chrissa needs to find a way to stand up for herself and speak up to the bullies.

Clements, Andrew. *Jake Drake, Bully Buster.* New York: Aladdin Paperbacks, 2007. 67pp. $3.99pa. ISBN 1416939334pa.

Jake Drake knew that at school, he was on his own. He didn't have an older brother, so he'll have to use his smarts to get by, especially when class bully Link Baxter arrives and the teacher assigns Jake and Link as partners.

Langan, Paul. *The Bully.* New York: Scholastic, 2007. 208pp. $3.99pa. ISBN 0439865468pa.

There are a lot of new things in Darrell Mercer's life right now: a new home in California, a new school, and unfortunately, a new bully to deal with. After weeks of hoping things will get better by themselves, Darrell has a decision to make: fight or flight. Should he keep on running from the bully or take a stand?

Ludwig, Trudy. *Just Kidding.* Berkeley, CA: Tricycle Press, 2005. 32pp. $15.95. ISBN 1582461635.

Every day, D. J. gets a knot in his stomach. That's because a bully at school can't wait to "tease" him. Of course the bully says he's "just kidding" if anyone tells him to stop. But with the help of his family and a teacher, D. J. finds a way to stop that verbal bully.

Ludwig, Trudy. *My Secret Bully.* Berkeley, CA: Tricycle Press, 2005. 32pp. $15.95pa. ISBN 1582461597pa.

Monica hated going to school. She knew that Katie would be waiting there. Monica knew going to school would mean listening to the names Katie would call her and that Katie had already told the girls in the school not to be Monica's friend. But this day was different. Monica talks with her mother, and together they plan how to deal with Katie's bullying.

Nagda, Ann Whitehead. *Tarantula Power!* New York: Holiday House, 2007. 93pp. $15.95. ISBN 0823419916.
Richard knew there could be trouble when he got assigned to work with the class bully on a project. But as Richard got to know the bully, he learned how to keep him from picking on younger children at school. All it took was his mysterious "tarantula power" and the help of his classmates and teacher.

Philbrick, W. Rodman. *Freak the Mighty.* New York: Scholastic Paperbacks, 2001. 176pp. $6.99pa. ISBN 0439286069pa.
Max just didn't fit in. He was big, so nobody bothered him much, but everyone called him dumb, stupid, and slow. But then Max met Freak. Freak was everything that Max wasn't. Freak was really smart, but he walked with crutches and lots of kids picked on him. But then Max and Freak became friends. Working together, they became "Freak the Mighty."

Pixley, Marcella Fleischman. *Freak.* New York: Farrar, Straus & Giroux, 2007. 144pp. $16.00. ISBN 0374324530.
You'd think that liking poetry and being smart in school would be a good thing, but not for middle schooler Miriam. Popular kids in school brand her a "freak." They make fun of her, until she stands up for herself.

Roy, James. *Max Quigley: Technically Not a Bully.* Boston: Houghton Mifflin Harcourt, 2009. 202pp. $12.95pa. ISBN 0547152639pa.
Turnabout is fair play when Max, after picking on a "geeky" classmate, Triffin Nordstrom, discovers that the target of his prank is the student who will now be his tutor. It's all part of a parental plan to help Max with his schoolwork and Triffin with his social skills. Does it work? You decide.

Shreve, Susan Richards. *Joshua T. Bates Takes Charge.* New York: Yearling (Random House), 1995. 102pp. $5.50pa. ISBN 0679870393pa.
Joshua used to be a target. A gang of kids bullied him when he got held back in third grade. But now the bullies have a new target, a new kid in school. Joshua wants to help, because he remembers what it was like to be bullied. If he helps the new kid, will the bullies set their sights on him again?

Shreve, Susan Richards. *Joshua T. Bates in Trouble Again.* New York: Alfred A. Knopf, 1997. 128pp. $8.50pa. ISBN 0-679-88520-xpa.
When Joshua got moved up to fourth grade in the middle of the year, he thought that his troubles were over. Unfortunately, he's in a class with Tommy, and Tommy wants to make everyone's life difficult in fourth grade, no matter where they come from.

Sinykin, Shery Cooper. *The Shorty Society.* New York: Viking, 1994. 144pp. $12.00pa. ISBN 0140367241pa.
After repeated bullying from bigger students, three seventh graders decide to form "The Shorty Society" and get back at their tormentors. The plan works. The only problem is, will they become bullies themselves?

Tacang, Brian. *Bully-Be-Gone.* New York: HarperCollins, 2006. 224pp. $16.99. ISBN 0060739118pa.
Kid inventor Millicent Madding sets to work on the "Bully-be-gone" bully repellant. The only problem is that instead of repelling bullies, it seems to attract them! Talk about product safety warnings! Millicent doesn't have long to get the formula right, stop the school bullies in their tracks, and save her friends.

Zeier, Joan T. *Stick Boy.* New York: Atheneum, 1993. 135pp. ISBN 0689318359pa.
Eric doesn't like to stick out. But that is just what happens when he grows seven inches during sixth grade. Now he can't help but stick out, especially to the class bully. When Eric moves to a new school, things don't get any easier. For that to happen, he has to change how he approaches the world.

Nonfiction Books (Grades 4–8)

Frankel, Fred. *Good Friends Are Hard to Find.* Glendale, CA: Perspective Publishing, 1996. 242pp. ISBN 096220-367Xpa.

> Making and having good friends can help a child avoid or better deal with problems like bullying and teasing. This book gives kids a step-by-step approach for making new friends and solving problems with current friends.

Hipp, Earl. *Fighting Invisible Tigers.* Minneapolis, MN: Free Spirit Publishing, 1995. 154pp. $12.95pa. ISBN 0-915793-80-6pa.

> Children deal with stress every day. If stress boils over, it can lead to conflicts, violence, and bullying. This book helps children understand what stress it and how to get control of their emotions and their lives.

Romain, Trevor. *Bullies Are a Pain in the Brain.* Minneapolis, MN: Free Spirit Publishing, 1997. 106pp. $8.95pa. ISBN 1-57542-023-6pa.

> An easy-to-read guide that helps children identify if they have a bullying problem and gives them simple, safe, and assertive ways of dealing with bullies. The "Do's and Don'ts for Dealing with Bullies" section is especially good at providing children with real-world responses to bullying situations.

Romain, Trevor. *Cliques, Phonies, & Other Baloney.* Minneapolis, MN: Free Spirit Publishing, 1998. 129pp. $8.95pa. ISBN 978-1-57542-045-5pa.

> In this easy-to-read book, Romain uses humor and down-to-earth good advice to show children what to do about social bullying and cliques at school. He also gives children good advice about how to find and make good friends and steer clear of situations that might put them at risk for social or emotional bullying.

Adult Resources

Beane, Allan L. *The Bully Free Classroom.* Minneapolis, MN: Free Spirit Publishing, 2005. 168pp. $24.95pa. ISBN 1-57542-194-1pa.

> A good resource for classroom teachers who are looking to add regular bullying prevention and conflict resolution activities into their classroom curriculum. Includes classroom reproducible activity sheets and an extensive bibliography.

Coloroso, Barbara. *The Bully, the Bullied, and the Bystander: From Preschool to High School—How Parents and Teachers Can Help Break the Cycle of Violence.* New York: HarperCollins, 2003. 218pp. $13.95pa. ISBN 0-06-001430-Xpa.

> If I had to recommend just one adult book about school bullying, this would be it. Coloroso covers the issue with real-life examples and just enough research to make her point, but not so much that the reader gets lost in the studies.

Olweus, Dan. *Bullying at School: What We Know and What We Can Do.* Cambridge, MA: Blackwell Publishers, Inc., 1993. 140pp. $28.95pa. ISBN 0631-19241-7pa.

> This is one of the seminal works in the modern bullying prevention movement. Many of the bullying prevention programs in the United States use at least some of the techniques Olweus describes in this book. It describes what elements a schoolwide bullying prevention programs needs to succeed.

Strauss, Kevin. *Building Heroes/Blocking Bullies: The Teacher and Parent Guide to Simple, Repeatable, Assertive Techniques That Anyone Can Use to Stay Safe and Stop Bullies.* Eden Prairie, MN: Trumpeter Press, 2010. 204pp. $25.00pa. ISBN 978-0-9814667-4-3pa.

> This book focuses on teaching children and teens the skills they need to be heroes in school and in the community. It takes a "bottom-up" approach to bullying prevention, training students how to deal with the bullying problem so that they will be able to stay safe while adults work to address community-wide issues and to implement a comprehensive solution to bullying problems at their school.

References

Coloroso, Barbara. 2003. *The Bully, the Bullied, and the Bystander: From Preschool to High School—How Parents and Teachers Can Help Break the Cycle of Violence.* New York: HarperCollins. 218pp. $13.95pa. ISBN 0-06-001430-Xpa.

Obama, Barack. 2009. *Prepared Remarks of President Barack Obama: Back to School Event.* Washington, DC: GPO. Available at http://www.whitehouse.gov/mediaresources/PreparedSchoolRemarks/. Accessed November 11, 2009.

Ross, Julia. 2002. *The Mood Cure: The 4-Step Program to Take Charge of Your Emotions Today.* New York: Penguin Books. 386pp. $16.00pa. ISBN 978-0-14-200364-0pa.

Strauss, Kevin. 2010. *Building Heroes/Blocking Bullies: The Teacher and Parent Guide to Simple, Repeatable, Assertive Techniques That Anyone Can Use to Stay Safe and Stop Bullies.* Eden Prairie, MN: Trumpeter Press. 204pp. $25.00pa. ISBN 978-0-9814667-4-3pa.

U.S. Department of Health & Human Services. 2008. *Myths About Bullying.* Washington, DC: GPO. Available at http://stopbullyingnow.hrsa.gov/HHS_PSA/pdfs/Fact_sheet_Myths_32.pdf. Accessed November 11, 2009.

U.S. Department of Health & Human Services. 2009. *Steps to Address Bullying at Your School: Tips for School Administrators.* Washington, DC: GPO. Available at http://stopbullyingnow.hrsa.gov/adults/tip-sheets/tip-sheet-15.aspx. Accessed November 11, 2009.

Chapter 5

Alcohol, Tobacco, and Other Drugs Suck

Unbeknownst to most people, there is an ad war going on in our schools and communities. Its operatives are sneaky, because their actions are illegal. They are attempting to suck the money, time, and health of our children by selling them alcohol, tobacco, and other drugs. While the operatives really only want our children's money, they usually take their time and health as well. The real reason that children and teens are attracted to alcohol, tobacco, and other drugs is that pushers are better at their jobs than we are at ours. This chapter can help level the playing field and give you the tools to keep children and teens away from these dangerous, mood-altering chemicals.

Definitions

- **Drug** (dr-UG). *noun.* Any chemical substance that, in small amounts, has a significant impact on mind or body functions. This includes medical and prescription chemicals like antibiotics and aspirin, as well as recreational chemicals like alcohol, tobacco, and marijuana.

- **Drug Abuse** (dr-UG ah-BUSE). *noun.* The use of a medical or recreational chemical substance in an unhealthy, harmful, or life-disrupting manner (Schwebel 1998).

- **Drug Dependence** (dr-UG de-PEND-ants). *noun.* A state of body and/or mind in which a person feels that he or she cannot stop consuming a particular chemical without suffering physical and/or mental pain (Schwebel 1998).

- **Recreational Drug** (REC-ree-ation-al dr-UG). *noun.* A chemical substance consumed for mood-altering or mind-altering entertainment purposes (e.g., caffeine, alcohol, tobacco, marijuana, methamphetamines).

How Big Is the Adolescent Drug Abuse Problem?

Before you can take action to resolve any social problem, you first need to know how big the problem is and where it is concentrated. Then you can develop coordinated strategies to address it. There is both good news and bad news in the drug ad war.

Good News/Bad News

The good news is that substance abuse is declining among adolescents. The bad news is that even lower levels of use pose a problem for communities, because adolescent users are much more likely to become teen and adult substance abusers.

According to the Partnership for a Drug-Free America (www.drugfee.org) in *The Partnership Attitude Tracking Study* (2008), alcohol use among seventh to twelfth graders in the previous thirty days fell from 46 percent in 1995 to 29 percent in 2008. Tobacco use fell from 42 percent in 1998 to 19 percent in 2008. The use of other illegal (for teens) drugs shows similar declines. But these numbers still mean that almost one in three adolescents has consumed alcohol in the previous month and almost one if five has used tobacco products like cigarettes. What's more, the numbers look even worse if you consider how many teens have ever tried alcohol, tobacco, or other drugs.

According to the Robert Wood Johnson Foundation in *Substance Abuse: the Nation's Number One Health Problem*, by eighth grade, one in two adolescents (52 percent) has consumed alcohol and almost one in two (41 percent) has smoked cigarettes. One in five (20 percent) has used marijuana. By twelfth grade, four out of five (80 percent) have tried alcohol, almost two out of three (63 percent) have smoked cigarettes, and almost one out of two (49 percent) has used marijuana (Robert Wood Johnson Foundation 2001).

Tobacco and Alcohol, the Real "Gateway" Drugs

More than 80 percent of adult smokers began smoking before age eighteen, the legal age to start smoking. The average age to begin smoking is 12.5, just after entering middle school. And while smoking brings with it a host of health and addiction problems, that isn't the worst part. Smoking also seems to put young people at increased risk for other alcohol and drug use behaviors as well. Those who smoke are sixteen times more likely to drink alcohol heavily (five or more drinks on each of five or more days in the past month), and ten times more likely to use other illegal drugs, than their peers (Robert Wood Johnson Foundation 2001).

Alcohol remains the number one drug of choice among both adolescents and adults, and it is the most widely available drug. Rates of alcohol dependency are significantly higher than for other illicit drugs. Alcohol kills 6.5 times more youth than all other illicit drugs combined. One out of two high school seniors (50 percent) reports drinking alcohol in the previous thirty days and 32 percent report being drunk in the previous thirty days (Robert Wood Johnson Foundation 2001).

Access is a key ingredient to substance abuse, so it is obvious why the "easy to obtain" drugs like alcohol and tobacco have the highest use among adolescents. Almost two out of three students who use alcohol (65 percent) report that they get the alcohol from their own homes or the homes of friends (Robert Wood Johnson Foundation 2001). Unfortunately, many drug prevention programs in the United States focus on "harder drugs" like marijuana and methamphetamines, ignoring the real (and adult-legal) gateway drugs like alcohol and tobacco in our communities.

Unique Risks for Adolescents

Tobacco companies have known for decades that it is far easier to get children "hooked" on tobacco than it is to hook adults. Until recently, tobacco companies engaged in practices that specifically targeted illegal teen consumers with the use of flavored cigarettes, cartoons in marketing materials, logo product giveaways, and other, now illegal, techniques.

The reason that adolescents are so susceptible to dependence and addiction to mind- and mood-altering substances is that teen brains are still developing, which means it is chemically and physically more difficult for teens to resist drug addiction when using mood-altering chemicals (Newsam 1992). Those same chemicals (alcohol, tobacco, caffeine) seem to pose a lower addiction risk to adult users. In some cases, alcohol/tobacco/ other drug use damages teen brain development, making a teen drug user even more susceptible to drug addiction in the future.

According to The Center for Applied Research in Education, it can take an adult user five to ten years to develop dependency (addiction) to a mood-altering drug. By comparison, it can take an adolescent (ages thirteen to seventeen) five to ten *months* to develop dependency, and preadolescents (ages ten to twelve) only five to ten *weeks* to develop alcohol/tobacco/other drug dependency (Newsam 1992).

According to the Partnership for a Drug-Free America, nine out of ten (90 percent) of those with substance abuse and addiction problems now started abusing those chemicals as a teenager. In contrast, if a person reaches age twenty without abusing those recreational chemicals, it is "highly unlikely" that he or she will develop a problem later in life (*Parents: You Matter!* 2009). According to one study, about two in five (40 percent) of those who start drinking before age fifteen develop alcohol dependence (addiction), compared to only one in ten (10 percent) of those who start drinking alcohol after age twenty (Robert Wood Johnson Foundation 2001).

Clearly, recreational drugs pose a much larger risk to developing child and teen brains than they do to adult brains. That's why it is especially important to keep children and teens from experimenting with these dangerous chemicals.

What Do Drugs Do?

Alcohol, tobacco, and other mood-altering drugs all make you feel good. That's why people take them, to "relax," "have fun," "feel energized," "chill out," or any of a hundred other euphemisms. These mood-altering substances give people an easy way to feel good. They also trigger the release of dopamine, the "feel-good" chemical in our brains.

Other activities, like exercise, romantic activities, dancing at a party, playing a favorite game, competing in sports, and eating a favorite food, also release dopamine, but mood-altering drugs release a lot more dopamine than these "natural" highs. The problem is that when your brain gets flooded with dopamine, it naturally creates brain roadblocks that reduce some of this artificial "good feeling" and help the brain return to its natural state. This means that your body develops "tolerance" of alcohol, tobacco, and other mood-altering drugs, and eventually you need to take more and more of the substance to get the same good feeling. Unfortunately, some of these mood-altering chemicals are much more dangerous in larger quantities, even leading to heart attacks or strokes (Kuhn et al. 2002).

Drug Categories

While levels of addiction to a particular chemical substance can vary dramatically depending on age at first use, genetics, family history, medical history, and other factors, there are some chemical substances that are, on average, more addictive than others. Also keep in mind that the adolescent developing brain is far more prone to addiction than the adult brain (Newsam 1992).

Based on researcher data, the chemicals are categorized below from "mildly addictive," meaning it may take heavy use or use over a long period of time to develop dependence, to "highly addictive," which indicates it may only take low-level use or a short period of time to develop dependence. These ratings are generalized. They do not imply that chemicals that are rated as "mildly addictive" are "safer" than "highly addictive" chemicals. It just might be easier for some people to stop using "mildly addictive" substances, or stopping use, on average, may have fewer side effects for many people.

Depressants: slow you down, calm you down, can put you in a coma from large doses

Alcohol (addictive)

Tranquilizers/Sleeping Pills (highly addictive)

Cough/Cold Medicine (mildly addictive)

Stimulants: speed you up, make you feel excited, keep you awake, can cause a seizure from large doses

Caffeine (mildly addictive)

Tobacco (highly addictive)

Methamphetamine (highly addictive)

Ritalin® ADHD Prescription Medication (addictive)

Extasy (addictive)

Hallucinogens: change your "state of mind"; may change how you see, hear, or feel the world

LSD (addictive)

Opiates: cause relaxation and euphoria

Marijuana (addictive)

Heroin (highly addictive)

Body Builders: help you build muscle and shrink your brain (and other body parts)

Anabolic Steroids (mildly addictive)

Sources: Robert Wood Johnson Foundation (2001); Hilts (1994); Kuhn et al. (2002)

Use, Abuse, and Addiction

There is a fair amount of debate about what constitutes substance use versus abuse. One way to think about it is to compare it to consumption that you already do. Most children (and many adults) like cookies. Because cookies are a treat, most families limit the amount of this treat or "junk food" that a child can eat. For instance, in our family, two cookies is an appropriate dessert "use" of chocolate chip cookies. But what if I really like cookies? Could I have another one? How about eight more? What if I ate so many that I got sick and threw up? What if I wanted to eat those same ten cookies before dinner, rather than as a dessert? It seems clear that eating so many cookies that you feel sick is a form of "cookie abuse." The same could be true of eating cookies at an inappropriate time, like right before dinner.

So "abuse" is when you use any product in a way that is dangerous to yourself or to someone else. For example, as an adult, I can legally drink beer. One or two beers with dinner could be termed reasonable "alcohol use." But drinking twelve beers alone in my bedroom, or drinking twelve beers and then driving a car, would both be cases of abuse, because both of those activities could make me sick, and driving while drunk could endanger others as well.

Addiction is the physical and psychological state in which a person thinks and feels that he or she needs a particular recreational chemical in order to function or survive. Though it is true that drug addicts can probably survive without their recreational chemical of choice, the absence of that chemical can cause actual physical and psychological pain, anxiety, nervousness, and other negative effects that make functioning difficult. In some cases, when someone is addicted, the chemical use has actually changed the functioning of his or her brain. Many experts classify addiction as a physical and/or mental disease. Addicts usually need medical help to stop using the chemical and may be at risk for a relapse into recreational chemical abuse for the rest of their lives (Kuhn 2002; Schwebel 1998).

What Skills Do Youth Need to Avoid Using Alcohol, Tobacco, and Other Drugs?

Researchers have identified several skills that help young people resist and avoid alcohol, tobacco, and other drugs. By teaching children drug resistance and avoidance skills, you are armoring them against these dangerous and life-changing substances. Numerous studies (Schwebel 1998; Solter 2006; Kuhn et al. 2002) have shown that children and teenagers use harmful substances for three main reasons:

1. To relieve boredom or to "have fun."

2. To relieve stress, anxiety, or depression.

3. To "fit in" with peers.

Any program that seeks to help students resist and avoid harmful or illegal substances needs to teach students the skills they need avoid boredom, stress, depression, and the pressure to "fit in." Those skills include the following:

- **Self-Control.** Children who have a positive sense of self and good control of their emotions are more likely to be able to deal with boredom and stress in healthy ways, so they won't feel a need to use mood-altering chemicals. They also have the ability to resist peer pressure to use recreational drugs.

- **Problem Solving.** Children who can take a problem apart in their heads and generate several options for dealing with it can much more effectively learn and practice the words and behaviors that help them resist peer pressure and avoid mood-altering chemicals. They also have the ability to come up with several ways to entertain themselves so they won't have to turn to recreational chemicals to have fun.

- **Kindness.** Children who care about others and have a lot of friends are less likely to feel a need to use mood-altering chemicals to "fit in." Kindness skills also help students to have positive relationships with their family members, who can provide factual information about the dangers of alcohol, tobacco, and other drugs.

- **Goal Setting.** Children who can set goals for the future and imagine themselves achieving their goals are usually too busy to "waste time" with mood-altering chemicals (or television and video games, for that matter). By the law of "opportunity cost," a child who is busy with sports, art projects, or volunteering simply doesn't have time to use harmful substances.

The stories and activities in chapters 6 and 7 are organized by the avoidance skills listed above, making it easy to choose stories and activities for your library or classroom.

Five Things Everyone Should Know About Alcohol, Tobacco, and Other Drugs

1. **Alcohol, Tobacco, and Other Drugs All Have the Potential to Be Addictive.** Mood-altering chemicals like those in alcohol, tobacco, and other drugs cause your brain to release large doses of "feel-good" dopamine chemicals. This is the "reward circuit" in our brains. This release of dopamine gives us that feel-good, intoxicated feeling (*Brain and Addiction* 2010). The problem is that we can become physically or mentally dependent on (addicted to) these good feelings. Whether or not a person will become addicted to a particular substance depends on a number of factors, including age at first use, genetics, and the substance itself. But there are no totally "safe" mood-altering chemicals. Statistically speaking, tobacco (nicotine) is one of the most addictive substances available. According to addiction medicine specialist Dr. Michael M. Miller, about 15 percent of regular alcohol users will develop an addiction to alcohol (alcoholism). In contrast, about 45 percent of those who smoke cigarettes on a regular basis will get addicted (Miller 2009). In short, there are no "safe drugs," no matter what people try to tell you. All recreational drugs carry risks, including short-term risks like lifelong addiction, memory problems, and lack of concentration and long-term risks like permanent brain damage or damage to lungs and other internal organs (Kittleson 2005).

2. **Recreational Drug Use Is Especially Dangerous for Teens and Children Because of How Adolescent Brains Develop.** The reason that adolescents are so susceptible to drug dependence and addiction is that teen brains are still developing, making it chemically and physically more difficult for teens to resist addiction when using mood-altering chemicals like alcohol, tobacco, and marijuana. According to the Center for Applied Research in Education, it can take an adult alcohol/tobacco/other drug user 5–10 years to develop dependency (addiction) on a mood-altering drug. By comparison, it can take an adolescent (ages 13–17) 5–10 *months* to develop dependency and preadolescents (ages 10–12) 5–10 *weeks* to develop alcohol/tobacco/other drug dependency (Newsam 1992).

   According to the Partnership for a Drug-Free America, nine out of ten (90 percent) of those with an alcohol, tobacco, or other drug use addiction problem today started abusing those chemicals as a teenager. In contrast, if a person reaches age 20 without abusing those recreational chemicals, it is "highly unlikely" that he or she will develop a problem later in life (*Parents: You Matter!* 2009).

3. **Legal Drugs Like Tobacco, Alcohol, and Prescription Drugs Are the Real "Gateway Drugs."** Though many "drug prevention" programs in the United States focus on illegal drugs like marijuana, methamphetamines, and cocaine, it is also true that the vast majority of youth will never use those "hard" drugs. Marijuana is often classified as a "gateway drug," but that gateway is rather narrow. Many studies have shown that only about 20 percent of teens use marijuana by eighth grade, and fewer than 10 percent use other hard drugs like methamphetamines and cocaine.

   The real "gateway drugs" are easy-to-access drugs that are legal for adult use: alcohol and tobacco. Over half of all teens (52 percent) report drinking alcohol, and almost half of all teens (41 percent) have smoked cigarettes, by eighth grade. Smoking also seems to put young people at increased risk for other alcohol/drug use. Those who smoke are sixteen times more likely to drink alcohol heavily (five or more drinks on each of five or more days in the past month) and ten times more likely to use other illegal drugs than their peers (Robert Wood Johnson Foundation 2001).

4. **Legal Drugs Like Tobacco, Alcohol, and Prescription Drugs Are Far More Dangerous to Both Children and Adults Than All Illegal Drugs Combined.** In terms of deaths caused by drug use, the numbers aren't even close. Even though "illegal drugs" like marijuana, methamphetamines, cocaine, and heroine get all of the headlines and much of the drug prevention funding, those addictive chemicals have a relatively small impact on national health. All of those "illegal drugs" combined cause only about 16,000 deaths per year. By comparison, alcohol use leads to about 100,000 deaths per year, and tobacco leads to 430,000 deaths per year (Robert Wood Johnson Foundation 2001).

5. **Alcohol, Tobacco, and Other Drug Use Causes Both Short- and Long-term Damage to Your Brain and Body.** Although many teens have heard how tobacco use can lead to lung cancer and alcohol use can lead to liver damage, fewer know about the short-term impacts of these mood-altering chemicals. Early alcohol use and abuse can lead to permanent memory problems. The nicotine in tobacco stains your teeth and fingers yellow and damages your lungs with the first puff. Other drugs can lead to paranoia, depression, and other psychological problems (Schwebel 1998).

What Are the Best Ways to Address Alcohol/Tobacco/Other Drug Abuse in Children and Teens?

According to the U.S. Department of Health & Human Services (National Institute on Drug Abuse 2003), the most effective drug prevention programs should do the following:

1. Address all kinds of recreational chemical use, including the underage use of alcohol and tobacco; abuse of prescription medications; use of illegal drugs (e.g., marijuana, cocaine); and illegal use of inhalants and other recreational chemicals. The most effective programs should focus on the kinds of drugs children and teens will actually encounter in their communities. In most cases, this includes an emphasis on alcohol and tobacco use.

2. Start early, as early as preschool, to address risk factors for later alcohol/tobacco/other drug use, including poor social skills, aggressive behavior, and academic difficulties, especially poor reading skills. If schools and communities address these risk factors early, they can reduce the risk of children experimenting or self-medicating with recreational drugs as teenagers.

3. Teach elementary school students social skills like self-control, problem solving, emotional intelligence, drug refusal, and effective communication. Schools should also provide extra academic support for struggling students, especially in reading, because difficulty in school has been linked to later drug use in children and teens.

4. Teach middle and high school students effective communication skills, friendship management skills, goal-setting skills, and drug resistance skills linked to personal values and life goals.

5. Be long-lasting, with repeated presentations and activities in every grade level to reinforce alcohol/tobacco/other drug use prevention messages. Drug prevention education is like every other kind of education. If students don't practice drug prevention activities and skills, the impact of programs seems to fade in a few years.

The stories and activities in chapters 6 and 7 give librarians, teachers, and parents the help they need to accomplish many of the goals outlined by the U.S. Department of Health & Human Services.

Sample Drug Use Prevention Curriculum

Educators can use the stories and activities in this book to enrich an alcohol/tobacco/other drug prevention program, as a stand-alone drug prevention unit, or as a way to help young people develop specific skills like self-control or goal setting. Following is an example of a week-long drug prevention unit for children in grades 4 to 5 and a unit for students in grades 6 to 8. The stories are in chapter 6 and the activities are in chapter 7.

Grades 4–5 Drug Prevention Unit

Day 1: Drugs—A Pandora's Box of Problems

Story: "Pandora's Box" (Greece)

Activity 7-1: What You Know About Alcohol, Tobacco, and Other Drugs Is Probably Wrong

Day 2: Healthy Values

Story: "The City Mouse and the Country Mouse" (Aesop)

Activity 7-3: The Healthy Values Barometer

Day 3: Getting Good Advice About Drugs

Story: "The Man, the Boy, and Their Donkey" (Aesop)

Activity 7-4: Getting Advice

Day 4: Setting Goals

Story: "The Wild Boar and the Fox" (Aesop)

Activity 7-6: Mapping the Future

Day 5: Saying No

Story: "Fox and Crow" (Aesop) or "Grasping at the Moon" (Tibet)

Activity 7-5: Saying "No" Like You Mean It

Grades 6–8 Bully Prevention Unit

Day 1: Drugs—A Pandora's Box of Problems

Story: "Pandora's Box" (Greece)

Activity 7-1: What You Know About Alcohol, Tobacco, and Other Drugs Is Probably Wrong

Day 2: Healthy Values

Story: "The Farmer and the Snake" (Aesop)

Activity 7-3: The Healthy Values Barometer

Day 3: Getting Good Advice About Drugs

Story: "Feed the People" (Romania)

Activity 7-4: Getting Advice

Day 4: Setting Goals

Story: "The Peddler of Swaffham" (England)

Activity 7-6: Mapping the Future

Day 5: Saying No

Story: "The Lotus-Eaters" (Greece)

Activity 7-5: Saying "No" Like You Mean It

References

Brain and Addiction. 2010. National Institute on Drug Abuse for Teens. Washington, DC. Available at http://teens.drugabuse.gov/facts/facts_brain1.php. Accessed May 25, 2010.

Hilts, Philip J. 1994. "Is Nicotine Addictive? It Depends on Whose Criteria You Use. Experts Say the Definition of Addiction Is Evolving." *New York Times*, August 2, 1994. Available at http://www.nytimes.com/ref/membercenter/nytarchive.html (search for the article by title) and http://www.drugsense.org/tfy/addictvn.htm. Accessed May 25, 2010.

Kittleson, Mark, ed. 2005. *The Truth About Drugs*. New York: Facts On File. 194pp. $35.00. ISBN 0-8160-5299-9.

Kuhn, Cynthia, Scott Swartzwelder, and Wilkie Wilson. 2002. *Just Say Know: Talking with Kids about Drugs and Alcohol*. New York: W.W. Norton & Co. 159pp. $14.95pa. ISBN 0-393-32258-0pa.

Miller, Michael M. 2009. "An Addiction Specialist Explains Nicotine's Powerful Hold Over Cigarette Smokers." *Health.com*. Available at http://www.health.com/health/condition-article/0,,20210696,00.html. Accessed October 28, 2009.

National Institute on Drug Abuse. 2003. *Preventing Drug Use Among Children and Adolescents: A Research-Based Guide for Parents, Educators, and Community Leaders*. Bethesda, MD: NIDA. 47pp.

Newsam, Barbara Sprague. 1992. *Complete Student Assistance Program Handbook: Techniques and Materials for Alcohol/Drug Prevention and Intervention in Grades 7–12*. West Nyack, NY: The Center for Applied Research in Education. 373pp. ISBN0-87628-878-6pa.

Parents: You Matter! Drugs/Alcohol, Your Teen and YOU. 2009. New York: Partnership for a Drug-Free America. Available at http://www.drugfree.org (search "Parents: You Matter!"). Accessed October 28, 2009.

The Partnership Attitude Tracking Study: Teens. 2008. New York: Partnership for a Drug-Free America. Available from http://www.drugfree.org (search "PATS study"). Accessed October 28, 2009.

Robert Wood Johnson Foundation. 2001. *Substance Abuse: The Nation's Number One Health Problem: Key Indicators for Policy*. Princeton, NJ: Robert Wood Johnson Foundation. 128pp. ISBN 0-942054-13-X.

Schwebel, Robert. 1998. *Saying No Is Not Enough: Helping Your Kids Make Wise Decisions About Alcohol, Tobacco, and Other Drugs*. New York: Newmarket Press. 290pp. $16.95pa. ISBN 1-55704-318-3pa.

Solter, Aletha. 2006. *Raising Drug-Free Kids: 100 Tips for Parents*. Cambridge, MA: DaCapo Lifelong Books. 223pp. $13.95pa. ISBN 978-0-7382-1074-2pa.

The Peddler of Swaffham (England)

Skills: Goal Setting, Self-Control, Problem Solving

In the old days, when London Bridge had shops and inns from one end to the other, a peddler named William lived in the far off village of Swaffham. He didn't get to London very often, because he made his living traveling from village to village, selling ribbons and tools and pots and pans from his peddler's pack. He was also the sort of man who didn't think money was the most important thing in the world.

If he saw a family who were too poor to afford a metal pot, but their old pot was too cracked to hold anything but the thickest stew, he would set his price low enough so the family could afford it. Usually he could make up the difference from those who could pay more. But as time went on, it got harder and harder to find people who could afford his wares at any price. And when sales dropped off, it got harder and harder for William to make enough to fill his belly.

Now people say that when a person is really hungry, that is when he dreams. And one night, William dreamed that he was standing on London Bridge. In the dream he heard a voice in his head say, "Go to the bridge, and you'll see what you're to see and hear what you're to hear and you'll fill your belly year by year."

When he awoke the next morning, William shrugged off the dream.

"It was only a dream, after all," he thought. "And dreams aren't real, not the way that bread and rain are, at least."

And that day it did rain when William made his rounds trying to sell knives and bowls to the people in the next village. When he returned home, he was soaked right through and hoping for some thick meat stew. But he hadn't sold anything, so he couldn't buy any food. He drank some fresh well water, ate an apple from his backyard apple tree, and went to sleep.

That night William had that same dream, in which he saw himself standing on London Bridge. He heard the voice in his head say, "Go to the bridge and you'll see what you're to see and hear what you're to hear and you'll fill your belly year by year."

The next morning William awoke and once again shook off the dream.

"After all, London is so far away. If it were the next town over, perhaps I would go, but it isn't. It's over a hundred miles to London, and I've got work to do."

So saying, the peddler set off once again to sell his wares in the rain. When he returned home that night, his clothes were soaked and his stomach rumbled.

That night William had the same dream, in which he saw himself standing on London Bridge. Once again he heard the voice say, "Go to the bridge and you'll see what you're to see and hear what you're to hear and you'll fill your belly year by year."

Now this was too much.

"If a dream comes three times, then it must be a sign," thought William. "Besides, I'm not making any sales here. Perhaps I can make some sales along the road to London."

William packed some apples from his backyard tree and set off down the road. Three days later he walked into London and stood in the middle of London Bridge. He saw all

From *Story Solutions: Using Tales to Build Character and Teach Bully Prevention, Drug Prevention, and Conflict Resolution* by Kevin Strauss. Santa Barbara, CA: Libraries Unlimited. Copyright © 2011.

the inns and shops that lined the bridge and all the merchants and farmers who crossed the bridge with their wares. He spent the whole day standing in the middle of the bridge waiting to, "See what he's to see and hear what he's to hear." But all day long, nothing happened.

Finally, as the sun was setting in the west, an innkeeper came out of his restaurant and walked up to William.

"My good man, at first when I saw you, I thought you were a beggar. But I've been watching you, and all you've been doing is standing there like you're waiting for something. Now I'm curious, so I'll make you a deal. I'll give you a free meal if you'll tell me your story. If you feed my curiosity, I'll feed your stomach."

The peddler agreed and sat down for a warm meal of stew, cheese, and bread. It was the first hot meal he had eaten in weeks. Then he told the innkeeper the story of his dreams. When he finished his story, the innkeeper burst out laughing.

"No wonder your life is so hard, peddler. If you had kept to your business you'd have made enough money to weather this hard time, but you didn't. And as for that dream . . . ha! What a fool you are! If I followed every dream that I had, I wouldn't have enough time to run my business. Why, I had a dream last night. In that dream, I stood at the edge of the village of Swaffham in a backyard garden. For some reason, I dug at the base of an apple tree and found a pot of gold. Now did I go running off to Swaffham to see if my dream were true? No. I stayed here, did my job, and cared for my family, like all the **responsible** business owners in town."

William smiled and stood up.

"Thank you for the meal," he said.

William set off for home. He walked all through the night and the very next day. Around sunset he arrived home and went straight to work. He borrowed a shovel and dug at the base of his apple tree until his shovel struck something hard. He kept digging until he unearthed a huge black pot full of gold.

People say that after that day, the peddler was always able to fill his belly "year by year," but he didn't stop there. He made sure that everyone in his village always had plenty to eat. And whenever people asked where he got his wealth, he would always tell them, "I had a dream, and I listened to what it said."

And that's the end of the story.

Discuss

1. This is a story about setting goals. If William had allowed himself to be distracted by worries, fears, or alcohol, how might this story have turned out differently?

2. In many stories, those who do good deeds like the peddler run into trouble down the road. But if they are brave, they usually overcome those problems and are better off in the end. Can you think of a time when you faced a challenge and turned out better because of it? What happened?

3. If William never went to London, would he have discovered the treasure in his own backyard? Why or why not?

Sources

Briggs, Katherine. *British Folk Tales.* New York: Pantheon Books, 1977. 315pp. ISBN 0-394-41589-2.

Colwell, Eileen. *Round About and Long Ago: Tales from English Counties.* Boston: Houghton-Mifflin, 1972. 124pp. ISBN 0395185157.

Yolen, Jane, ed. *Favorite Folktales from Around the World.* New York: Pantheon Books, 1986. 498pp. $18.95pa. ISBN 0-394-75188-4pa.

King Midas and the Gift of the Golden Touch (Greece)

Skills: Self-Control, Kindness

Glossary:

Dionysus (die-o-NIE-sus). *noun.* The Greek god of wine, parties, and merrymaking. Dionysus is called "Bacchus" in Roman legends.

Satyr (SAY-ter). *noun.* A creature who from the waist up looks like a human and from the waist down looks like a two-legged goat. These creatures are known for singing, dancing, and drinking with Dionysus.

Silenus (SY-leen-us). *noun.* A satyr and the guardian of the Greek god Dionysus, often pictured as overweight and often drunk.

King Midas was a king like any other, with one difference. While all kings like gold, Midas loved it. He loved it more than his friends and more than his family. He would spend days at a time sitting in his treasury counting his gold coins, and he always felt sad when he came to the end of his counting.

"No, no, this will never be enough," he muttered as he walked up the stairs to his throne room. "I need more gold."

One day a tipsy satyr named Silenus rode into Midas's throne room on the back of a donkey. The captain of the guard asked if he should throw out the satyr. But Midas would have none of it. He knew that Silenus was the friend and guardian of Dionysus, the Greek god of wine and parties. Instead, the king ordered ten days of feasting in honor of Silenus.

On the eleventh day Dionysus came to the palace looking for his friend. When he saw how well Midas had cared for Silenus, Dionysus took Midas aside.

"For the care you have given my friend, I grant you one wish, to use as you will. But you must use it now. What will it be?"

Midas didn't have to think.

"Gold, I want gold," said Midas. "I want everything that I touch to turn to gold."

"Are you sure that is what you want? Such a wish may lead to problems," said Dionysus, with a frown.

"That is what I want, with all my heart and all my soul. All I really want is gold," said the king.

"So be it," said Dionysus and thunder boomed in a clear sky. "I grant you the 'Gift of the Golden Touch.'"

After bidding the god good-bye, Midas set to work trying out his new power. He touched his throne, and it turned to solid gold. Then he touched the pillars in his throne room, and they too turned to gold. He began cheering and running through the palace, touching everything he saw, doors, statues, and walls. Everything turned to gold.

"I'm rich, I'm rich!" he shouted.

And then, realizing that he was hungry from all his running, he shouted, "Bring me food. We shall have a feast!"

He sat down to eat at his now golden table, but when he touched the ham, or grapes, or bread, they all turned to gold. He tried to drink his wine, but the moment the cup touched his lips, the wine turned to solid gold.

"Arrgh! Am I to die of hunger and thirst amid riches?" Midas shouted.

Just then his young daughter came into the room.

"Father, what's the matter, and what has happened to our palace?"

Midas reached out to hug the girl, but once he touched her, she, too, turned into a golden statue.

"What have I done?" shouted Midas. "I need to find Dionysus."

Midas set off into the woods, looking for the god. After a day of searching, he found Dionysus, eating and drinking with his companions in a clearing.

"Ah, Midas, how do you like the gift I gave you?" asked the god.

"Dionysus, I have been a fool," said Midas. "Please take back your gift. Now I see what a curse it is."

"I am sorry, I can't take away a gift you freely accepted," said Dionysus. "But I can tell you how to free yourself. You must do exactly as I say."

"Yes, please tell me," said Midas.

"Travel to the source of the river Pactolus. Wash your head and hands in that water, and it will relieve you of the Golden Touch and undo its magic, changing everything back to the way it was before."

After a two-day journey, the hungry and thirsty king stumbled onto a spring pool and dunked his head in the water. At once he felt the magic leave his body, and he saw bits of gold at the bottom of the pool. The old Midas would have waded in and gathered that gold, but not this Midas. He hurried home to find his palace exactly as it had been a few days before. His daughter ran out to greet him, and he held her in his arms for a long, long time.

Discuss

1. Midas thought that having a lot of gold would make him happy. Was he right?

2. You could say that Midas's desire for more and more gold was like an addiction. What are some of the things that Midas lost when he received the "Golden Touch?"

3. If someone gave you a magical wish, what would you wish for?

Sources

Evans, Cheryl, and Anne Millard. *Greek Myths and Legends.* London: Usborne Publishing, 1985. 64pp. $10.95pa. ISBN 0-86020-946-6pa.

Hamilton, Edith. *Mythology.* New York: Little, Brown, 1942. 498pp. ISBN 0-316-34151-7pa.

Leipold, L. E. *Folk Tales of Greece.* Minneapolis, MN: T. S. Denison & Co., 1970. 123pp. ISBN 0-513-01097-1.

The Goose That Laid the Golden Eggs (Aesop)

Skills: Self-Control, Problem Solving

Long ago, a farmer went to the barn to collect eggs from his chickens and his goose. But this day was different; as he collected the eggs from the nest boxes, he saw something glint in the sunlight. He reached down and picked up something cold and heavy. It was a golden goose egg.

The farmer was so excited about the gold that he built the goose a special house, with a strong fence to keep out foxes.

"With this gold, I can build a grand mansion," said the farmer. He went to town that morning and sold the egg and bought wood and nails and paint. But the money didn't buy as much as he thought it would.

"I'm going to need five more eggs before I can build my new house," thought the farmer.

Each day after that, the farmer searched through the straw for another golden egg. But days went by, weeks went by, and no more eggs appeared. Finally, a month later, he found another egg.

"At this rate, I'll never get my house built," thought the farmer.

But then he had an idea.

"If all that gold is in this goose, maybe I can get it all at one time," he thought.

He took his ax to the barn and killed his goose.

But when he cut the goose open, it was just a regular goose on the inside, and he never saw another golden egg.

Discuss

1. Think of a time when you were impatient for something. What happened? How did you deal with feeling impatient?

2. Self-control and goal setting are important components of a healthy lifestyle. In this story, the farmer was greedy and lost a source of gold. What does that lesson mean in your life?

Sources

Handford, S. A. *Aesop's Fables.* New York: Puffin, 1994. 212pp. $4.99pa. ISBN 0-14-130929-6pa.

Strauss, Kevin. *Tales with Tails: Storytelling the Wonders of the Natural World.* Westport, CT: Libraries Unlimited, 2006. 231pp. $35.00pa. ISBN 1-59158-269-5pa.

Zipes, Jack. *Aesop's Fables.* New York: Signet Classic, 1992. 288pp. $4.95pa. ISBN 0-451-52565-5pa.

The Boy and the Jar of Raisins (Aesop)

Skills: Self-Control

Once a young boy saw a huge jar of sweet raisins sitting on his dining room table. Now this was a long time ago, when raisins were a special treat, much like candy bars are today. He reached in to grab a handful of the tasty treats. But as he tried to pull his hand out of the jar, he realized that it was stuck tight. At first the boy thought the jar was a magical trap.

"Help, help, this mean jar won't let go of me!" cried the boy.

His mother walked into the room and smiled.

"It's not the jar that has you, but your own greed. The jar traps a closed fist, but admits and releases an open hand. Open your hand and drop the raisins. Then you can take the raisins one at a time at your leisure."

After that, the boy ate the raisins slowly, but he ate as much as he wanted, and he never got stuck.

Discuss

1. Have you ever been in a situation where your greed led you into trouble? What happened?

2. Why do you think it was hard for the boy to let go of his fistful of raisins so that he could free himself?

3. We aren't really greedy for "things" (money, food, cars, etc.). What we really want is how these things make us feel. Drugs can make us feel good, and they can trap us, just like the jar of raisins. Describe two ways to avoid the traps that alcohol/tobacco/other drugs can set for us.

Sources

Bennett, William J., ed. *The Book of Virtues: A Treasury of Great Moral Stories.* New York: Simon & Schuster, 1993. 832pp. ISBN 0-671-68306-3.

Handford, S. A. *Aesop's Fables.* New York: Puffin, 1994. 212pp. $4.99pa. ISBN 0-14-130929-6pa.

Zipes, Jack. *Aesop's Fables.* New York: Signet Classic, 1992. 288pp. $4.95pa. ISBN 0-451-52565-5pa.

The Wild Boar and the Fox (Aesop)

Skills: Self-Control, Persistence, Goal Setting

One day, Fox was walking through the forest when he noticed a wild Boar sharpening his tusks on a stone.

"My friend, why are you doing that right now? There are no hunters in the forest today, and I have seen no other dangers here," said Fox.

The Boar stopped for a moment and looked at Fox.

"My father always taught me, 'Prepare, prepare, prepare'," said Boar. "You're right that we are safe today. But tomorrow the hunters may return. And when the hunting dogs are chasing me, there is no time to sharpen my tusks."

Discuss

1. Describe a time when you had to prepare for some event. How did it go?

2. When do you think that Fox would prepare to deal with hunters? Why?

3. This is a story about goal setting. Describe a goal you would like to accomplish in the next year. Describe three steps you'll take to accomplish that goal.

Sources

Handford, S. A. *Aesop's Fables.* New York: Puffin, 1994. 212pp. $4.99pa. ISBN 0-14-130929-6pa.

Jacobs, Joseph, ed. *The Fables of Aesop.* Mineola, NY: Dover Publications, 2002. 196pp. $2.50pa. ISBN 0-486-41859-6pa.

Zipes, Jack. *Aesop's Fables.* New York: Signet Classic, 1992. 288pp. $4.95pa. ISBN 0-451-52565-5pa.

The Lotus-Eaters (Greece)

Skills: Self-Control, Goal Setting, Problem Solving

Now you may have heard of the great Trojan War and how wily Odysseus tricked the Trojans by hiding his soldiers inside the huge wooden Trojan Horse. The Trojans dragged the wooden horse into their city, and when night fell, the Greek soldiers sneaked out of the horse, opened the city gates for their fellow soldiers, and destroyed the city. But after Troy was nothing but ashes, some of the gods were so angry at what the Greeks had done that they sent a storm to wreck their ships and drown their men.

Odysseus was lucky in that his ship was only blown across the sea. But some say he would suffer more than those who drowned that day. Low on food and water, the tired Greeks dropped anchor at a lonely green island. Warily, Odysseus sent a party of armed soldiers ashore to look for food and fresh water. The men never returned. He sent another party. They disappeared as well. Finally Odysseus led a party of warriors onto the island himself. But instead of being met with soldiers, those who lived on the island met Odysseus and his men at the edge of the forest and invited them to a banquet. The islanders brought them to a clearing, where Odysseus saw the rest of his men, lying on their backs and eating a large white flower. Odysseus approached one of the men.

"Cyrus, what are you doing lying there? I ordered you to find food and water and return to the ship!"

"Odysseus? It is good you are here. We've found food! These lotus flowers taste like summer honey. Taste one!" said Cyrus.

As Odysseus looked around, he saw that all of his men were picking and eating the lotus flowers in that field. Not all of the men were there. At the edge of the field there were blood-stained clothes, as if some wild animal had devoured a sailor.

"What happened to that man over there?" said Odysseus, pointing to a pile of clothes.

"Oh, him; some creature may have eaten him during the night. Who knows? Did you try a lotus flower yet? They taste so good," said Cyrus.

Odysseus couldn't believe what he was seeing. Battle-hardened soldiers reduced to lazy children at the mere taste of this flower.

"It is time to go. We need to find water and meat for our journey."

"Journey? Why would anyone want to leave this wonderful field? Everything we want is right here, a freshwater stream, warm weather, and all the lotus flowers we can eat. Try one, they're wonderful."

Odysseus knocked the flower from Cyrus's hand.

"Get up! We're leaving. That's an order," yelled a red-faced Odysseus.

But Cyrus simply reached out and picked another lotus flower.

"There's nothing as good as a lotus flower. Did I tell you that they taste just like summer honey, all warm and sweet? You should really try one," said Cyrus.

Odysseus grabbed Cyrus by the arm, but Cyrus pulled out his dagger.

"Leave me alone!" he screamed.

"Grab them! Drag them back to the ship if you have to!" shouted Odysseus.

The lotus-eaters tried to fight and claw their way back to the flowers, but after hours of dragging, Odysseus got most of his men back onto the ship and chained them to their seats. Still, it took days before those men did anything but cry for the taste of their lotus flowers, the flowers that tasted just like honey on a warm, summer's day.

Discuss

1. In this story, the lotus flowers were so tasty that they made the sailors forget everything else. What would have happened if Odysseus hadn't taken action?

2. We could say that sailors like Cyrus were "addicted" to the lotus flowers. What do you think it is like to be addicted to something? How do you think Cyrus would describe his experience?

Sources

Hamilton, Edith. *Mythology.* New York: Little, Brown, 1998. 498pp. ISBN 0-316-34114-2pa.

Lupton, Hugh, and Daniel Morden. *The Adventures of Odysseus.* Cambridge, MA: Barefoot Books, 2006. 96pp. $19.99. ISBN 1-84148-800-3.

McCaughrean, Geraldine. *Odysseus.* Oxford, England: Oxford University Press, 2003. 128pp. ISBN 0192741985pa.

Never Enough (Greece)

Skills: Self-Control

Glossary:

Demeter (dee-MEET-er). *noun.* The Greek goddess of the growing plants and the harvest.

Erys (AIR-iss). *noun.* A cruel king from Greece.

Long ago, there lived a wicked king name Erys. This king was the sort of king who thought that everything in his kingdom belonged to him, personally. So when it was time to build his new palace, he ordered his workmen to cut trees from the goddess Demeter's sacred grove. When the king's workmen entered the grove, they heard voices and saw shapes that frightened them. They ran back to the king, to beg him not to cut down those sacred oak trees. The king sent his soldiers to the grove, but they returned with similar stories. Finally he went to the grove himself and, grabbing an ax, set to work cutting down the tallest tree in the center of the grove. As his ax cut into the tree, the tree bled.

A voice rang out in the grove, "Demeter will punish any who harm this grove!"

The soldiers and workmen ran in fear, but King Erys kept cutting.

Before long the great oak came crashing to the ground. The king used the wood to fashion the largest banquet table in the world, with seats for 300 visitors.

"What do I have to fear from a goddess of crops?" scoffed King Erys. "What's she going to do, bury me in wheat?"

But Demeter's vengeance was not so easy. She sent her servants to ask the old woman Famine to visit the king.

"I wish that no amount of food shall ever satisfy this king. Let him starve in the very act of eating," commanded the angry goddess.

That night Famine walked unnoticed through the palace and entered the king's bedroom. Famine approached the king and wrapped her bony arms around him. She leaned close and breathed her foul breath into his mouth. She filled the king with a hunger that would never end. Then she turned and slowly walked away.

King Erys awoke almost immediately, famished. He ordered his servants to feed him an extravagant meal of pork and lamb and apples and grapes. When his family awoke the next day, they saw the king devouring his sixth meal, and still he was hungry. He couldn't sleep, because of the hunger. He stopped talking to his wife and his daughter, because of the hunger. Soon the food stores in the palace were empty. The servants hurried to buy more food in town. Then they sent wagons to the neighboring towns. The king sold all of his gold and jewels to buy more food. When his treasury was empty, he sold his daughter into slavery to buy a cow that he could eat. But the king's hunger was so great that when a servant came to him with the news that there was no more food to eat, King Erys drew his sword and chased the servant, bellowing, "I can still eat you!"

Even the king's family, the servants, and guards abandoned the king to his empty castle. Fearing for their lives, the guards blocked the palace gates with wagons and boxes so "mad King Erys" couldn't escape and devour them.

Some say that the king starved to death in that palace. Others say that Famine's magic wouldn't let him die. Those people say that the king devoured himself, one piece at a time. He ate his left hand and then his left arm. Then his legs. Then his belly and his skin. Soon all that was left were his jaws.

Some say that those jaws still travel the roads on dark nights in Erys's kingdom, looking for even more food. So if you're ever walking down the road in the dark and hear the sound of chomping teeth, run!

Discuss

1. Erys's desire to eat more and more food is similar to a drug addict's need for more and more of a recreational chemical. Who got hurt by Erys's compulsion? Was it only Erys?

2. Do you think that Erys was a good king in this story? Why or why not?

3. How could Erys have changed?

Sources

Hamilton, Edith. *Mythology.* New York: Little, Brown, 1998. 498pp. $13.99pa. ISBN 0-316-34114-2pa.

Ovid. *Metamorphoses.* New York: Oxford University Press, 1998. 528pp. $8.95pa. ISBN 978-0192834720pa.

Strauss, Kevin. *Building Heroes/Blocking Bullies: The Teacher and Parent Guide to Simple, Repeatable, Assertive Techniques That Anyone Can Use to Stay Safe and Stop Bullies.* Eden Prairie, MN: Trumpeter Press, 2010. 204pp. $25.00pa. ISBN 978-0-9814667-4-3pa.

Grasping at the Moon (Tibet)

Skills: Problem Solving, Self-Control

The King of the Monkeys woke up one night to see the full moon reflected in the pond below his royal tree.

"Treasure!" he shouted. "There is golden treasure in my pond!"

The Monkey King didn't know it was only a reflection. He called together all of his monkey subjects.

"I must have that golden moon for my throne," said the Monkey King. "I order you to reach down and lift that treasure into the tree."

The monkeys tried to reach the moon from shore, but it was too far away. So they walked out onto a strong branch that hung right over the pond. The strongest monkey held onto the branch with his feet and hung down, but he couldn't reach it. The second-strongest monkey grabbed the strongest monkey's paw, and the third- and the fourth-strongest monkeys grabbed on as well. The monkey chain almost reached the water. When the king saw how close they were, he shouted out, "I must be the first to touch the treasure!"

He climbed over each of the monkeys, but his added weight was so much that the strongest monkey couldn't hold on any more, and they all fell, "Splash" into the pond. Some say that all those monkeys drowned. Others say they didn't. But I know for sure that the Monkey King never returned. When he fell into the water, he just kept swimming deeper and deeper, hoping to reach the golden moon that was never really there.

Discuss

1. Was the Monkey King a good leader? Why or why not?

2. Have you ever had a friend who tried to get you to do something that seemed like a bad idea? What did you do?

3. Sometimes people might ask you to do something that isn't very smart, like trying alcohol/ tobacco or other drugs. Those people are like the Monkey King in this story. What could the other monkeys have done to avoid this calamity?

Sources

Hyde-Chambers, Frederick, and Audry Hyde-Chambers. *Tibetan Folk Tales*. Boston: Shambhala, 2001. 208pp.$21.00pa. ISBN 1570628920pa.

MacDonald, Margaret Read. *Peace Tales*. Hamden, CT: Linnet Books, 1992. 116pp. $14.95pa. ISBN 0-208-02329-1pa.

Strauss, Kevin. *The Reading Ranger Guide to 55 Fabulous Five-Minute Folktales That Everyone Should Read and Hear*. Eden Prairie, MN: Trumpeter Press, 2010. 196pp. $25.00pa. ISBN 978-0-9814667-3-6pa.

The City Mouse and the Country Mouse
(Aesop)

Skills: Self-Control, Goal Setting

Once upon a time, Sid the City Mouse came to visit his cousin Fern at her home in the country. Fern cooked her cousin a meal of wheat soup and served him a glass of water from the creek. After dinnerthey went for a walk through the field and into the woods before retiring for the evening.

The next day when Sid was leaving, he turned to Fern.

"It was restful here, but I miss the excitement of the city. When you visit me, I'll take you to fine restaurants and concerts, and you'll meet all of my friends."

Fern thanked Sid for his invitation and went back to her work baking hard oat bread.

Time went by, and one day Fern decided to go visit her cousin in the city. It was a long journey, full of strange sights and smells. She saw buildings bigger than country hills and people wearing bright-colored clothes. The roads were a noisy jumble of horses and wagons and people moving in all directions. It was a wonder she wasn't trampled crossing the street! She heard yelling voices and laughing and talking wherever she went.

When she finally arrived at Sid's house, she was exhausted. Sid led her into his fine parlor and let her rest a while. When evening arrived, Sid returned.

"We're going out to eat this evening," he said with a smile.

The two mice crept through a crack in a wall and into a brightly lit dining room. Fern had never seen crystal goblets that sparkled so in the candlelight. She had never seen so many different kinds of cakes and dumplings and fruits. The mice scurried up the tablecloth and began eating their fill. But as she was eating, Fern looked up to see a large furry creature staring right at her from the floor. The creature moved silently across the room. Then it stopped. Fern felt her neck hair stand on end.

"Run!" shouted Sid as he grabbed her paw and pulled her across the table. The cat leaped and landed just inches from Fern, but it slid across the table, landing in a cake. In the confusion, the mice scurried down the tablecloth and climbed back into that crack in the wall.

"W-w-w-what was that?" panted Fern as they lay resting inside the wall.

"That, my dear cousin, is a cat," said Sid. "The last one at that house was so old that he slept all night. But now I see the family that lives there has a younger cat. I'll have to be more careful from now on. We'll have to dine somewhere else tonight. Come on."

"I'm sorry, cousin," said Fern. "I won't be staying much longer. My life might have been plain in the country, but at least it was free of cats!"

Discuss

1. This is a story about taking risks and setting goals in life. Sid was willing to risk the danger of a cat for the reward of eating cake. Why wasn't Fern ready to take that risk?

2. Tell a story about a time when you visited a place very different from the place where you live. What happened?

3. Sid thought that the country was "boring," and he longed for the excitement of the city. Adolescents sometimes use mind-altering chemicals for fun and excitement. Describe four ways to entertain yourself that don't include mind-altering chemicals, junk food, or electronic devices. Was this difficult? Why or why not?

Sources

Handford, S. A. *Aesop's Fables.* New York: Puffin, 1994. 212pp. $4.99pa. ISBN 0-14-130929-6pa.

Jacobs, Joseph, ed. *The Fables of Aesop.* Mineola, NY: Dover Publications, 2002. 196pp. $2.50pa. ISBN 0-486-41859-6pa.

Zipes, Jack. *Aesop's Fables.* New York: Signet Classic, 1992. 288pp. $4.95pa. ISBN 0-451-52565-5pa.

The Money Fish (Finland)

Skills: Self-Control, Goal Setting, Problem Solving

Glossary:

    Pukko (PU-ko). *noun.* A sheath knife that boys and men carry in Finland.

A long time ago, a young man named Mika had a sweetheart named Kari, who lived in a village in Finland. Mika couldn't get married until he had worked and saved up enough money to build a cottage. The problem was that no matter how hard he worked on the farms in the valley, he couldn't save much money. One Sunday he was talking with Kari about this problem.

"Why don't you ask Luck for some money? People always say that Luck gives them money. Maybe he would do that for you," said Kari.

The next day Mika traveled high into the mountains, to the forest where Luck lived. After searching for most of the day, Mika discovered an old cabin covered in moss. He knocked on the door. No one answered. So he opened the door and walked inside. There in the gloom he saw a bed, and there slept a blonde-haired young man under a green netting. Mika knew from what people said that this must be Luck. People said that Luck was usually sleeping.

Mika cleared his throat. Nothing happened.

"Um, excuse me, Mr. Luck. Could I have a word with you?"

Luck stirred. He opened his blue eyes and raised his head an inch above the pillow.

"Huh? What do you want?" said Luck in a sleepy voice.

"Um, I need some money to build a cottage for my sweetheart so we can get married. Could you give me some money?" asked Mika.

"No," said Luck.

"No? But I thought that Luck always gave money to those who found him."

"You are mistaken. At most, I provide people with a way to get money. I don't give it outright. That would be far too much work and I'm (he yawned) a little tired right now."

"Well, how can I get enough money for a cottage?" asked Mika.

"You must do exactly what I say. Go to the next valley to the north and find a deep, dark, shaded pond. Make a fishing pole and catch a copper fish. It should be worth enough for a fine little cottage," said Luck as he yawned again and closed his eyes. A moment later he was snoring softly.

Mika traveled to the valley and found the pond. Using his pukko knife, he cut a branch for a fishing pole and carved a wooden hook. After finding some worms, he sat down on one of the jagged black rocks that surrounded the pond and watched the water. Every once in a while, a copper-colored perch leapt out of the water. Sun glinted on its scales, and it flashed like a new penny.

Mika's hook had barely touched the water when a copper fish bit it. Mika pulled the fish to shore and when the fish touched the rocks, it turned into a stiff, solid copper fish. He put the fish in his pocket and prepared to go.

"Do you want more fish like that?" boomed a deep voice. Mika looked around. At first he thought that someone was there. But he didn't see anyone.

"It must have been my imagination," thought Mika.

Then he said out loud, "Of course I want more. After all, I can't build much of a cottage with just one copper perch. I should catch at least two or three."

You see, he had already forgotten Luck's instructions.

Mika caught three more copper perch and stuffed them into his bulging coat pockets. But then he caught a silver carp. It was bigger than two perch put together! Mika emptied his pockets of the copper fish and stuffed them with the silver one.

"Do you want more fish like that?" boomed a deep voice. Mika looked around again. But look as he did, he still didn't find anyone around the pond. Shrugging his shoulders, he said, "Of course I want more."

Soon Mika had his pockets stuffed with silver carp. But then he pulled up his line and there on the end hung a golden pike.

"A fish of gold!" laughed Mika. "With fish like this I could build a mansion for my sweetheart!"

He dumped the stiff silver fish onto the rocks and stuffed the golden pike into his pocket.

"Do you want more fish like that?" boomed a deep voice. Mika looked around yet again. But look as he did, he still didn't find anyone around the pond. Shrugging his shoulders, he said, "Of course I want more."

Mika kept catching fish of gold. After he had filled his coat pockets, Mika thought, "Whoever is talking to me isn't on the land. He must be in the pond." Mika crept forward to look into the water. There he saw a terrible face with a bald head and white beard. Its eyes were sunken deep into its skull, and its teeth were old and broken.

"Eeew! You are ugly, guardian of the pond," said Mika.

Then he headed for home. When he got to his village, it seemed different. There were new houses and new roads, and lots of people he didn't recognize.

Mika walked up to one of those strangers.

"Have you seen my young sweetheart, Kari?" he asked.

The man gave him a strange look.

"I don't know of any 'young' girl named Kari. But old Kari lives at the edge of town, old man." And then he walked off.

"Who's he calling old?" thought Mika as he walked to the edge of town. He didn't recognize any of the people that he passed along the way.

"That's strange; I thought I knew everyone in this village."

Mika knocked on the door of an old, weather-beaten house at the edge of town.

"Who is it?" came an old woman's voice.

"Grandmother, I am looking for my sweetheart, Kari. Do you know where she is?"

The old woman opened the door just a crack.

"I am Kari, but I don't know you and I already have a husband. He's out in the forest cutting wood."

There was something familiar about the woman, old though she was.

"I talked with Kari just this morning," said Mika. "I told her I was going to the forest to look for Luck. She said she would wait for me. Look here, I have fish made of solid gold!"

The woman's eyes grew wide, but she didn't open the door any wider.

"I had a sweetheart once," said the woman. "But he went off into the woods to ask Luck for money, and he never came back. That was a long time ago, old man."

Then she slowly closed the door.

"Humph!" stamped Mika as he turned and walked away. "Has everyone gone crazy around here? I'll go ask Luck what to do. Perhaps I lost my way in the woods and I am in the wrong village. My sweetheart must be waiting for me still."

Mika walked back into the mountain forest. It took him a week to find Luck's cabin. He walked right up to the sleeping figure on the bed and shook him.

"Luck, where is my sweetheart? Have you hidden her somewhere?"

Luck slowly opened his eyes. "Did you do as I said? Did you catch a copper fish and build her a cottage?"

"Well . . . I did fish, but I didn't stop with the copper perch. I caught silver carp and golden pike. I'm going to build her a palace! That is, once I find her again."

"I told you nothing about gold fish or building a palace. You will never find your young sweetheart."

With that, Luck yawned deeply, turned to the wall, and fell back to sleep under the green netting. Soon he was snoring softly.

Shaking with rage, Mika stomped out of the cabin. As the sun shown down on him, for the first time he noticed that his hands were covered with the wrinkles of an old, old man.

Discuss

1. Why did Mika keep fishing when he had enough fish to build a cottage?

2. In this story Mika got so focused on catching more and more valuable fish that he lost all track of time. The same thing happens when people use alcohol/tobacco/other drugs. That's why we say that drugs "suck your time." What did Mika lose when he caught that golden fish?

3. How do you think Mika feels at the end of this story? How would you feel if this happened to you?

Sources

Strauss, Kevin. *The Reading Ranger Guide to 55 Fabulous Five-Minute Folktales That Everyone Should Read and Hear.* Eden Prairie, MN: Trumpeter Press, 2010. 196pp. $25.00pa. ISBN 978-0-9814667-3-6pa.

Uchida, Yoshiko. *The Dancing Kettle and Other Japanese Folk Tales.* New York: Harcourt, Brace & World, 1949. A similar "time passing quickly" tale from Japan.

Vaananen-Jensen, Inkeri, trans. *The Fish of Gold and Other Finnish Folk Tales.* Iowa City, IA: Penfield Press, 1990. 126pp. ISBN 0-94-101678-1pa.

Pandora's Box (Greece)

Skills: Self-Control, Problem Solving

Glossary:

    Pandora (pan-DOR-ah). *noun.* The first woman in the world. Her name means "all gifts."

    Prometheus (pro-MEETH-e-us). *noun.* A titan, or giant, in ancient Greece. His name means "forethought."

Long ago, the people say, a giant named Prometheus stole fire from the gods on Mount Olympus and gave it to the humans. With fire, the people could cook their food, heat their homes, make tools, and travel more safely at night. This self-sufficiency angered the gods.

Zeus, the king of the gods, came up with a way to punish the people. He took a beautiful magical box, filled it with "gifts" for the humans, and then presented it to a woman named Pandora as a wedding present. Pandora couldn't take her eyes off the box. Zeus, in disguise, whispered into her ear, "Whatever you do, don't open the box." Pandora agreed.

As time passed, she became more and more curious about what was in that box. Finally she couldn't take it any more. She opened the latch and lifted the lid on the box. Suddenly a rush of spiky, snarly, sickly creatures poured from the box. It was filled with hate and illness, problems and trouble. Pandora tried to grab the creatures and throw them back into the box, but they were too quick. Finally she slammed the lid and latched it.

"Wait," came a soft voice.

"Who are you?" asked Pandora.

"I am the one that you must set free."

"Why is that?" asked Pandora.

"Because I am Hope. Without me, all the hatred and illness and problems of the world will destroy the people. While I can't destroy the problems you set loose in the world, I can give people the feeling that they can overcome those problems, if they work together and work hard."

Pandora lifted the lid.

And that is how it is today. We still have trouble in the world. But we also have Hope.

Discuss

1. What could Pandora have done if she really didn't want to think about or open that box?

2. In this story, Pandora's box is a symbol for something "forbidden," like alcohol, tobacco, and other drugs. Describe some of the problems that people encounter if they open the Pandora's box of alcohol/tobacco/other drugs.

3. Can you think of a time when you wanted to do something that your parents or friends warned you not to do? What happened?

From *Story Solutions: Using Tales to Build Character and Teach Bully Prevention, Drug Prevention, and Conflict Resolution* by Kevin Strauss. Santa Barbara, CA: Libraries Unlimited. Copyright © 2011.

Sources

Evans, Cheryl, and Anne Millard. *Greek Myths and Legends.* London: Usborne Publishing, 1985. 64pp. $10.95pa. ISBN 0-86020-946-6pa.

Hamilton, Edith. *Mythology.* New York: Little, Brown, 1942. 498pp. ISBN 0-316-34151-7pa.

Leipold, L. E. *Folk Tales of Greece.* Minneapolis, MN: T. S. Denison & Co., 1970. 123pp. ISBN 513-01097-1.

The Farmer and the Snake (Aesop)

Skills: Self-Control, Problem Solving, Kindness

One cold morning, a farmer was walking down the road when he saw a snake nearly frozen to death on the side of the road.

"P-p-p-please help me. I am so cold," hissed the snake.

"Poor thing," thought the farmer.

"I can't pick you up," he said. "Snakes are dangerous."

"Who told you that foolish thing?" said the snake. "We're p-p-perfectly harmless. Besides, if you help me now, I'll let all those other, 'dangerous' snakes know that you are a friend, and they won't hurt you either."

The farmer liked the sound of that, and maybe he had misjudged the snake, so he said, "If you promise not to hurt me, then I'll help you."

"I promise," said the snake.

The farmer picked up the creature and put it in his warm coat.

The warmth of the farmer's body warmed the snake, and it began to move and stretch. For a while the farmer felt good about the deed he had done.

But then the farmer felt a sharp pain in his side. It was the fangs of the snake. He felt the venom burn in his blood.

"What did you do that for?" yelled the farmer as he yanked the snake out of his coat and threw it on the ground.

"What are you complaining about?" hissed the snake. "You knew I was a snake when you put me in your coat."

Discuss

1. In many cases, being kind to another seems like a good thing. Why wasn't that the case in this story?

2. In this story, the snake represents mind-altering drugs like alcohol, tobacco, and other drugs. Some people will tell you that those chemicals "won't hurt you." Are they right? Can anyone make that promise to you? Why or why not?

3. Did the farmer deserve his fate? Why or why not?

Sources

Handford, S. A. *Aesop's Fables.* New York: Puffin, 1994. 212pp. $4.99pa. ISBN 0-14-130929-6pa.

Jacobs, Joseph, ed. *The Fables of Aesop.* Mineola, NY: Dover Publications, 2002. 196pp. $2.50pa. ISBN 0-486-41859-6pa.

Zipes, Jack. *Aesop's Fables.* New York: Signet Classic, 1992. 288pp. $4.95pa. ISBN 0-451-52565-5pa.

Elders Feed the People (Romania)

Skills: Problem Solving, Kindness

Long ago in Romania, life was hard for the people. There often was not enough food to go around during the cold, cold winters when snow fell in heaps upon the land. In that land, the king looked at his starving people and had to make a terrible choice. He sent his soldiers far and wide with the announcement that from now on, anyone too old to work must be left on the mountain to die.

Many families cried when they heard this announcement. They loved their grandfathers and grandmothers and didn't want to see them go. But the law was the law, they thought. At first the soldiers escorted the old people up to the mountain, but as time went on, the soldiers ordered the families to do it themselves, under penalty of death.

Now there was one family who had a gray-haired grandmother who loved to tell stories to her grandchildren around the evening fire. But as she grew too old to cook or knit, her son knew that soon she too must go to the mountain. If the soldiers found her in the house, they might all be in danger.

One winter's day, the man and his son, crying, set the grandmother on a sled and began pulling her up the mountain. When the neighbors saw what was happening, a few thought, "It's about time they leave her on the mountain." Others thought, "It is too bad that we have this law." But nobody did anything to change the law.

When they arrived at the high mountain valley, the man dropped the rope and turned to walk away, tears in his eyes.

Just then his son called out, "Father, we can't leave the sled up here."

"Why not?"

"Because how will I take you to the mountain when you are old?"

The man burst out crying and hugged his mother and son.

"You are right. No one will stay on the mountain this night."

"But that is dangerous," said the old woman. "Leave me here. It is my time to die."

"When one breathes, it is never your time to die," said the man. "We will wait until dark, then we will cover the sled with wood and sneak you back into our house."

So that's what they did. They made room for the old woman in the basement food cellar and brought her bread to eat every night. And while her life was not comfortable, it was a life, and the old woman could still tell stories to her grandchildren at night.

The next year a terrible famine struck the land. Many people starved, and those who lived ate all their seed grain just to stay alive through the winter. The man knew that with no seeds to plant, soon the grim reaper would be at their door as well.

One night, when he went to visit his mother in the cellar, she saw the concern on his face.

"What is the matter, my son?"

"Mother, we have eaten our seed grain and we'll have nothing to plant in the spring. I fear that we will starve this year."

"Nonsense," she said. "Where're there's breath, there's hope. Do you still have thatch on the barn? Is there still that turn in the road near the south field?"

"Yes and yes, mother, but what does that have to do with anything?"

"Don't you remember? When we thatched the barn roof, we used bundles of wheat stalks. Some of those stalks still have grain on them. What's more, that curve by the south field is so tight that wagons often spill a bit of grain there. Thresh the roof and plow the road and you'll have plenty to plant this year."

The man did as his mother suggested and sure enough, he had seeds to plant and crops to feed his family and his neighbors. When news of this reached the palace, the king ordered the man to come to his castle.

"Where did you find seeds to plant this year?" asked the king.

"My lord, I got them from the roof of my barn and the road by my farm."

"And how could one as young as you be smart enough to do that?"

The man stopped for a moment. Lying to a king was a capital crime. But so was caring for an old person.

"My king, I didn't know how to do that. The only reason we survived the famine was because we have kept my mother hidden in our basement all these years. Her memory of the last famine saved us from this one. You see, my lord, the old ones feed the people with their wisdom and their stories. They don't use their hands, but the harvest is just as great."

The king first turned red with anger, but then cooled. He looked at the floor and then slowly raised his head.

"I command that from this day forth, all families should care for their grandmothers and grandfathers as this family has done."

And that is the end of the story.

Discuss

1. At the start of this story, people thought old people weren't worth much. Although some elders aren't physically strong, what strengths do they have?

2. Talk about a time when you learned something from someone who is older than you.

3. No one knows everything. Make a list of the people you trust to tell you the truth about issues like alcohol/tobacco/other drug use, school bullies, and making new friends. Make a plan to ask one of these people for advice in the next two days. Write a half-page report on how it went.

Sources

DeSpain, Pleasant. *Thirty-Three Multicultural Tales to Tell.* Little Rock, AR: August House, 1993. 128pp. $15.00pa. ISBN 0874832667pa.

Deutsch, Babette, and Avraham Yarmolinsky. *More Tales of Faraway Folk.* New York: Harper & Row, 1963. 93pp.

Strauss, Kevin. *The Reading Ranger Guide to 55 Fabulous Five-Minute Folktales That Everyone Should Read and Hear.* Eden Prairie, MN: Trumpeter Press, 2010. 196pp. $25.00pa. ISBN 978-0-9814667-3-6pa.

The Three Impossible Gifts (China)

Skills: Problem Solving, Kindness

Long ago in ancient China, there lived a wealthy family with four sons. Now the oldest three sons had already married. But after years went by, the three wives were feeling sad. They missed their home villages. So they asked their father-in-law, Chang, if they could have permission to visit their home villages. At first he said no.

"My sons and I need you here," he explained.

But the women kept asking and asking. Soon going to visit their families was the only thing they could think of. They went to ask their father-in-law again. This time Chang thought about this for a while and then replied, "You may visit your homes if you each promise to bring me back the special gift that I request."

"Oh yes, yes, we promise," said the women.

"I will make a list of the gifts I want and seal it with wax. Open the letter when you reach the river. And just to make sure you are serious, you must either bring me these gifts, or never return!"

The women were a little worried about Chang's demand, but they were so excited to see their parents and families again that they soon forgot all about the letter. Before long they were riding in a sedan chair carried by servants. They talked and talked about who they wanted to see in their own villages. But as they reached the river, they remembered Chang's demand. The oldest daughter-in-law opened the letter.

"When you return, I want you to bring me three gifts: fire in paper, wind in paper, and music in paper," said the letter.

Each woman read the letter. But none of them knew how to solve the riddle that Chang had given them. They began wailing and crying, "Now we can never return to our husbands!"

A farmer's daughter named Jin was leading her water buffalo to the river for a drink of water when she heard all the noise.

"What's the problem?" she asked.

"We must find three impossible things," wailed the youngest woman.

"Really, what are they?" said Jin.

"It doesn't matter. They're impossible!" wailed the oldest woman.

"Come now," said Jin. "Usually impossible is just a word for something we haven't figured out yet. Now tell me the problem."

So the three sobbing women told Jin what they had to bring to their father-in-law if they were to return to their husbands.

"A week from now, meet me here and I will have the solution to this riddle," said Jin.

So the women continued their journey, happy to visit their families again. In a week's time the women met Jin at the river, and she told them how to solve the riddle. When the women returned to their father-in-law's house, they presented him with three gifts.

"Here is 'fire in paper'," said the oldest daughter-in-law, holding up a paper lantern with a candle glowing inside.

"Here is 'wind in paper'," said middle daughter-in-law, holding up a paper fan and fanning up a small wind in the room.

"And here is 'music in paper'," said the youngest daughter-in-law, holding up a set of ornate paper wind chimes that made a rustling, ringing sound in the wind.

Chang was impressed.

"I always knew that you were kind and hard-working daughters-in-law, but now I also know that you are as clever as the rivers are long."

The sisters looked at each other.

"Father, we wouldn't want to lie to you," said the oldest daughter-in-law. "We didn't solve your riddles."

"Really? Then who did?" said a surprised Chang.

"It was a farm girl that we met at the river. She solved the riddles," said the oldest woman.

Chang smiled.

"You are even more clever than I imagined," said Chang. "A fool relies on what she knows. A wise person asks for help with a problem."

Later that day Chang asked his youngest son to look for this farmer's daughter and invite her to the house. On the long journey to the house, Jin and the youngest son took a liking to each other.

When Chang met Jin, he asked her, "Would you like to marry my son?"

Jin blushed and said, "I would like that very much, but my family has no money to pay for my marriage."

"Ha! money, what use it that when you are as clever as you are?"

So it was settled. Jin married Chang's youngest son. And after that, all of the wives and husbands lived long and happy lives, and the women visited their parents whenever they wanted to.

Discuss

1. Think of a time when you asked someone for advice. Was the advice that you received good or bad? Did you follow the advice? Why or why not?

2. How do you know whom to trust when asking for advice?

3. What thoughts or feelings might prevent a person from asking for advice about a problem?

4. What thoughts or feelings might inspire a person to give bad or selfish advice?

Sources

Gruenberg, Sidonie. *Favorite Stories Old and New.* Garden City, NY: Doubleday, 1955. 512pp.

Strauss, Kevin. *Building Heroes/Blocking Bullies: The Teacher and Parent Guide to Simple, Repeatable, Assertive Techniques That Anyone Can Use to Stay Safe and Stop Bullies.* Eden Prairie, MN: Trumpeter Press, 2010. 204pp. $25.00pa. ISBN 978-0-9814667-4-3pa.

Yang, Dori Jones. *Bring Me Three Gifts!* Carmel, CA: Hampton-Brown, 2008. 32pp. ISBN 0-73622495-5pa.

The Man, the Boy, and Their Donkey (Aesop)

Skills: Problem Solving, Goal Setting

One day, a man and his son were leading their donkey to market. They passed a group of people on the road, and the people began to murmur, "They are foolish. Why aren't they riding their donkey?" So the man and his son climbed up on the donkey's back. They passed another crowd and heard those people say, "Look at what they are doing to that poor beast. They are riding it to death." Not wanting to insult those people or ride their donkey to death, the man and son got off the donkey and lifted it up on their shoulders.

As they were crossing a bridge over a river, the donkey, nervous at being carried, began to kick. Before they knew what was happening, the man his son accidentally dropped the squirming donkey into the river, where it drowned.

As the man and his son stared sadly into the river, a crowd gathered around them. When they heard what had happened, one old man said, "Sometimes you have to choose who you listen to."

Discuss

1. Think of a time when someone gave you some advice. Was the advice that you received good or bad? Did you follow the advice? Why or why not?

2. What is a good way to determine the best choice among several pieces of conflicting advice?

3. In this story, the man and his son couldn't decide what advice to listen to. What would have been a better choice in this situation?

Sources

Handford, S. A. *Aesop's Fables.* New York: Puffin, 1994. 212pp. $4.99pa. ISBN 0-14-130929-6pa.

Jacobs, Joseph, ed. *The Fables of Aesop.* Mineola, NY: Dover Publications, 2002. 196pp. $2.50pa. ISBN 0-486-41859-6pa.

Zipes, Jack. *Aesop's Fables.* New York: Signet Classic, 1992. 288pp. $4.95pa. ISBN 0-451-52565-5pa.

Why Bear Has a Stumpy Tail (Sweden)

Skills: Problem Solving, Goal Setting

One winter's day, Bear was hungry. He sniffed the air and gazed over the snowy woods. Then he smelled it.

"Mmmm, I love fish," said Bear. He could see Fox coming up the hill with three fish on her back. Bear hid behind a bush, hoping to surprise Fox and steal some fish. As Fox climbed the hill, she noticed Bear's long black tail sticking out from behind the bush. Fox knew that she needed a plan.

"I didn't steal these fish from that fisherman just to lose them to Bear," thought Fox.

When Fox was almost to the bush, she called out, "Boy, these fish are heavy. I wish I had some help carrying them back to my den. I'd be happy to share them with anyone who helped me."

Just then Bear came out from behind the bush, looking for a free meal.

"Hey Fox, I can help carry your fish," said Bear. "I'm very strong."

"Bear, I was just thinking of you," said Fox. "I was thinking that I have so many fish that I should really share some with my good friend Bear. But then I thought to myself that that wouldn't be a very nice thing to do."

Bear frowned.

"Why wouldn't that be a nice thing to do, Fox?"

"Well Bear, I could give you a fish now, and you would be hungry in a couple hours," said Fox. "Or I could teach you how to fish, and then you would never be hungry again. But I don't have much time, so I can only do one or the other. Which will it be, Bear?"

Bear thought about that for a moment and finally decided that he should learn how to fish.

"Wonderful, Bear, wonderful," smiled Fox. "All you have to do is go down to the frozen pond, break a hole in the ice with your paw, and put your long, furry tail into the water. When you feel fish nibbling on your tail, pull it out, and you'll have all the fish you want."

Of course, that wasn't how Fox got his fish, but Bear didn't know that. Bear did as he was told, and Fox went home to eat his stolen fish.

After Bear had stuck his tail in the icy water, he waited and waited. Finally he tried to pull it out. But it wouldn't move.

"I must have caught a really big fish on my tail!" thought the excited Bear.

He pulled and pulled until he heard a snap and fell forward on his nose. When Bear looked behind him, he saw that his tail was no longer attached to his rear end. It was still frozen in the lake.

After that, Bear decided that he didn't want to eat fish anyway. He went off to his den and went to sleep. From that day on, bears have had stumpy tails, and from that day on, when snow falls and ice forms on the lakes, rather than going ice fishing, bears sleep all winter long.

Discuss

1. In this story Bear got some bad advice. How can you avoid getting (or listening to) bad advice about alcohol/tobacco/other drugs?

2. Why might someone lie to you about a plan or a product (like drugs)? Where can you go to "check out" advice you might get from other kids?

Sources

Blecher, Lone Thygesen, and George Blecher. *Swedish Folktales and Legends.* New York: Pantheon Books, 1993. 383pp. $25.00; $17.00pa. ISBN 0-394-54791-8; 0-697-75841-0pa.

Brooks, Kaarina. *Foxy: Finnish Folk Tales for Children.* Beaverton, ONT: Aspasia Books, 2002. 62pp. $12.95pa. ISBN 0-9689054-7-1pa.

Deutsch, Babette, and Avrahm Yarmolinsky. *More Tales of Faraway Folk.* New York: Harper & Row, 1963. 93pp.

Good News, Bad News (China)

Skills: Problem Solving, Self-Control

Long ago in ancient China, there lived a farmer and his son. Now it so happened that this farmer was able to save up enough money to buy a handsome white stallion. The farmer's son trained the horse and used it to help plow the fields. One night a storm came up and frightened the horse. Before the son could put the horse into the barn, it broke out of its paddock and ran off into the woods.

The next day the farmer's neighbors came by. "What bad news," they all said when they heard the story.

To each visitor, the farmer said, "Good news, bad news, who knows? We'll see."

The next day the white stallion returned with a wild black mare. Now the farmer had two horses. When his neighbors walked by, they saw two horses in the paddock and congratulated the farmer.

"What good news," they all said.

To each visitor, the farmer said, "Good news, bad news, who knows? We'll see."

The next week the son began to train the wild mare, but since she had been a wild horse, she didn't like the saddle or the bridle. One day when the son was riding her, she threw him and he broke his leg.

"Oh, what bad news," said the neighbors when they came by to visit.

To each visitor, the farmer said, "Good news, bad news, who knows? We'll see."

The next week, a troop of soldiers marched into town to round up all the able-bodied young men and draft them into the army. The emperor needed them to fight in a new war on the border. Since the farmer's son had a broken leg, they left him behind.

"What good news," said the neighbors, many of whom had to give up their own sons.

The farmer just looked at his neighbors and said, "Good news, bad news, who knows? We'll see."

Because the farmer's son couldn't plow the fields and plant crops, the farmer and his family couldn't make much money, and they had to get by on just one meal of rice per day.

"What bad news," said the neighbors, many of whom had plenty to eat.

The farmer just looked at his neighbors and said, "Good news, bad news, who knows? We'll see."

Discuss

1. Usually, nothing in life is always completely good. For instance, if your parents offer to take you to a movie, that might also mean that you can't play with your neighborhood friends. Think of a time when you got some really good news. Was there any "bad news" that came along with it?

2. Alcohol/tobacco/other drug use is usually a case of "good news/bad news." Although a particular recreational chemical may make you feel good and make your problems seem to "go away" (at least for an hour or so), every one of those chemicals have "bad news" that comes with them. Make a list of the immediate negative effects of alcohol/tobacco/other drug use on your time, money, and health.

3. Write a sequel to this story, starting at the end and going through two more cycles of "good news/bad news." For instance, what could be good about a family that has little to eat?

Sources

Asbjornsen, Peter Christen, and Jorgen Moe. *Norwegian Folk Tales.* New York: Pantheon, 1982. 192pp. $15.95pa. ISBN 0394710541pa.

Forest, Heather. *Wisdom Tales from Around the World* . Little Rock, AR: August House, 1996. 160pp. $17.95pa. ISBN 0874834791pa.

Yolen, Jane, ed. *Favorite Folktales from Around the World.* New York: Pantheon Books, 1986. 498pp. $18.95pa. ISBN 0-394-75188-4pa.

Cat and Parrot (Denmark)

Skills: Self-Control, Problem Solving

Once upon a time, Cat and Parrot were best friends. And one day Cat invited Parrot over for dinner. When Parrot arrived at Cat's house, she saw only a pint of milk, a thick slice of fish, and a biscuit on the table. Parrot couldn't lap up the milk like Cat, so Cat drank it all. Parrot tried to pick up a piece of fish, but the scales got caught on her tongue, and the biscuit was so old and dry that Parrot couldn't even break off a piece to eat.

While some guests might have complained about the dinner, Parrot was too polite to do that.

"Perhaps my friend never learned how to host a guest," thought Parrot as she flew home. "I'll invite Cat over and show him how it's done."

The next week Parrot invited Cat to dinner. Parrot spent the whole day preparing the meal. She brewed a pot of blueberry tea; baked a ham; assembled a basket of apples, oranges, and pears; and baked 500 spicy cakes to eat. Since Parrot knew that Cat was bigger than she was, she put 498 of the spicy cakes in front of Cat and took only two for herself.

Cat grinned as he entered the dining room. He sat down at the table and began shoveling food into his mouth with both paws! First he ate the ham, then he drank the tea. Then he ate all the apples, oranges, and pears. Then he ate all 498 spicy cakes without even taking a breath. "Slurp, gobble, burp!"

Cat's eyes narrowed.

"That was pretty good food, Parrot. Do you got some more?" said Cat, licking his chops.

"W-well, I have these two little cakes," said Parrot, sliding her plate across the table.

"Slurp, gobble, burp!" the cakes and the plate disappeared down Cat's throat.

"That was pretty good food, Parrot. Do you got some more?" said Cat, licking his chops again.

"I'm sorry to say, my friend. You have eaten all of the food in my house," said Parrot.

"Not quite," said Cat.

"What do you mean?" said the nervous Parrot, glancing at the door.

"I could still eat YOU!" said Cat as he pounced on Parrot and swallowed her whole. "Slurp, gobble, burp!"

As Cat walked down the street, he still had some of Parrot's tail feathers hanging out of his mouth. A passing woman recognized the tail feathers.

"Shame on you, Cat! You shouldn't eat your friend Parrot," said the woman.

"What's a friend to me when I'm hungry?" said Cat, and he opened his mouth and "Slurp, gobble, burp!" swallowed the woman whole.

Cat walked down the street and met a man driving a donkey to market.

"Out of my way, Cat, or my donkey might step on you," called the man.

"What's a donkey to me when I'm hungry?" said Cat, and he opened his mouth and "Slurp, gobble, burp!" swallowed the man and the donkey whole.

Now this much larger cat kept walking down the street until he met the king, his new bride, 100 soldiers, and a dozen elephants walking toward him.

The king called out, "Be careful, Cat, or my elephants might step on you."

"What's an elephant to me when I'm hungry?" said Cat, and he opened his mouth and "Slurp, gobble, burp!" swallowed the king, his bride, the soldiers, and the elephants whole.

The street ended at a sandy beach, and as Cat walked across the beach, he met two crabs. The crabs heard the "Help, help!" calls from Cat's now much larger stomach. Mother Crab got an idea. She walked up to Cat.

"Watch out, Cat, this is our beach!"

Cat's eyes narrowed. "What's a crab to me when I'm hungry?" said Cat, and he opened his mouth and "Slurp, gobble, burp!" swallowed Mother Crab and her son whole.

When the crabs got used to the dark in Cat's belly, they could make out the king holding his bride in his arms, and the soldiers and elephants trying to line up. They could see the man and his donkey and the woman, and in one corner of that enormous stomach there was Parrot, sitting on a pile of 500 spicy cakes.

At night, when Cat went to sleep, Mother Crab told everyone in the stomach, "Get ready."

She cut a hole in Cat's stomach big enough for the king and his bride and his soldiers and the elephants, donkey, man, woman, and Parrot to pass through. Parrot flew out of the stomach holding a spicy cake in each foot. Mother Crab replaced the people and animals with rocks and sewed up that hole (mothers can do that, you know).

When Cat awoke the next morning, he had the worst stomachache ever, and with all of those rocks in his stomach, he never ate more than a pint of milk, a thick piece of fish, and a single biscuit again.

Discuss

1. This is a story about excessive behavior. Now to the Cat, this behavior seemed normal. He was hungry, so he ate. How did he react when the woman criticized him for his behavior? Why do you think he acted that way?

2. In this story, food is more important to Cat than anything else in the world. You could say that Cat was "addicted" to eating in this story. What are some downsides to the addiction in this story? What are some downsides to forms of addiction in real life?

Sources

Asbjornsen, Peter Christen, and Jorgen Moe. *Norwegian Folk Tales.* New York: Pantheon, 1982. 192pp. $15.95pa. ISBN 0394710541pa.

Bennett, William J., ed. *The Moral Compass: A Companion to the Book of Virtues.* New York: Simon & Schuster, 1995. 825pp. $30.00. ISBN 0-684-80313-5.

MacDonald, Margaret Read. *Fat Cat: A Danish Folktale.* Little Rock, AR: August House, 2001. 32pp. $15.95. ISBN 9780874836165.

Fox and Crow (Aesop)

Skills: Self-Control, Problem Solving

Once there was a Fox who saw a Crow fly up to a tree with a piece of cheese in her mouth. Fox said to himself, "Boy, I'd like to get a piece of that cheese. Hmmm, what can I do?"

Fox walked up to the tree.

"Hello there, fine Crow. Boy, it is a beautiful day, don't you think?"

Crow didn't say anything. She just looked for a place where she could set down her piece of cheese.

"Hey Crow, where did you find such a fine piece of cheese?"

Crow didn't say anything.

"My oh my, look at that beautiful coat of feathers you have. You know, I think that you are the most beautiful bird I have ever seen. What do you think of that?"

Crow didn't say anything. But she did smile, just a bit.

"You know, I have head that crows have some of the most beautiful voices in the animal world. I'm sure that someone with such a beautiful coat of feathers must have an equally beautiful voice to match."

At that, the proud Crow opened her beak to "Caw! Caw!," but as she did, she dropped her piece of cheese. Fox ran up and grabbed it.

"I'd be careful about who I listen to, Crow. Sometimes people just tell you what you want to hear, so they can take what's really dear. And as for me, if you please, I'll be enjoying this piece of cheese."

Discuss

1. How do you know whether someone means a compliment or is just saying it to get something from you?

2. How do you think Crow will act from now on? Why?

3. Sometimes people compliment you to win your friendship and get you to do something that they want you to do (like trying drugs). What can you do to protect yourself from these "false friends?"

Sources

Bennett, William J., ed. *The Book of Virtues: A Treasury of Great Moral Stories*. New York: Simon & Schuster, 1993. 832pp. ISBN 0-671-68306-3.

Handford, S. A. *Aesop's Fables*. New York: Puffin, 1994. 212pp. $4.99pa. ISBN 0-14-130929-6pa.

Zipes, Jack. *Aesop's Fables*. New York: Signet Classic, 1992. 288pp. ISBN 0-451-52565-5.

Chapter 7

Drugs Suck Activities

When I talk with children and teens about alcohol, tobacco, and other drug abuse issues, they all know why I'm there. They all know that I'm going to tell them that drugs are dangerous and they should not use drugs. Because they already know that part of the conversation, I skip right over it and tell them that, "Drugs suck."

They suck your **money**, because alcohol, tobacco, and other drugs are expensive, especially if you have to pay a supplier (or pusher). They suck your **time**, because every minute that a child or teen is spending looking for drugs, using drugs, or covering up the fact that he or she is using drugs is a minute he or she isn't spending learning, reading, and preparing for the adult world he or she will soon be joining.

They suck your **health** because mood-altering drug abuse has short-term and long-term negative impacts on a person's body and mind. Early alcohol use makes it harder to remember things and can eventually cause serious health problems like liver and heart disease, and tobacco use gives you stained teeth and fingers, takes your breath away, gives you bad breath, and ultimately causes diseases like cancer and emphysema. "Harder" drugs like methamphetamines make you look old in just a few years, cause your teeth to fall out, make your skin scab over, and can cause permanent brain damage. They suck your **friends** because either your friends will use drugs, and possibly get addicted, or they won't want to use drugs and won't want to hang out with people who do.

The activities in this chapter give adults who work with youth the tools they need to help children and teens reject recreational chemicals like alcohol, tobacco, marijuana, and other drugs.

Activity 7-1: What You Know About Alcohol, Tobacco, and Other Drugs Is Probably Wrong

Objective: Students will learn that many of the things that they have heard about alcohol, tobacco, and other drugs are either partly incorrect or completely wrong. They will explore ways to find accurate information about these substances.

Skills: Problem Solving

Grade Level: 4–8

Materials: "The Brain Chemistry Quiz," paper, pencils

Background

It seems like every other day, kids hear more "facts" about alcohol, tobacco, and other drugs. They hear them from their parents, the media, the Internet, their teachers, and their friends. The thing is, even well-meaning people may not be giving children the facts they need to make responsible, long-term decisions about alcohol, tobacco, and other drugs. This quiz and its answers give students a crash course in the effects of mood-altering substances on their bodies and minds.

Activity

1. Hand out the "The Brain Chemistry Quiz" and have students complete it either on the handout or on a machine-scored form.

2. After completing the quiz, collect and score the results. At a later class time, go over the answers with the students, using the answer sheet. Discuss why students may have gotten the answers wrong, even if they thought they "knew" the correct answers.

Evaluation

Have students write a half-page reflection paper on how they get information about the food, beverages, and in some cases, chemicals (like caffeine, alcohol, tobacco, or other drugs) that they might choose to put into their bodies.

The Brain Chemistry Quiz

1. Which is the most common "gateway drug" for children and teenagers? (A "gateway drug" is the first mood-altering substance that a person might use in his or her lifetime. Some users of "gateway drugs" go on to use more dangerous drugs in the future.)

    A. Marijuana

    B. Alcohol

    C. Tobacco

    D. They are all used by equal numbers of teens.

2. What is the most addictive drug in common usage (more than 8 percent of the population) by children and teenagers today?

    A. Marijuana

    B. Alcohol

    C. Tobacco

    D. Cocaine

3. What is the most dangerous drug in use today in terms of the number of annual deaths that it causes?

    A. Marijuana

    B. Alcohol

    C. Tobacco

    D. All illegal drugs combined (marijuana, methamphetamines, cocaine, heroine, and all the rest of the "hard drugs," i.e., NOT alcohol, tobacco, or prescription drugs)

4. In surveys, what do adults list as the most common reason that children and teens try alcohol, tobacco, and other drugs?

    A. Media images that alcohol, tobacco, and other drugs "are cool"

    B. Their peers pressure them to try alcohol, tobacco, and other drugs.

    C. They're "bored" or think drugs would be "fun to try."

    D. Both A and B

5. In surveys, what do children and teens list as the most common reason that they try alcohol, tobacco, and other drugs?

    A. Media images that alcohol, tobacco, and other drugs "are cool"

    B. Their peers pressure them to try alcohol, tobacco, and other drugs.

    C. They're "bored" or think drugs would be "fun to try."

    D. Both A and B

6. Why do you think that adults like teachers, doctors, and parents are working hard to keep children and teens from using alcohol, tobacco, and other drugs?

   A. Because they don't want you to have any fun.

   B. Because they think it is morally wrong to use mood-altering chemicals like alcohol, tobacco, and other drugs.

   C. Because they get paid to tell kids not to use drugs, so they're just doing their job.

   D. Because alcohol, tobacco, and other drugs are far more dangerous and addictive for children and teens than they are for adults, and because they care about children and teens and want them to be healthy.

7. What is the main reason that some people (including some who advertise alcohol and tobacco products) want to get adolescents to try alcohol, tobacco, and other drugs before they turn eighteen?

   A. Because they care about you and want you to have lots of fun.

   B. Because they don't think it is morally wrong to use mood-altering chemicals like alcohol, tobacco, and other drugs.

   C. Because alcohol, tobacco, and other drugs are far more addictive for children and teens than they are for adults, and if they hook teens before they turn eighteen, they could have addicted customers for life.

   D. Because they want to make sure that teens can make their own choices about alcohol, tobacco, and other drugs.

The Brain Chemistry Quiz Answers

1. Which is the most common "gateway drug" for children and teenagers? (A "gateway drug" is the first mood-altering substance that a person might use in their lifetime. Some users of "gateway drugs" go on to use more dangerous drugs in the future.)

   B. Alcohol

   Alcohol is the most common gateway drug of children and teens today. In a survey of eighth graders, 52 percent had used alcohol, 41 percent had used tobacco, and 20 percent had used marijuana (Robert Wood Johnson Foundation 2001).

   Many drug prevention programs focus on marijuana as the most prevalent gateway drug. That is because marijuana is the most prevalent *illegal* (for everyone) gateway drug. Multiple surveys of youth report that because alcohol and tobacco are so easily accessible in our society, adolescents use those drugs first. Some of them go on to use marijuana and other drugs afterward.

2. What is the most addictive drug in common usage (more than 8 percent of the population) by children and teenagers today?

   C. Tobacco

   In some studies, almost two-thirds (60 percent) of smokers report physical and/or mental withdrawal symptoms when they try to stop using tobacco. This compares to just 42 percent of marijuana users, 38 percent of cocaine users, and 23 percent of alcohol users. Almost seven in ten smokers (68 percent) want to quit, almost five in ten (46 percent) try to quit, but half of those fail. It usually takes three or more attempts to quit smoking (Robert Wood Johnson Foundation 2001).

   Like it or not, the nicotine in tobacco is a highly addictive substance, and it is more addictive than many "hard drugs" like cocaine (Hilts 1994).

3. What is the most dangerous drug in use today in terms of the number of annual deaths that it causes?

   C. Tobacco

   Tobacco consumption leads to about 430,000 U.S. deaths per year, or two out of every ten deaths in the country (20 percent). Because it can take decades for the effects of tobacco smoking to show up, many children and teens don't consider tobacco as dangerous a drug as methamphetamines or cocaine.

   Alcohol consumption leads to about 100,000 deaths per year. This includes deaths from both alcohol-related diseases and car accidents. This is a conservative figure, since a high proportion of deaths from falls, fires, and drownings are also alcohol-related.

   Illicit drugs like marijuana, methamphetamines, and cocaine cause about 16,000 deaths annually from the fatal effects of overdosing or mixing drugs and alcohol. If you add to this number the deaths from drug-using hazards like AIDS, hepatitis, and other diseases spread through illegal drug use, the death toll rises to about 25,000 deaths annually (Robert Wood Johnson Foundation 2001). This is still small compared to the half a million Americans killed by tobacco and alcohol use every year.

4. In surveys, what do adults list as the most common reason that children and teens try alcohol, tobacco, and other drugs?

   D. Both A (media) and B (peers)

   Parents often blame the media and a child's peers for that child's experimentation with alcohol, tobacco, or other drugs. Although media, advertising, and the portrayal of alcohol, tobacco, and other drugs in movies and in songs do have an impact on drug use, they probably don't have the largest impact. Millions of children are exposed to these same movies and songs, but most of them don't go on to use alcohol, tobacco, and other drugs. Recent surveys seem to indicate that children choose a peer group based on whether or not that group includes users or nonusers. So in many ways, children self-select peers who reinforce their own beliefs about alcohol, tobacco, and other drug usage (Wilmes 1988).

5. In surveys, what do children and teens list as the most common reason that they try alcohol, tobacco, and other drugs?

> C. They're "bored" or think drugs would be "fun to try."

Children and teens often see alcohol, tobacco, and other drug use as an adventure and a response to boredom (Schwebel 1998; Solter 2006; Kuhn et al. 2002; Wilmes 1988). While having peers or family members who use alcohol, tobacco, and other drugs can encourage someone to use these substances, surveys seem to indicate that children choose a peer group based on whether or not that group includes users or nonusers. So in many ways, children self-select for peers who reinforce their own beliefs about alcohol, tobacco, and other drug usage (Wilmes 1988). Some teens may also view mind- and mood-altering chemicals as more enticing because adults keep telling them not to use those chemicals.

6. Why do you think that adults like teachers, doctors, and parents are working hard to keep children and teens from using alcohol, tobacco, and other drugs?

> D. Because alcohol, tobacco, and other drugs are far more dangerous and addictive for children and teens than they are for adults, and because they care about children and teens.

The fact is that the growing child and adolescent brain is especially susceptible to the effects of alcohol, tobacco, and other drugs. Children and teens who experiment with and abuse mood-altering chemicals at this early age are far more likely to become addicted to those substances and run a much higher risk of brain damage from them than adults who engage in the same behaviors.

Studies indicate that if a person doesn't start using alcohol, tobacco, or other drugs until he or she turns twenty, he or she is far less likely to develop addiction than if he or she tried them as a teenager (Newsam 1992; *Parents: You Matter!* 2009).

7. What is the main reason that some people (including some who advertise alcohol and tobacco products) want to get adolescents to try alcohol, tobacco, and other drugs before they turn eighteen?

> C. Because alcohol, tobacco, and other drugs are far more addictive for children and teens than they are for adults, and if they hook teens before they turn eighteen, they could have addicted customers for life

The reason that alcohol, tobacco, and other drugs are so easy to obtain and use is that someone can make a lot of money selling them. Even "legal" (for adults) substances like alcohol and tobacco are multi-billion-dollar industries in this country. Some companies use their economic power to keep the government from restricting their advertising and marketing projects. Until recently, it was common for some tobacco companies to target children and teenagers with their ad campaigns. One internal tobacco company document from the 1970s even focused on working with schools to identify third graders who could become teen smokers (Gallogly 2005).

The tobacco companies know that if you didn't start smoking before you turned eighteen, it isn't likely that you will ever smoke. They also know that more than eight out of ten adult smokers (80 percent) today started smoking before they turned eighteen (the legal age to buy and smoke cigarettes). There have been numerous reports of how tobacco companies manipulate the amount of nicotine in cigarettes and add flavors to cigarettes to hook new customers and keep their current customers addicted (Tobacco-Free Kids 2010; National Cancer Institute 2010).

Activity 7-2: School Safety Survey 2

Objective: Students anonymously describe their interactions with alcohol, tobacco, and other drugs.

Skills: Problem Solving, Goal Setting

Grade Level: 4–8

Materials: "School Safety Survey 2" forms for each student, pencils,

Background

Keeping in mind that alcohol, tobacco, and other drug use is probably underreported in many schools, a short survey can give educators a sense of the size of the problem and the drug use "hotspots" at their school and community.

Activity

1. Ask students to complete the "School Safety Survey 2" form (p. 146). Tell children that this form will help teachers and administrators improve student education and safety at school. Remind them not to put their names on their surveys.

2. Collect and review the surveys. Look for patterns of where alcohol, tobacco, and other drug use is occurring.

3. Discuss the results with your students and ask students to come up with ways to make school safer for everyone. "I see that according to our surveys, some children don't feel as safe on the playground. Can anyone think of a way we could work together to make the playground safer?"

Evaluation

Have students complete a one-page reflection paper or create an 8½-by-11-inch poster that completes the statement: "If I ran the school, I would make it safer by . . . ." Did each student think of two or three ways to make school safer?

School Safety Survey 2

Answer the following questions on a scale of 1-5, where 1 = never (0-10% of the time), 2 = seldom (10-40% of the time), 3 = sometimes (40-60% of the time), 4 = often (60-90% of the time), 5 = always (90-100% of the time), and NA = Does Not Apply to Me

1. I feel safe at school.

    1   2   3   4   5   NA

2. I feel safe on the playground.

    1   2   3   4   5   NA

3. I feel bored.

    1   2   3   4   5   NA

4. I feel "stressed out."

    1   2   3   4   5   NA

5. I see kids using alcohol, tobacco, or other drugs at school.

    1   2   3   4   5   NA

6. I see kids using alcohol, tobacco, or other drugs in my neighborhood.

    1   2   3   4   5   NA

7. I see people using alcohol, tobacco, or other drugs in my home.

    1   2   3   4   5   NA

8. I am comfortable saying "no thanks" when someone offers me alcohol, tobacco, or other drugs.

    1   2   3   4   5   NA

9. I have a friend who uses alcohol, tobacco, or other drugs.

    1   2   3   4   5   NA

10. When I see other children using alcohol, tobacco, or other drugs at school, I report it to the teacher or principal.

    1   2   3   4   5   NA

11. I feel safe on the school bus.

    1   2   3   4   5   NA

12. I see alcohol, tobacco, or other drug use every week at school.

    1   2   3   4   5   NA

13. To help me know what to do about drug abuse, I would like to learn about (circle all that apply):

    responding to social pressure   how to report dug use to a teacher or parent

    how to walk away from drug use   how to say "no" to a bad idea

    how to feel good about myself   how to help someone who is using drugs

Activity 7-3: The Healthy Values Barometer

Objective: Students will decide whether they agree with, disagree with, or are uncertain about statements relating to mood-altering drug use.

Skills: Problem Solving, Kindness, Goal Setting

Grade Level: 6–8

Materials: lesson plan, "Strongly Agree" and "Strongly Disagree" signs

Activity

1. Put a sign that says "Strongly Agree" on one side of the room and one that says "Strongly Disagree" on the other side. Ask students to stand on the line between the two signs in response to statements that the teacher or librarian will read.

2. Discuss student responses. Ask students to defend their position on the "values barometer." Emphasize that are were no "right" or "wrong" answers in this activity. We are just exploring people's opinions and values.

Evaluation

Ask students to write a half-page reflection paper in which they describe something that surprised them about their answers or a friend's answers in this activity.

Have older students research the answers to some of these questions. What do researchers say about them?

The Healthy Values Barometer Statements

1. Teenagers should be able to make up their own minds about alcohol, tobacco, or drug use.

2. "Smoke free" areas are unfair and infringe on the rights of smokers.

3. Drug use is a personal decision, not a government or parental decision.

4. It is okay to use alcohol, tobacco, or other drugs at home as long as you don't use them at other times.

5. Legalizing drugs would end many of the drug problems in our country.

6. Parents and teachers use unfair "scare tactics" to frighten kids into staying off alcohol, tobacco, or other drugs.

7. Smokers shouldn't be allowed to use taxpayer-funded health care for lung cancer treatment.

8. Most drugs are much safer than parents, teachers, and police officers think they are.

9. Using alcohol, tobacco, or other drugs is just a normal part of growing up.

10. Only "morally weak" people get addicted to alcohol, tobacco, or other drugs.

11. Alcohol, tobacco, or drug users are mostly loners who have low self-esteem and don't have many friends.

12. If you "ignore" an alcohol, tobacco, or drug use problem, it will probably go away.

13. Bystanders have a moral obligation to tell a child or teenager to stop using alcohol, tobacco, or other drugs.

14. Bystanders have a moral obligation to report any alcohol, tobacco, or other drug use they see to a teacher, principal, their parents, or another responsible adult.

15. Alcohol, tobacco, or other drug use is something that only affects the user, not the community.

16. If someone is using alcohol, tobacco, or other drugs, it is okay for that person to keep it a secret.

17. Alcohol, tobacco, or other drug users deserve to suffer from the side effects of chemical use. We shouldn't help them "get clean."

Activity 7-4: Getting Advice

Objective: Students learn how to find people who can give good advice.

Skills: Kindness, Self-Control

Grade Level: 4–8

Materials: paper and pencil for each student

Activity

1. Read or tell, "The Three Impossible Gifts" (in chapter 6) to the students. Answer the questions as a class. Children often don't know whom to turn to when they need help. Children who are the targets of alcohol, tobacco, or other drug pushers (or "supplier friends") often feel embarrassed if they're not sure what to say, making them even less likely to ask for help or advice. As a class, brainstorm what makes an adult "safe" to talk to. Parents and other close relatives are often good people to talk to because they love their children (nephews, nieces, or grandchildren) and want them to succeed in life. Other adults, like librarians, teachers, clergy, medical staff, and police officers, can also qualify since their jobs include the responsibility to help children. Who else could provide a student with good advice?

2. Have children make a list of adults in their own lives whom they could ask for advice. Are there some things you would talk about with a parent, but not with a teacher? Are there some questions that you would rather ask a doctor or religious leader?

3. Have children make an anonymous (no names on it) list of questions that they might want to ask their teacher on topics like "alcohol, tobacco, or other drug use," "setting goals," or "making friends."

Evaluation

Review the papers that students turn in. Collect the question pages and use them to plan future classroom life skills lessons.

Activity 7-5: Saying "No" Like You Mean It

Objective: Students will learn four ways to say "No" to someone and practice how to say "No" to friends who want them to do something they don't want to do.

Skills: Self-Control, Problem Solving, Goal Setting

Grade Level: 4–8

Materials: "Ways To Say No" cards, "No Practice" cards for each student

Background

Drug pushers and other "fake friends" often try to control their friends and classmates by getting them to do things they don't want to do. Keep in mind, one way to know if someone is really your friend or not is to watch how he or she responds when you say "No" about something really important. A real friend will listen to you and try to understand you. Real friends care about your feelings. A false friend will try to convince you to change your mind without regard for how you are feeling.

Also remember, saying "No" is a complete sentence. You don't need to explain yourself or defend your decision. If someone is your real friend, he or she will respect your choice, even if he or she doesn't understand or agree with it. People who aren't your real friends will keep trying to get you to change your mind so they can get you to do something or buy something that you don't initially want to. Don't listen to them.

Four Ways to Say "No" and Walk Away

1. The Plain (Vanilla) No: "No." (Or "No, thank you.") Then walk away.

2. The Reasoned No: "No, because I don't think that's the right thing to do." Or "No, I just don't feel like it right now." Then walk away.

3. The Authority No: "No, the teacher is watching. We'd better wait for a better time." Or "No, I've got a game this week." (Then make sure that the "better time" never arrives.) Then walk away.

4. The Better Idea No: "I'm getting tired of that. (or "That's getting boring.") How about we . . . (play football, ride our bikes to the park, go play a video game, etc.)." Then walk away.

Saying "No" is a skill that far too few of us practice. Saying "No" to someone gets easier the more we do it. Often we worry that someone won't like us if we say "No," but the opposite is usually true for real friends. Real friends tend to respect you more when you say how you really feel, rather than just "going along with the crowd."

Role-playing Activity

1. Assign students to work with a partner. Have them decide who will be Student A and who will be Student B. Student A's job is to get Student B to say "Yes." Student B has to be creative about finding new says to say "No." (Remember, the goal here is to practice saying "No", even if Student A suggests something Student B really would want to do. Also remember the idea of "opportunity cost." This is the idea that when you choose to do one thing, you also choose against doing something else at that same time.) "You can't dance at two weddings at the same time" (Jewish proverb).

2. Discussion:

   Was it difficult to say "no?" Why or why not?

   Did it get easier the more you did it? (It usually does.)

Evaluation

Ask students to think of a time when they felt pressure to agree to something even though they didn't want to do it. Then have them write down a list of ways they could say "No" to that pressure the next time it happens.

Ways to Say "No"

1. The Plain (vanilla) No: "No" (or "No thank you"). Then walk away.

2. The Reasoned No: "No, because I don't think that's the right think to do." Or "No, I just don't feel like it right now." Then walk away.

3. The Authority No: "No, the teacher is watching. We'd better wait for a better time." (Then make sure that "better time" never arrives.) Then walk away.

4. The Better Idea No: "I'm getting tired of that" (or "That's getting boring.") "How about we … (play football, ride our bikes to the park, go play a video game, etc.)." Then walk away.

(©2010 Kevin Strauss, www.bullyblockers.com)

Ways to Say "No"

1. The Plain (vanilla) No: "No" (or "No thank you"). Then walk away.

2. The Reasoned No: "No, because I don't think that's the right think to do." Or "No, I just don't feel like it right now." Then walk away.

3. The Authority No: "No, the teacher is watching. We'd better wait for a better time." (Then make sure that "better time" never arrives.) Then walk away.

4. The Better Idea No: "I'm getting tired of that" (or "That's getting boring.") "How about we … (play football, ride our bikes to the park, go play a video game, etc.)." Then walk away.

(©2010 Kevin Strauss, www.bullyblockers.com)

Ways to Say "No"

1. The Plain (vanilla) No: "No" (or "No thank you"). Then walk away.

2. The Reasoned No: "No, because I don't think that's the right think to do." Or "No, I just don't feel like it right now." Then walk away.

3. The Authority No: "No, the teacher is watching. We'd better wait for a better time." (Then make sure that "better time" never arrives.) Then walk away.

4. The Better Idea No: "I'm getting tired of that" (or "That's getting boring.") "How about we … (play football, ride our bikes to the park, go play a video game, etc.)." Then walk away.

(©2010 Kevin Strauss, www.bullyblockers.com)

Ways to Say "No"

1. The Plain (vanilla) No: "No" (or "No thank you"). Then walk away.

2. The Reasoned No: "No, because I don't think that's the right think to do." Or "No, I just don't feel like it right now." Then walk away.

3. The Authority No: "No, the teacher is watching. We'd better wait for a better time." (Then make sure that "better time" never arrives.) Then walk away.

4. The Better Idea No: "I'm getting tired of that" (or "That's getting boring.") "How about we … (play football, ride our bikes to the park, go play a video game, etc.)." Then walk away.

(©2010 Kevin Strauss, www.bullyblockers.com)

"No" Practice 1

Student A: Let's go get some ice cream.

Student B: No thanks.

Student A: Why not? I thought you like ice cream.

Student B: I do. But I just don't want it now. I'd rather go for a walk.

Student A: Going for a walk is boring. I'm hungry.

Student B: OK, I'll see you later.

"No" Practice 2

Student A: Let's go do _____ (fill in the blank).

Student B: No thanks.

Student A: Why not? I thought you liked _____ (fill in the blank).

Student B: No thanks.

Student A: Are you sure you don't want to _____ (fill in the blank)?

Student B: No thanks.

"No" Practice 1

Student A: Let's go get some ice cream.

Student B: No thanks.

Student A: Why not? I thought you like ice cream.

Student B: I do. But I just don't want it now. I'd rather go for a walk.

Student A: Going for a walk is boring. I'm hungry.

Student B: OK, I'll see you later.

"No" Practice 2

Student A: Let's go do _____ (fill in the blank).

Student B: No thanks.

Student A: Why not? I thought you liked _____ (fill in the blank).

Student B: No thanks.

Student A: Are you sure you don't want to _____ (fill in the blank)?

Student B: No thanks.

Activity 7-6: Mapping the Future

Objective: Students will learn how important it is to set goals and work to accomplish them.

Skills: Goal Setting, Self-Control, Problem Solving

Grade Level: 6–8

Materials: "Mapping the Future" worksheets and pencils for each student

Background

Everyone understands the process of mapping your neighborhood or your town. Maps, whether they are sketched on a napkin or part of a modern GPS system, help us to get where we need to go.

In this activity, each student will make a map of his or her future, starting with brainstorming a list of "long-term" (three-year) goals and then dividing them into short-term (a few months to one-year) goals.

Activity

1. Have students make a list of ten things they would like to have accomplished in the next three years. Examples include make the varsity basketball team, win a music competition, write a poem and get it published, get 500 people to subscribe to my blog, etc.

2. Have each student choose one three-year goal and then, working with two partners, brainstorm a list of twenty-five things that the student must do to achieve this goal. Don't let the students stop with just five ideas; have them continue brainstorming until they reach twenty-five. The best ideas usually come at the end of a brainstorming session.

3. Have students use the "Mapping the Future" worksheet to develop short-term objectives to help them reach their long-term goals.

4. Repeat this activity until students have outlined four or five goals. Each month, have students write a half-page reflection paper on how they are working toward one of their goals.

Evaluation

Collect and review participants' goals worksheets and follow-up reflection papers.

Mapping the Future: Three-Year Goals

In the next three years I will _____ (your goal).

To accomplish this goal, I will:

Year 2 to Year 3

Year 1 to Year 2

Start to Year 1

Activity 7-7: Salesperson

Objective: Students will practice defensive techniques to protect themselves and their classmates from someone who wants to sell them a dangerous and/or unhealthy product.

Skills: Self-Control, Problem Solving

Grade Level: 4–8

Materials: Pusher Scripts

Background

Practicing how to deal with peer pressure makes it easier to handle that pressure in real life. In most cases, the most effective defensive technique to help a child avoid alcohol/tobacco/other drugs is to say "No" and walk away (Somdahl 1996). Walking away is the key here. As I like to say in my presentations, both rattlesnakes and mood-altering chemicals are perfectly safe when they are fifty feet away. You need to get distance to get safe.

Activity

1. Assign children to work with a partner or have them choose partners. Let them decide who will be Student A (the salesperson) and who will be Student B (the target). The salesperson might offer "free samples," tell the target that "Everyone's doing it," or say "What are you scared of?" The goal of the salesperson is to get the target to agree to try the drugs. The goal of the target is to say "No" and walk away. The scripts will help students know what to say.

2. After two minutes, switch roles.

3. Discuss what it was like to be the salesperson and what it was like to be the target. What tricks could a salesperson use to make a sale? What defenses were effective against the salesperson?

Evaluation

Have students create a poster of "ways to stop the drug pusher."

Alcohol/Tobacco/Other Drugs Pusher Scripts

Pusher Role-play 1

Pusher: Hey, want a smoke?

Target: No thanks.

Pusher: Why not? Are you afraid?

Target: No, I just don't like cigarettes.

Pusher: How about chewing tobacco?

Target: No thanks.

Pusher: Come on, everybody's doing it.

Target: Actually, fewer than one in five teens use tobacco products.

Pusher: What are you, some kind of goody-two-shoes?

Target: No, I just don't like tobacco. Bye. (Turn and walk away.)

Pusher Role-play 2

Pusher: Hey, buddy, want a beer?

Target: No thanks.

Pusher: Why not? Are you afraid?

Target: No, I just don't like beer.

Pusher: How about a wine cooler?

Target: No thanks. I prefer to have fun without alcohol.

Pusher: Come on, everybody's doing it.

Target: Actually, most kids don't drink. And those who do drink don't report being any happier overall than those who don't.

Pusher: What are you, some kind of goody-two-shoes?

Target: No, I just don't need drugs to have fun. Bye. (Turn and walk away.)

Activity 7-8: Good News, Bad News

Objective: Students will learn both the benefits and the many disadvantages of using alcohol/tobacco/other drugs. They will also develop a list of alternatives to recreational chemical use.

Skills: Problem Solving, Goal Setting

Grade Level: 4–8

Materials: paper and pencils

Activity

1. People use drugs for a number of reasons, and it is true that some people get a lot of pleasure out of that use. Review the reasons that adolescents give for using alcohol/tobacco/other drugs: to feel "good," to "relax," to "forget my problems," to "stay awake and focused," to "have fun," to "be social," to be "a part of a group."

2. That was the good news. Now let's look at the bad news. Have children research the negative effects of alcohol, tobacco, marijuana, and methamphetamine use. Challenge them to find at least ten short-term negative effects of each of these recreational chemicals.

3. Now have children make a list of ten ways they could relax, feel good, forget their problems, have fun, be social, and be part of a group without using alcohol/tobacco/other drugs.

Evaluation

Have students write a one-page paper on the relative advantages and disadvantages of using alcohol/tobacco/other drugs to have fun or fit in.

 From *Story Solutions: Using Tales to Build Character and Teach Bully Prevention, Drug Prevention, and Conflict Resolution* by Kevin Strauss. Santa Barbara, CA: Libraries Unlimited. Copyright © 2011.

Activity 7-9: A Family Healthy Living Contract

Objective: Children and parents develop and agree to a "Healthy Living Contract" with clear guidelines and consequences for unhealthy or dangerous behavior.

Skills: Kindness, Self-Control, Goal Setting

Grade Level: 4–8

Materials: "Healthy Living Contract" sample (p. 160), paper and pencils

Activity

1. Community and school "Drug-free Pledge" events don't seem to have much effect on student drug use, probably because no one holds students accountable to that pledge, and there are no clear consequences for breaking the pledge (Surgeon General 2010). It is a bit like having adults pledge to follow the speed limit and then tell them that the police won't be patrolling the highways anymore.

   The results are more positive when a child and parent develop and sign a family pledge like a "Healthy Living Contract," with clear behavioral guidelines and parent-enforceable consequences (Somdahl 1996).

   Much of the benefit probably comes from the fact that completing a family contract requires parents to talk with children about drug use and creates a format for parents to set rules and consequences for drug use behavior. According to the Partnership for a Drug-Free America, when parents talk with their children about the dangers of alcohol/tobacco/other drug use, child drug use drops by 50 percent (*Parents: You Matter!* 2009).

2. As a take-home assignment, children and parents will review the sample "Healthy Living Contract" and decide if they need a contract like that to help them stay safe. Parents and children can edit the agreement until it fits the unique needs of their family. Students must either return with a signed copy of the contract (keep the original at home) or return a one-page letter written by the student and signed by a parent that explains why this sort of contract didn't work for their family. The letter needs to describe the other actions they are taking to keep their child safe in a world where many children and teens have easy access to alcohol, tobacco, and other drugs.

Evaluation

Review the contracts or papers that students turn in. Is it clear that families understood and discussed the assignment? Is it clear that both the parent and the student were involved in the activity?

Sample Family Healthy Living Contract

Definitions:

Prescription Drug—a chemical substance prescribed by a doctor and used to treat a medical condition

Recreational Drug—a chemical substance that people use to "feel good" or to get "buzzed" or "high"

Since illegal drugs like alcohol, tobacco, marijuana, and other "recreational" (mind-altering) chemicals can cause addiction, illness, apathy, brain damage, and other long-term consequences for children and young adults, I hereby promise that:

1. I will not use or spend time with people who use recreational chemicals like alcohol, tobacco, marijuana, or other mind- or mood-altering drugs.

2. If our family doctor prescribes a prescription medication, I will use it only as directed by our family physician (or the product label) and will not share medications with anyone else. The same rule applies to over-the-counter medications and other household products.

3. Since the peer pressure to use recreational chemicals increases when people around you are using those chemicals, I promise that I will not attend events where alcohol, tobacco, or other drugs are present. If I am at a party that I thought would be "drug free" and suddenly discover that people are using alcohol, tobacco, or other recreational drugs, I promise to leave right away. If I need I ride home, I can call my parents for a ride any time of the day or night. The only exception to this rule is for events in which I am accompanied by my father or mother (e.g., at a family event where the *adults* are legally drinking beer, for instance). While parents may give me permission to be at an event, under no circumstances does this mean I have permission to consume alcohol, tobacco, or other recreational drugs (see Rule 1 above).

4. Since mind-altering drugs like alcohol and marijuana impair a driver's ability to control his or her vehicle, I promise not to ride as a passenger in any vehicle driven by a person whom I know or suspect of using mind-altering chemicals. I have blanket permission to call my parents for a ride at any time (day or night), or to call a cab, so I can avoid riding with an impaired driver.

5. I will tell my parents where I am, whom I am with, and where I am going at all times. This information is part of the deal for the privilege of going out with friends.

6. I realize that my friends have a big influence on the choices that I make. For this reason, I agree to bring my friends home, introduce them to my parents, and give my parents a chance to learn about my friends. These introductions are part of the deal for the privilege of spending time with my friends.

7. I realize that many young adults make bad choices late at night. To reduce the likelihood that I will make bad choices like this, I agree to a curfew. I will be home no later than _____ on weekdays and _____ on weekends. If there is a special event that lasts later than my curfew, I will ask for special permission to stay out later at least twenty-four hours before the event takes place.

8. I have blanket permission to call my parents at any time (day or night) for advice or help. If I have made a bad choice, my parents will come get me and promise not to talk about the event until the next morning. They will support me as I accept the health, legal, and/or financial consequences of my actions.

9. Part of the privilege of going out with my friends involves taking responsibility for my behavior, including any legal consequences that may result from my bad choices. My parents will be there to support me, but it is not their job to help me avoid the consequences of my actions. If I am old enough to make bad choices on my own or with my friends, then I am old enough to take responsibility for those choices.

10. I have blanket permission to talk with my parents whenever I have a concern about alcohol/tobacco/other drugs or other health issues (pressure to have sex, reproductive health, weight, steroids). If my parents can't answer my questions, we will find a (medical, counseling, or religious) professional who can help.

11. My parents and I will each set two personal and two educational goals for ourselves for the coming year, and we will support each other in reaching our goals.

I understand that violating any of these agreements is a breech of trust and that I will have to earn my parent(s)' trust back in order to regain the privileges that I currently enjoy as part of this family. In addition, my parents have the right and responsibility to impose one or more of the following consequences for my actions:

A. No nonhomework computer use for one week (e.g., no e-mail, no social network sites).

B. Grounding in my room for _____ days.

C. Loss of telephone (texting, e-mail, and other communication) privileges for _____ days.

D. Loss of driving privileges for _____ weeks.

E. No television/video game use for _____ weeks.

F. Loss of other privileges (cell phone, etc.) for _____ weeks.

G. Extra work duties as assigned by a parent.

In addition, I agree to pay any financial costs that result from my bad choices. I will either get a job or do **extra** work around the house to earn that money.

Child's Signature _____

Parent 1's Signature _____

Parent 2's Signature _____

Date _____

Additional Readings

Fiction Books (Grades 4–8)

Anonymous. *Go Ask Alice*. New York: Simon Pulse, 2005. 224pp. $9.95pa. ISBN 978-1416914631pa.

    The anonymous author of this book invites you to read the diary of an awkward teenage girl who struggles to live up to the expectations of her high-achieving parents. She experiments with drugs and enjoys the escape, until she begins bouncing between the exciting highs and painful lows. Whether the book is memoir or fiction isn't clear. But what is clear is that over the past quarter century, this book has changed how we think about teen drug addiction.

Harazin, S. A. *Blood Brothers*. New York: Delacorte Press, 2007. 224pp. $15.99pa. ISBN 038573364Xpa.

    It wasn't supposed to be this way. But it is. Seventeen-year-old medical technician Clay watches his friend lying in a hospital bed on life support. It looks like an overdose. But as Clay thinks about their friendship and their last argument, he is also looking for clues about what led to the overdose and who's responsible.

Hill, Kirkpatrick. *Do Not Pass Go*. New York: Margaret K. McElderry Books, 2007. 229pp. $15.99. ISBN 9781416914006.

    Deet thought he lived a pretty normal life for a native kid in Alaska. His stepdad worked too much, but that was normal, too. But then police arrest his stepdad for taking pills to keep himself awake at work. Deet worries about how jail might change his dad and what people in town will think when they hear that his dad is in jail. Life does get harder for his family with his stepfather in jail and less money coming in. But Deet also learns that everybody has problems, and the jail where his father goes isn't like the prisons on television.

Hinton, S. E. *That Was Then, This Is Now*. New York: Puffin, 1998. 159pp. $4.99pa. ISBN 40389660pa.

    Mark and Byron have been friends for as long as they could remember, but that all starts to change when these sixteen-year-olds get involved with girls, the local gangs, and drugs. Suddenly friendship doesn't seem to mean as much anymore.

Kern, Peggy. *No Way Out*. West Berlin, NJ: Townsend Press, 2009. 140pp. $4.95pa. ISBN 9781591941767pa.

    Harold Davis feels trapped under the weight of his grandmother's medical bills and an uppity social worker who thinks Harold would be better off in a foster home. Unfortunately, local drug pusher Londell James has an "easy" solution to all of Harold's problems, easy money. Before long Harold is dealing and looking for a way to stay out of trouble at home and in school.

Koertge, Ron. *Stoner and Spaz*. Somerville, MA: Candlewick, 2004. 176pp. $6.99pa. ISBN 978-0763621506pa.

    Ben doesn't have many friends. He thinks it's because of his cerebral palsy. But then he meets Colleen. The class "stoner" (drug addict) falls asleep on his shoulder at the movie theater. Suddenly Ben's social life gets a lot busier as the two of them address his biology and her chemical escape route.

Lurie, April. *The Latent Powers of Dylan Fontaine*. New York: Delacorte Press, 2008. 211pp. $15.99pa. ISBN 9780385731256pa.

    If you think you've had a hard day, take a look at Dylan's world. At fifteen, he's starring in his friend Angie's documentary. But as the camera rolls, Dylan's family starts to come unglued. His brother is playing in a band and using drugs, his mother has just moved out, and all the while, Dylan's trying to get up the nerve to ask his friend Angie out on a date. Too bad her ex-boyfriend is also on the film crew. So much for showbiz.

Mezinski, Pierre, with Melissa Daly and Françoise Taud. *Drugs Explained: The Real Deal on Alcohol, Pot, Extasy, and More*. New York: Amulet Books, 2004. 112pp. ISBN 0-8109-4931-8pa.

    Using a teenage journal as a format, *Drugs Explained* shows readers how alcohol/tobacco/other drugs affected Emily and her friends. Then the authors go on to explain how alcohol/tobacco/other drugs affect the human body and brain, using examples from the journal narrative. Unlike many drug prevention guides, this book actually explains how it feels to consume alcohol/tobacco/other drugs while at the same time explaining the many downsides to alcohol/tobacco/other drug use and abuse. Readers get the sense that the authors want teens to get the facts about the advantages and disadvantages of using alcohol/tobacco/other drugs without some of the fear tactics used by anti-drug-use organizations. This is an anti-drug-use book, but it is written in a way that sophisticated teens can read and respect.

Myers, Walter Dean. *The Beast.* New York: Scholastic, 2003. 170pp. $6.99pa. ISBN 0439368413pa.

Anthony "Spoon" Witherspoon thought that he had it made when he got into Wallingford prep school. He figured that leaving Harlem would be a good thing. His neighborhood could be as dangerous as the wild beasts he'd read about in books. But when Anthony returns home for Christmas break, he finds out that one of his friends has dropped out of school, and his poet girlfriend Gabi is experimenting with drugs. Spoon is left straddling two worlds as he tries to decide what is best for him and his family and friends.

Wilhelm, Doug. *Falling.* New York: Farrar, Straus & Giroux, 2007. 241pp. $17.00. ISBN 9780374322519.

Matt Shaw seems to have it all. He is a star on the basketball court, has a close family, and gets good grades. But then things start to change. He doesn't join the junior high basketball team. He keeps to himself, and he's carrying a terrible secret: His older brother is a drug addict. Shaw doesn't know what to do, even after meeting a classmate named Katie in an online chat room. Can he tell her? Can he tell anyone?

Nonfiction Books (Grades 4–8)

Brynie, Faith Hickman. *101 Questions Your Brain Has Asked About Itself But Couldn't Answer—Until Now.* Brookfield, CT: Millbrook Press, 1998. 176pp. $23.90. ISBN 0761304002.

Have you even wondered how your brain works? Well, this book tells you. Learn about memory, senses, thinking and the effects of diseases and drugs on the brain. You'll be glad you did.

Hafiz, Dilara. *The American Muslim Teenager's Handbook: For Muslims and Non-Muslims Alike.* New York: Atheneum Books for Young Readers, 2009. 168pp. $11.99pa. ISBN 9781416985785pa.

Although this book focuses on Muslim values, the sections on peer pressure, drinking, and drugs give any teenager some ways to make good, healthy life choices. (This book also provides a good introduction to Muslim history, controversies, and celebrations.)

Packer, Alex J. *Highs!: Over 150 Ways to Feel Really, Really Good—Without Alcohol or Other Drugs.* Minneapolis, MN: Free Spirit Publishing, 2000. 251pp. $14.95pa. ISBN 1575420740pa.

In survey after survey, adolescents tell us that one of the reasons they use alcohol, tobacco, or other drugs is "for fun" or because they're "bored." This book can be a solution to those problems. It gives teens healthy ways to get those feel-good endorphin rushes through meditation, exercise, art, and sports.

Peacock, Nancy B. *Alcohol (Junior Drug Awareness).* Philadelphia: Chelsea House Publishers, 2000. 80pp. ISBN 0-7910-5174-9.

Gives age-appropriate information about what alcohol does to the human body, why people use alcohol, and how it can lead to addiction. It also addresses how advertising can affect underage drinkers. The book also includes a glossary and a list of additional organizations and resources.

Radev, Anna. *I've Got This Friend Who—: Advice for Teens and Their Friends on Alcohol, Drugs, Eating Disorders, Risky Behaviors and More.* Center City, MN: Hazelden, 2007. 188pp. $14.95pa. ISBN 9781592854585pa.

Teens have questions, and this book has answers. It goes beyond the "just say no" approach to giving teens realistic ways to have friends, be cool, and still not get hooked on alcohol, tobacco, or other drugs. The personal stories, self-quizzes, and fast facts make this an engaging and useful book for teens.

Rebman, Renee C. *Addictions and Risky Behaviors: Cutting, Bingeing, Snorting, and Other Dangers.* Berkeley Heights, NJ: Enslow Publishers, 2006. 104pp. $31.93. ISBN 9780766021655.

Rebman explores a wide range of addictive behavior, from alcohol and other drug addiction to eating disorders and Internet addiction. She explains how addiction is a form of mental illness and describes what teens can do to get help for themselves, their family members, or their friends.

Sheff, Nic. *Tweak: Growing Up on Methamphetamines.* Waterville, ME: Thorndike Press, 2008. 534pp. $9.99pa. ISBN 978-1416972198pa.

Everyone knows that the life of a meth head can be messy, but you have no idea how messy until you see it firsthand. Sheff walks you though his experience drinking alcohol at age eleven and then "graduating" to hard-core drugs like cocaine, meth, and heroine. Through his eyes, you'll get a sense of the mental and physical depths of drug addiction as Sheff struggles to get clean. He also shows us the violent relapse that finally made him serious about recovery. This book is not for the faint of heart.

Traynor, Pete. *Cigarettes, Cigarettes: The Dirty Rotten Truth About Tobacco.* Mount Airy, MD: Sights Productions, 1996. 32pp. $7.95pa. ISBN 978-1886366084pa.

Traynor pulls no punches with a children's book that describes the tobacco industry's practice of marketing cigarettes to children. And since righteous anger is an easy emotion for teens, this book could make them angry enough to stay off tobacco for good.

Adult Books

Aue, Pamela Willwerth, ed. 2006. *Teen Drug Abuse.* (Opposing Viewpoints® Series). Farmington Hills, MI: Greenhaven Press. 236pp. ISBN 0-7377-3336-5pa.

Wade into the alcohol/tobacco/other drug debate with this edition from the Opposing Viewpoints® Series. Medical, psychological, and policy experts present opposing view on issues like "Do Cigarette Ads Influence Teen Smoking?" and "Does Drug Testing Deter Teen Drug Use?" While drug-prevention organizations often have a specific approach to the issues surrounding alcohol/tobacco/other drug use, the authors of these articles challenge some of these viewpoints with research-based conclusions.

Benson, Peter, Judy Galbraith, and Pamela Espeland. *What Kids Need to Succeed.* Minneapolis, MN: Free Spirit Press, 1998. 243pp. $6.99pa. ISBN 1-57542-030-9pa.

This groundbreaking book describes the Search Institute study of over 100,000 young people in more than 200 communities to determine what "assets" (support, empowerment, boundaries) they had in their lives and how those assets helped youth resist alcohol, tobacco, drug use, and other risky behaviors. It also presents simple ways that parents, schools, and communities can help to build and develop these assets in their youth.

Schwebel, Robert. *Saying No Is Not Enough: Helping Your Kids Make Wise Decisions About Alcohol, Tobacco and Other Drugs.* New York: Newmarket Press, 1998. 290pp. $14.95pa. ISBN 1-55704-318-3pa.

Schwebel gives parents clear information about the history of alcohol/tobacco/other drugs and the effects they can have on bodies and minds. He then sets out a use prevention curriculum based on four pillars: high self-esteem, clear thinking, problem solving, and positive relationships. He includes activities that help parents and teachers develop these drug-resistance assets in children.

Solter, Aletha. *Raising Drug-Free Kids: 100 Tips for Parents.* Cambridge, MA: Perseus Books Group, 2006. 223pp. $13.95pa. ISBN 0-7382-1074-9pa.

This is one of the few comprehensive alcohol/tobacco/other drug use prevention books available. It looks at the underlying causes of adolescent drug use and provides parents with tips and techniques they can use starting at birth to build parent and family connections as well as child assertiveness, self-esteem, and decision-making skills. This book also includes tips for how to discuss alcohol/tobacco/other drugs with children and teens in age-appropriate ways.

Somdahl, Gary L. *Drugs and Kids: How Parents Can Keep Them Apart.* Salem, OR: Dimi Press, 1996. 261pp. ISBN: 0-931625-30-0pa.

      Somdahl presents a multitude of ways that parents can live up to their billing as "The Anti-Drug" with information about family antidrug contracts, refusal techniques, and real-life stories of families affected by alcohol/tobacco/other drug use and abuse.

References

Benson, Peter, Judy Galbraith, and Pamela Espeland. 1998. *What Kids Need to Succeed.* Minneapolis, MN: Free Spirit Press. 243pp. $6.99pa. ISBN 1-57542-030-9pa.

Gallogly, Meg. 2005. *Phillip Morris and Targeting Kids.* Washington, DC: Campaign for Tobacco-Free Kids. Available at www.tobaccofreekids.org. Accessed December 24, 2009.

Hilts, Philip J. 1994. "Is Nicotine Addictive? It Depends on Whose Criteria You Use. Experts Say the Definition of Addiction Is Evolving." *New York Times*, August 2, 1994. Available at http://www.nytimes.com/ref/membercenter/nytarchive.html (search for the article by title) and http://www.drugsense.org/tfy/addictvn.htm. Accessed November 14, 2010.

Kuhn, Cynthia, Scott Swartzwelder, and Wilkie Wilson. 2002. *Just Say Know: Talking with Kids about Drugs and Alcohol.* New York: W.W. Norton & Co. 159pp. $14.95pa. ISBN 0-393-32258-0pa.

National Cancer Institute. 2010. *Cancer Trends Progress Report—2009/2010 Update.* Washington, DC: National Cancer Institute. Available at http://progressreport.cancer.gov/doc_detail.asp?pid=1&did=2007&chid=71&coid=702&mid=#smoking. Accessed November 14, 2010.

Newsam, Barbara Sprague. 1992. *Complete Student Assistance Program Handbook: Techniques and Materials for Alcohol/Drug Prevention and Intervention in Grades 7–12.* West Nyack, NY: The Center for Applied Research in Education. 373pp. ISBN0-87628-878-6pa.

Parents: You Matter! Drugs/Alcohol, Your Teen and YOU. 2009. New York: Partnership for a Drug-Free America. Available at http://www.drugfree.org (search "Parents: You Matter!"). Accessed October 28, 2009.

The Partnership Attitude Tracking Study: Teens. 2008. New York: Partnership for a Drug-Free America. Available at http://www.drugfree.org (search "PATS study"). Accessed October 28, 2009.

Robert Wood Johnson Foundation. 2001. *Substance Abuse: The Nation's Number One Heath Problem.* Princeton, NJ: Robert Wood Johnson Foundation. 128pp. ISBN 0-942054-13-Xpa.

Schwebel, Robert. 1998. *Saying No Is Not Enough: Helping Your Kids Make Wise Decisions About Alcohol, Tobacco and Other Drugs.* New York: Newmarket Press. 290pp. $14.95pa. ISBN 1-55704-318-3pa.

Solter, Aletha. 2006. *Raising Drug-Free Kids: 100 Tips for Parents.* Cambridge, MA: Perseus Books Group. 223pp. $13.95pa. ISBN 0-7382-1074-9pa.

Somdahl, Gary L. 1996. *Drugs and Kids: How Parents Can Keep Them Apart.* Salem, OR: Dimi Press, 261pp. ISBN: 0-931625-30-0pa.

Surgeon General, 2010. *Youth Violence: A Report of the Surgeon General.* Washington, DC. Available at http://www.surgeongeneral.gov/library/youthviolence/chapter5/sec4.html. Accessed April 19, 2010.

Tobacco-Free Kids. 2010. *Big Tobacco's Guinea Pigs.* Washington, DC: Campaign for Tobacco-Free Kids. Available at http://www.tobaccofreekids.org/reports/products/. Accessed November 14, 2010.

Wilmes, David J. 1988. *Parenting for Prevention: How to Raise a Child to Say No to Alcohol/Drugs.* Minneapolis, MN: Johnson Institute Books. 197pp. ISBN 0-935908-46-3pa.

Chapter 8

Conflict Resolution Facts

Definitions

- **Conflict** (KON-flikt). *noun.* A disagreement between two or more people.

- **Mediate** (ME-de-ate). *verb.* To help others to solve a dispute or conflict.

- **Resolution** (rez-o-LU-shun). *noun.* A solution or a fix to a problem or disagreement.

What Does It Mean to "Resolve Conflicts?"

Conflicts are a part of everyday life because we all have different wants and needs, and we go about trying to satisfy those wants and needs in a world with limited resources (time, toys, money, land). And while conflicts might be inevitable, if we successfully resolve them, they don't have to result in broken friendships, anger, or violence. If we find ways to resolve conflicts with "win-win" negotiations, they may never escalate to the arguments, shoving matches, fistfights, or other conflicts that damage our schools and communities. To change a conflict into a "win-win" learning experience, librarians, educators, and parents can use the stories and activities in chapters 9 and 10 to teach children and teens the skills they need to resolve disagreements, either on their own or with the help of others.

How Big of a Problem Are Conflicts in Our Schools and Communities?

In her 2004 book *The Kid's Guide to Working Out Conflicts*, researcher Naomi Drew described her research interviewing over 1,000 middle-school students to see how conflicts affected their lives. In that survey, eight out of ten students (80 percent) said that they see arguments or fights every day at school. Almost half of students (45 percent) said that they have one or more conflicts every day. Nine out of ten students (90 percent) reported that they thought learning to solve conflicts was important (Drew 2004).

Thankfully, few of these conflicts lead to actual violence. But just because a conflict doesn't turn violent, it doesn't mean that it doesn't cause problems for students, teachers, and parents. Unresolved conflicts usually result in blaming, increased anger, and more conflicts down the road.

What Skills Do Children and Teens Need to Resolve Conflicts?

Researchers have identified several skills that help children resolve conflicts. Those skills include the following:

- **Self-Control.** Children who have good control of their thoughts and emotions and take responsibility for their actions are better able to control the fear or anger that often escalates conflicts into full-blown crises. These children will also be better able to harness their rational minds to help resolve a conflict (Drew 2004).

- **Teamwork.** Children who have the ability to work together to find common goals and develop "win-win" solutions to conflicts will have a much easier time resolving problems than those lacking teamwork skills (Drew 2004).

- **Problem Solving.** Children who can take a problem apart in their heads, generate several options for dealing with it, and then carry out a solution develop the reality-based idea that they can face life's challenges, a key building block for conflict resolution (Judson 2005).

- **Assertive Communication.** Children who can express themselves respectfully and assertively and can actively listen to someone else will be better able to describe, discuss, and resolve disagreements with others (Drew 2004).

The stories and activities in chapters 9 and 10 are organized by the conflict resolution building block skills listed above, making it easy for you to choose stories and activities for your classroom.

How Can We Resolve Conflicts?

Resolving conflicts is a social skill, similar to setting the table, writing a letter, or apologizing for a mistake. Like all social skills, it is teachable and learnable.

Three Ways to Approach a Conflict

There are at least three ways to approach a conflict: aggressively, assertively, and passively.

- **"The Lion" Aggressive Response (Win/Lose):** If someone jumps ahead of you in line, an aggressive response would be to hit or shove or yell at that person. You might frighten that person enough that he or she will go back to the end of the line, or that person might hit back, and the problem could escalate into a fight. Aggressive action is like a fire, hot and difficult to control.

- **"The Mouse" Passive Response (Lose/Win):** If someone jumps ahead of you in line, a passive response would be to just stand there and do nothing. You might even try to cut in line yourself at some time in the future (a passive/aggressive response).

- **"The Giraffe" Assertive Response (Win/Win):** If someone jumps ahead of you in line, an assertive response would start with taking a deep breath and making sure that your emotions are under control (Stop). Then you might think about the class rules about cutting in line (Think) and decide if you want to get involved in this issue. You might tap the student on the shoulder and remind him or her of the class rules about cutting in line. If that doesn't work, you could explain what you are seeing (Observe), how it makes you feel, and what you would like to see the student do (Plan). If the student still doesn't comply with the rule, you could then ask the teacher to intervene (Crawford and Bodine 1996).

Because an aggressive response escalates the conflict and a passive response ignores it and may even encourage the conflict-making behavior, the only response that has any hope of resolving the conflict is the assertive response.

S.T.O.P.

One way to deal with a problem is to implement the S.T.O.P. process. In this process, you:

- **Stop**—Stop what you are doing and focus on the problem. Look, listen, and pay attention to what you are thinking and feeling.

- **Think**—Think about what is going on around you. Ask yourself, "What is going on here?" "What are some possible solutions to this situation?"

- **Observe**—Look around at the situation. How are people feeling? (Look at their body language.) How are you feeling? Which one of the solutions would work best in this situation?

- **Plan**—Choose the best solution and take steps to implement the plan.

The Conflict Management Mindset

If you really want to resolve any sort of conflict, be it at school, at the library, at home, or at work, researchers have developed a set of steps to get you in the right "mindset" for solving conflicts. Although the process is "step-by-step," it isn't easy. You need to practice these skills several times, just like when you learned to read or drive a car, before the skills will become second nature.

1. Cool down; control your emotions.

Many small conflicts escalate into larger crises because one or both people involved in the conflict become angry and try to resolve the conflict with aggression. So the first step toward resolving any conflict is to calm down. Thomas Jefferson once said, "When angry, count to ten before you speak; if very angry [count to] a hundred." (Lloyd and Mitchinson 2008).

We have all had experiences in which we said or did something in anger and wished later that we could take it back. Avoid wasting that time by calming down before trying to solve a problem. We never think well when we're angry.

2. Talk to the other person in the conflict and use "I" messages to explain your thoughts and feelings.

We've all done this before. We get angry about something (forgetting step 1) and we say something like, "I hate it when YOU . . . ." We almost make it sound like the world would be perfect if that other person would just get it together and change to accommodate our needs. But try as we might, we can never control another person's behavior. We can only control our own behavior.

What's more, no one likes being told what to do. So a more effective conflict resolution approach is to always use "I" statements like, "When you cut in line ahead of me, I feel angry because that doesn't seem fair to me. I would like it if you would line up like everyone else."

3. Look the other person in the eyes and use "active listening" to hear his or her side of the story.

Many conflicts escalate when one person doesn't feel listened to and respected. One way to open the channels of communication is to make sure you are being a good listener. Good listeners listen with their eyes as well as their ears. They look for friendly or unfriendly body language. They repeat back what they think they have heard to make sure they heard what they think they heard.

4. Brainstorm at least five conflict solutions and choose the one that seems the "most fair."

There are an infinite number of solutions to most social problems. At this point, work together to think of at least five. Then work together to find the solution that works best for both of you. In the case of the "cutting in line" problem, you could agree to take turns being first in line. Other solutions could include flipping a coin to determine who gets to go in front or requiring the person who wants to be in front of the line to sing a song verse. Keep in mind, these don't all have to be "logical" solutions. Silly solutions can be just as effective if both people like them. Silly solutions may also help build friendly relationships that prevent future conflicts. The "work together" steps here also develop the teamwork skills you need to solve problems later.

For this process to work, people need to show **assertive communication** by listening to and thinking about what the other person thinks and feels. You demonstrate this by being respectful and not blaming or name calling the other person or putting him or her down with words or body language. You demonstrate **problem solving** by looking for several "win-win" solutions to the conflict and you demonstrate **teamwork** by attacking the problem, not the people involved, and by striving to come up with a fair solution for everyone involved.

Stories That Help Resolve Conflicts

Since self-control, teamwork, assertive communication, and problem-solving skills are key student building blocks for resolving conflicts, the stories and activities in chapters 9 and 10 help students develop those tools. The activities also provide some step-by-step models for resolving conflicts.

Sample Conflict Resolution Curriculum

Educators can use the stories and activities in this book to enrich a schoolwide conflict resolution program, as a stand-alone program or unit, or as a way to help children develop specific skills like self-control or teamwork. Following is an example of a week-long conflict resolution unit for students in grades 4–5 and a unit for students in grades 6–8. Alternatively, these programs could be offered in the library as a once-a-week program. The stories are in chapter 9, and the activities are in chapter 10.

Grade 4–5 Conflict Resolution Unit

Day 1: Understanding Others

Story: "The 'Missing' Ax and the 'Guilty' Boy" (China)

Activity 10-1: Empathy Role-play

Day 2: Listening and Talking Skills

Story: "Just Desserts" (Germany)

Activity 10-5: How Not to Listen or Activity 10-4: Emotion Charades

Day 3: Teaming Up

Story: "The Enormous Carrot" (Adapted from Russia)

Activity 10-3: Crossing the Delaware

Day 4: Finding Solutions

Story: "The Blind Hunter's Catch" (Zimbabwe)

Activity 10-2: Four Steps to Resolving a Conflict

Day 5: Steps to Resolve a Conflict

Story: "It's in Your Hands" (Jewish)

Activity 10-2: Four Steps to Resolving a Conflict

Grade 6–8 Conflict Resolution Unit

Day 1: Understanding Others

Story: "Four Blind Men and the Elephant" (India)

Activity 10-1: Empathy Role-play

Day 2: Listening and Talking Skills

Story: "How Rattlesnake Got Her Venom and Her Rattles" (Adapted African American Tale)

Activity 10-5: How Not to Listen or Activity 10-4: Emotion Charades

Day 3: Teaming Up

Story: "The Parable of the Stomach" (Aesop)

Activity 10-3: Crossing the Delaware

Day 4: Finding Solutions

Story: "The Difference Between Heaven and Hell" (Adapted Jewish Tale)

Activity 10-4: Four Ways to Face a Problem

Day 5: Steps to Resolve A Conflict

Story: "It's in Your Hands" (Jewish)

Activity 10-2: Four Steps to Resolving a Conflict

References

Canter, Lee, and Katia Petersen. 1995. *Teaching Students to Get Along.* Santa Monica, CA: Lee Canter & Associates. 166pp. $13.95pa. ISBN 0-939007-99-1pa.

Crawford, Donna, and Richard Bodine. 1996. *Conflict Resolution Education: A Guide to Implementing Programs in Schools, Youth-Serving Organizations, and Community and Juvenile Justice Settings.* Washington, DC: U.S. Department of Education, Office of Elementary and Secondary Education. 138pp.

Drew, Naomi. 2004. *The Kid's Guide to Working Out Conflicts: How to Keep Cool, Stay Safe, and Get Along.* Minneapolis, MN: Free Spirit Publishing. 150pp. $13.95pa. ISBN 1-57542-150-Xpa.

Judson, Karen. 2005. *Resolving Conflicts: How to Get Along When You Don't Get Along.* Berkeley Heights, NJ: Enslow Publishers. 112pp. ISBN 0-7660-2359-1.

Lloyd, John, and John Mitchinson. 2008. *If Ignorance Is Bliss, Why Aren't There More Happy People?* New York: Harmony Books. 400pp. $21.99. ISBN 978-0-307-46066-0.

Merriam-Webster. 2002. *The Merriam-Webster and Garfield Mini Dictionary.* Springfield, MA: Merriam-Webster. 501pp. $5.99pa. ISBN 0-87779-922-9pa.

Chapter 9

Conflict Resolution Stories

Resolving conflicts is a performance skill, like giving a speech, shooting a basketball, or riding a bicycle. These stories provide models for various ways to deal with conflicts. Reading and hearing these stories and answering the discussion questions can give young people the skills they need to resolve their own conflicts.

Conflict Resolution Building Block Skills

- **Self-Control.** Children who have self-control skills have the ability to monitor and adjust their emotions, thoughts, words, and actions to accomplish their short- and long-term goals.

- **Problem Solving.** Children who have problem-solving skills have the ability to look at a difficult situation, brainstorm several possible solutions, and then implement the best solution.

- **Teamwork.** Children who have teamwork skills have the ability to communicate with and cooperate with others to reach a common goal.

- **Assertive Communication.** Children with assertive communication skills have the ability to remain calm while listening and talking in a manner that is respectful to both the speaker and listener.

Ant and Magpie (China)

Skills: Teamwork, Problem Solving

Long ago, an Ant was carrying a seed back to her mound when a sudden rainstorm washed her down the hill and into a stream. She dropped the seed and began calling for help.

"Help, help!" Ant called.

Luckily for her, a resting Magpie bird heard her call and pulled a leaf off a branch and dropped it to Ant.

"Climb on this," she called.

Ant climbed onto the leaf "boat" and thanked the Magpie. Then she paddled to shore.

A week later, Ant was carrying another seed to her mound. She smiled as she heard Magpie singing in the tree above her.

"I know that bird," said Ant to her ant friends.

Just then, Ant saw a huge sandaled foot land right next to her. She looked up to see a hunter raising his gun toward Magpie.

Ant called out, "Sisters, sisters, bite and sting that man's foot!"

Just as he was about to pull the trigger, the hunter felt a burning pain in his foot. "Ow!" he yelled, frightening off Magpie. Magpie dove into a thick bush. From there she could see the hunter trying to stomp those angry ants.

The next day, Magpie found Ant walking down the trail, carrying a seed.

"Thank you for saving me yesterday," said Magpie.

"Think nothing of it," said Ant. "If you hadn't saved me last week, I wouldn't have been there to help you yesterday. What comes around, goes around, my friend."

Discuss

1. Describe a time when you helped someone. What happened? How did you feel afterward?

2. Describe a time when someone helped you. What happened? How did you feel afterward?

3. In many cases, helping people builds "social capital" and friendships that help prevent or resolve conflicts. List five ways you could help classmates at school.

Sources

Han, Carolyn. *Why Snails Have Shells: Minority and Han Folktales of China.* Honolulu: University of Hawaii Press, 1993. 74pp. ISBN 0-8248-1505-X.

Handford, S. A. *Aesop's Fables.* New York: Puffin, 1994. 212pp. $4.99pa. ISBN 0-14-130929-6pa.

Zipes, Jack. *Aesop's Fables.* New York: Signet Classic, 1992. 288pp. $4.95pa. ISBN 0-451-52565-5pa.

Just Desserts (Germany)

Skills: Self-Control, Assertive Communication

Glossary:

Spindle (SPIN-dell). *noun*. Short, pointed stick used to hold finished thread from a spinning wheel.

Long, long ago, there lived a widow who had two daughters. Her stepdaughter, Greta, was kind and hard-working, but her daughter, Helga, was mean and lazy. Unfortunately, the mother loved Helga best. The widow made Greta wash the dishes, cook the meals, tend the fire, cut the wood, and feed the animals. In short, Greta had to do everything. She even had to go out and sit by the well on the high road and spin wool into thread until her fingers bled.

Now it was Greta's bad luck one day to let some blood fall onto the spindle of thread. So she leaned over the well to get some water to wash it off. But the spindle fell out of her hand and dropped to the bottom of the well. Greta ran home crying to tell her mother what had happened. But the widow didn't care.

"Since you let the spindle fall, you should go and fetch it. If you can't find it, don't come back," she said with a scowl.

Greta thought and thought about what she should do. Since she could think of nothing else, she went back to the well, put her feet into the bucket, and jumped into the water. There was a terrific "Splash" and then everything went black.

The next thing Greta knew, she was lying in a flower-filled meadow looking up at a sunny blue sky. There were red, blue, yellow, and pink flowers everywhere she looked. Greta got up and walked across the meadow until she came to an outdoor baker's oven. The strange thing was, there were voices coming out of the oven.

"Little girl, we're the bread made of flour and ginger. Take us out or we'll be burnt to a cinder."

Greta knew about baking bread, so she took the loaves out of the oven and let them cool on a stone shelf. Then she set off until she came to a tree full of apples. But the tree talked to her as well.

"Shake me, shake me, with all your might. Then my apples will fall just right."

Greta knew about picking apples. She shook the tree until the apples fell all around her onto the soft ground. Greta gathered the apples into a pile and then set off again. She came to a cottage where a woman was sweeping the front step.

"Hello," said the woman.

Greta noticed that the woman's front teeth were so big they reminded her of a rabbit. That scared Greta, so she turned to run away, but the woman called after her.

"Please don't go! I get so few visitors here. I know that I look strange, but if you work for me, I'll care for you and I'll pay you well."

Greta thought about life with her stepmother and stepsister and figured that life with this strange old woman couldn't be worse. So she stopped running and went back to the cottage. The woman introduced herself as Mother Holle. First she gave Greta a warm meal of meat and potato stew. Then she took her around the cottage and garden to show Greta the work she would like her to do.

"Most of the jobs here, you can do any way you'd like, as long as you get the job done right. But one job I want you to do my way. I want you to make my bed by taking the feather blankets and tossing them into the air and shaking them so hard that the feathers go flying."

Greta thought that was a strange way to shake out a blanket, but she followed Mother Holle's directions. One day Greta got up the courage to ask Mother Holle why she wanted her blankets shaken so. Mother Holle smiled.

"Dear child, when you shake my blankets here, people say that snow falls back on earth. For that is one of my jobs, bringing snow to the world below."

Greta worked hard for Mother Holle, but as time went by, she missed her friends in the world below. After a year had gone by, Greta asked Mother Holle if she could return home.

"Of course you can, dear girl," said Mother Holle. "You had only to ask."

Mother Holle handed Greta the spindle she had dropped into the well. Then the two of them walked out of the garden gate and onto a path in the woods that Greta had never noticed before. It led to a silver oak tree.

"Put your hands out, girl," said Mother Holle.

And like magic, gold coins fell from the tree. Greta gathered them up in her hands and in her apron. But when she looked around, Mother Holle was gone, and she was once again standing by the well on the high road. She ran home to tell her stepmother and stepsister what had happened. At first the stepmother was angry. Then she saw the gold.

"Darling daughter, it is SO good to see you," she said, forcing a smile.

That was strange, because the widow had never called her "darling" before. But Greta told them her whole story, and the next morning, the widow sent Helga to spin thread on the high road and to drop her spindle into the well. Helga did as she was told and jumped into the well. When she arrived at the meadow, she walked right past the baking oven and the apple tree.

"I don't have time to dirty my hands for the likes of you! I'm looking for gold," she snorted.

When she came to the cottage, she saw Mother Holle.

"I want a job," Helga demanded.

"Well, if you work for me I'll care for you and I'll pay you well," replied Mother Holle, rather surprised that the girl wasn't afraid of her.

On Helga's fist day, she worked hard and followed directions, thinking she could get her gold and leave the next day. The second day, when Mother Holle wasn't looking, Helga dawdled over her work. On the third day, she didn't even get out of bed. She said she was ill, but Mother Holle knew she was just being lazy. Even when she did finally get out of bed, Helga never took Mother Holle's feather blanket outside to shake it around.

On the morning of the fourth day, Helga daubed her face with water to make it look like she was crying and she went to ask Mother Holle if she could go home to visit her friends, since she was so homesick.

"Yes, I think it is time for you to go," said Mother Holle.

Helga almost couldn't contain her joy. She thought, "That gold will soon be mine!"

Mother Holle handed Helga the spindle she had dropped into the well. Then the two of them walked out of the garden gate and onto a path in the woods that Helga had never noticed before. It led to a silver oak tree.

"Put your hands out, girl, and you'll get what's coming to you," said Mother Holle.

And like magic, lumps of sticky black tar fell from the tree. They stuck to Helga's hands and hair and dress and face. When the shower ended, the tar-covered Helga found herself standing by the well on the high road. But when she returned home, her mother pretended not to recognize her. When Helga grabbed onto her mother's arm, some of the tar stuck to her mother as well.

"Ahh!" they both screamed, running down to the lake to wash the stuff off.

Greta waited for her stepmother and stepsister to return, but days went by and they never came back. So she packed up her gold and set off down the road. Now some people say that Greta bought a farm of her own, and when the time was right, she found a kind young man to be her partner. Others say that she married the prince of a faraway country. You can decide which is true. From now on, the story is up to you.

Discuss

1. What was different about Greta and Helga? Which do you think you would like to have as a friend? Why?

2. What does this story have to say about being a guest in someone's house?

Sources

Grimm, Jacob, and William Grimm. *Grimm's Complete Fairy Tales.* New York: Barnes & Noble Books, 1993. 628pp. ISBN 0-88029-519-8.

Magoun, Francis P., Jr., and Alexander H. Krappe, trans. *The Grimm's German Folk Tales.* Carbondale: Southern Illinois University Press, 1960. 674pp. ISBN 0-8093-0356-6pa.

Stotter, Ruth. *The Golden Ax and Other Folktales of Compassion and Greed.* Tiburon, CA: Stotter Press, 1998. 183pp. $22.95pa. ISBN 0943565162pa.

The Enormous Carrot (Adapted from Russia)

Skills: Teamwork, Assertive Communication

Once upon a time, an old man and an old woman went out to plant vegetables in their garden. All of the vegetables grew well, thanks to generous amounts of fertilizer, but by midsummer, it was clear that one carrot in their garden was growing extremely well. When fall arrived, the old woman was harvesting the garden and she got to that carrot. It was so large that the carrot greens looked like a small bush.

"Well, I'll have to work to get this one out," said the old woman. So she set down her basket and grabbed onto the carrot, and she pulled and she pulled and she pulled with all her might, but that stubborn carrot stayed stuck all right.

So the old woman went behind the barn, where she found the old man chopping wood. "Dear husband, could you please help me pull up that enormous carrot in our garden?"

The husband, who loved carrot salad and carrot sticks and carrot cake, and most of all loved his hard-working wife said, "Of course, dear."

The old man grabbed onto the old woman, and the old woman grabbed onto the carrot, and they pulled and they pulled and they pulled with all their might, but that stubborn carrot stayed stuck all right.

"I've got an idea," said the old man, and he went and found his granddaughter working in the field.

"Granddaughter, could you please help us pull up that enormous carrot in our garden?"

"Sure, grandpa," said the granddaughter, who was very helpful.

She came to the garden, and she grabbed onto the old man, and the old man grabbed onto the old woman, and the old woman grabbed onto the carrot, and they pulled and they pulled and they pulled with all their might, but that stubborn carrot stayed stuck all right.

"I've got an idea," said the granddaughter, and she went and found the dog sleeping on the porch.

"Dog, could you please help us pull up that enormous carrot in our garden?"

"Sure, granddaughter," said the dog.

He trotted over to the garden, and he grabbed onto the granddaughter, and the granddaughter grabbed onto the old man, and the old man grabbed onto the old woman, and the old woman grabbed onto the carrot, and they pulled and they pulled and they pulled with all their might, but that stubborn carrot stayed stuck down tight.

"I've got an idea," said the dog, and he trotted into the barn, where he found the cat sleeping in the window.

"Cat, could you please help us pull up that enormous carrot in our garden?"

"Sure, dog," said the cat.

She stretched and sauntered over to the garden, and she used her mouth to grab dog's tail, and the dog grabbed onto the granddaughter, and the granddaughter grabbed onto the old man, and the old man grabbed onto the old woman, and the old woman grabbed onto the carrot, and they pulled and they pulled and they pulled with all their might, but that stubborn carrot stayed stuck all right.

This time the family pulled so hard that they fell right down. Puffing to catch her breath, the old woman said, "Maybe we won't be able to pull this carrot out after all."

"Nonsense," said the cat, who was very wise for her age. "We just need the right help."

"I've got an idea," said the cat, and she sauntered over to the haystacks in the field, and there she found mouse.

"Mouse, could you please help us pull up that enormous carrot in our garden?"

"Sure, Cat," said the mouse.

Mouse hopped up and scurried over to the garden. She grabbed onto the cat's tail, cat grabbed onto the dog's tail, and the dog grabbed onto the granddaughter, and the granddaughter grabbed onto the old man, and the old man grabbed onto the old woman, and the old women grabbed onto the carrot, and they pulled and they pulled and they pulled with all their might, and suddenly, that carrot took flight. They had pulled so hard that the carrot flew up into the air and landed, "Splash" in the pond.

"I knew I could do it," squeaked the mouse. "I knew I could do it."

The old woman took the rowboat out onto the pond and washed the enormous carrot. Then she borrowed the old man's ax and she cut the giant carrot into pieces for carrot sticks and carrot salad and carrot cake. That night, the old woman and the old man and the granddaughter and the dog and the cat and the mouse had the biggest and best carrot dinner ever.

And that's the end of the story.

Discuss

1. "Persistence" means trying and trying, even when it is hard and you want to give up. Describe examples of persistence from this story.

2. Who was the most important person or animal in this story? Is there a "most important" helper, or were they all important in accomplishing this task?

3. What does this story teach you about how to get help with solving a problem?

Sources

Afanas'ev, Aleksandr. *Russian Fairy Tales*. Trans. by Norbert Guterman. New York: Pantheon Books, 1945. 663pp. ISBN 0-394-73090-9pa.

Haviland, Virginia. *The Fairy Tale Treasury*. London: Hamish Hamilton Ltd., 1972. 192pp. ISBN 024102207X.

Pearmain, Elisa Davy. *Once Upon a Time: Storytelling to Teach Character and Prevent Bullying*. Greensboro, NC: Character Development Group, 2006. 377pp. $25.00pa. ISBN 1-892056-44-5pa.

The "Missing" Ax and the "Guilty" Boy (China)

Skills: Self-Control, Assertive Communication

One day a farmer left his house to chop some wood. When he turned the corner, the woodpile was still there, but his ax wasn't.

"I'm sure I left my ax here yesterday."

Then it dawned on him. "Someone has stolen my ax!"

He looked next door to see his neighbor's son working to move pieces of firewood.

"I've never trusted that boy," thought the farmer. "And now that he's older, I trust him even less. He has the look of a thief about him. Look how he won't meet my gaze or wave to me. I think he has something to hide. He even moves like he's guilty of something."

The farmer stomped back into the house. "That no-good boy next door has stolen my ax, I'm sure of it," said the farmer.

"Perhaps, dear," said his wife. "But before you accuse anyone of anything, make sure you didn't leave it somewhere else on the farm. You know how forgetful you can be sometimes, especially when you're busy. And you were very busy yesterday."

Grumbling, the farmer began walking around his property. Whenever the boy next door looked his way, the farmer would glare at him, but the boy didn't seem to notice.

As the farmer was just about to give up looking, he saw something glint in the sunlight. He walked closer and saw that it was his ax, still lying where he left it. It was next to a tree he wanted to cut down yesterday before he had been called away to help his wife with a sick calf. The farmer set to work chopping down the tree and cutting it up for firewood. As he carried the wood from the woods to his house, he saw that the neighbor boy was still carrying firewood. Then he realized why the boy had never met his gaze. The wood that the boy was carrying was so heavy, that he had to concentrate on his work.

"My what a good, honest, hardworking boy that is," thought the farmer.

Discuss

1. Have you ever been "sure" that someone took something of yours? How did that make you feel? What happened?

2. What changed about the boy in this story? What changed about the farmer? Why?

3. We sometimes imagine that a person is mean or that he or she doesn't like us, when in reality, that person is just busy. How would this story have been different if the farmer had simply asked the boy if he had seen the farmer's ax?

From *Story Solutions: Using Tales to Build Character and Teach Bully Prevention, Drug Prevention, and Conflict Resolution* by Kevin Strauss. Santa Barbara, CA: Libraries Unlimited. Copyright © 2011.

Sources

Forest, Heather. *Wisdom Tales from Around the World.* Little Rock, AK: August House, 1996. 160pp. $17.95pa. ISBN 0874834791pa.

Strauss, Kevin. *The Reading Ranger Guide to 55 Fabulous Five-Minute Folktales That Everyone Should Read and Hear.* Eden Prairie, MN: Trumpeter Press, 2010. 196pp. $25.00pa. ISBN 978-0-9814667-3-6pa.

Yolen, Jane, ed. *Favorite Folktales from Around the World.* New York: Pantheon Books, 1986. 498pp. $18.95pa. ISBN 0-394-75188-4pa.

The Blind Hunter's Catch (Zimbabwe)

Skills: Assertive Communication, Teamwork, Self-Control

Once, a young man married a woman. And this woman had a wise brother who lived with her. While the brother could see into men's hearts, his eyes were blind to this world.

The young man longed to get to know his brother-in-law, so he invited him to go hunting.

"You know that I cannot see," said the blind man. "But if you help me, I will come."

They traveled into the forest with the young man leading his blind brother-in-law. The blind man told the young man all the things he could hear around him. "There is a snake slithering over there. Listen to that bird as it feeds its young in the nest above us."

The young man hadn't noticed those sounds before, and he was impressed with his brother-in-law's hearing. Finally they came to a pond where birds came to drink. The young man set a trap near the water, disguising it so the birds couldn't see it. He set a second trap so his blind brother-in-law could catch a bird. He didn't bother to hide that trap very well.

"What does it matter?" he thought to himself. "He can't tell if I've hidden his trap or not. Besides, it is getting late and I must get back to my wife."

The two hunters returned the next day. Even before they reached the pond, the blind hunter knew that they had caught something.

"I hear the birds flapping in our traps!"

When they arrived at the young man's trap, he saw that he had captured a small brown bird. "It would make part of a meal," he thought as he put the bird in his pouch.

But when they reached the blind man's trap, the young man's heart filled with envy. There in the trap was a large, bright-colored bird with red and green and blue feathers. That bird would be worth a lot of money. Then he had an idea.

"Here is your bird," said the young man, handing the blind hunter the small brown bird.

The blind hunter took the bird and felt its feathers and beak and a strange look came over his face. But he said nothing.

On their way home, the two men sat under a tree to rest. As they were resting, they saw two monkeys screeching at each other.

"Sometimes they almost act like people," said the young man.

"Yes, sometimes," said the blind man.

"Now people in the village say you are a wise man, and I have always wondered why monkeys, or people, fight the way they do. Can you tell me?" asked the young man.

The blind man sat silently for several minutes until the young man wasn't sure if he had heard the question. But then the blind man turned to look him straight in the eye. It was almost as though the blind man could see into his heart.

"People fight because of greed and pride and because of what you have just done to me today."

From *Story Solutions: Using Tales to Build Character and Teach Bully Prevention, Drug Prevention, and Conflict Resolution* by Kevin Strauss. Santa Barbara, CA: Libraries Unlimited. Copyright © 2011.

The young man was shocked. He tried to deny the charge, but no words came to his dry throat. Finally, he got up and fetched his pouch and gave the bright-colored bird to his brother-in-law.

"Do you have any other questions?" said the blind man.

"Yes. How can people become friends again after they have fought with each other?"

"Ah, that is easy," said the blind man as he smiled. "They simply do what you have just done now. It is both the easiest and the hardest thing in the world to do."

Then the two men stood up and walked home together.

Discuss

1. This is a story about honesty. What lesson did the hunter learn about honesty?

2. Do you think the hunter would have tried to cheat his brother-in-law if his brother-in-law could see? Why or why not?

Sources

MacDonald, Margaret Read. *Peace Tales.* Hamden, CT: Linnet Books, 1992. 116pp. $14.95pa. ISBN 0-208-02329-1pa.

Smith, Alexander McCall. *Children of Wax: African Folk Tales.* Northampton, MA: Interlink Publishing Group, 1999. 128pp. $9.95pa. ISBN 1566563143pa.

Strauss, Kevin. *The Reading Ranger Guide to 55 Fabulous Five-Minute Folktales That Everyone Should Read and Hear.* Eden Prairie, MN: Trumpeter Press, 2010. 196pp. $25.00pa. ISBN 978-0-9814667-3-6pa.

Waters, Fiona. *Kingfisher Treasury of Five-Minute Stories.* London: Kingfisher, 2000. 151pp. $5.46pa. ISBN 978-0-7534-1156-8pa.

The Third Friend (Greece)

Skills: Self-Control, Teamwork

Glossary:

Amarantos (A-ma-RAN-tos). *noun.* A king in the ancient Greek colony of Sicily, in what is now modern Italy.

Damon (DAY-mon). *noun.* A friend of Pythias.

Pythias (PITH-e-us). *noun.* A friend of Damon.

Long ago in the ancient Greek colony of Sicily there lived two friends, Damon and Pythias. They had known each other all their lives and could always be trusted to lend a hand when the need arose. But back in those days, a cruel king named Amarantos ruled the island. The king was always afraid of being overthrown, so he sent his guards into the cities to root out even the smallest sign of disloyalty. Hundreds of innocent men and women filled the king's prisons and work camps.

Finally, Damon could take it no longer. He began making speeches in the town square, urging the people to rise up and get rid of Amarantos. The king's guards grabbed Damon and dragged him before the king.

"I sentence you to death by the executioner's ax for your treason!" roared the king.

"If the truth be treason, then I welcome my fate," said Damon. "But before I die, I have one favor to ask."

"And what is that?" bellowed the king.

"Could I have a week to put my affairs in order and to take money to my parents, so they won't have to live in poverty? I promise to return."

"Haw, haw, haw," laughed the king. "Why should I trust you to return? Doubtless you'll use the time to spread more lies about me. No, you stay in prison until the day you die."

Then a shout went up from the crowd. It was Damon's friend, Pythias.

"My king, I volunteer to take Damon's place. I will sit in his cell, and if he doesn't return, I will die in his place," said Pythias.

The king liked the sound of this. In his mind, the only thing more interesting than executing a guilty man was executing an innocent man in his place.

"Agreed," snapped the king. "But at sundown seven days from today, one of you will die." He leered at Damon. "I guess you can decide which it is to be."

Damon thanked his friend and set off to sell all his possessions and sail on a ship to visit his parents with the money and the bad news. But as he was visiting them, a storm arose. When Damon retuned to the docks, the captain refused to sail until the storm broke. Damon paced up and down the docks.

"I must reach my friend," he thought. "I must reach my friend."

On the morning of the seventh day, King Amarantos visited Pythias in his cell.

"I see that you are still here," laughed the king. "It seems that your friend loves his own life more than he loves you."

From *Story Solutions: Using Tales to Build Character and Teach Bully Prevention, Drug Prevention, and Conflict Resolution* by Kevin Strauss. Santa Barbara, CA: Libraries Unlimited. Copyright © 2011.

"That is not true, my king," said Pythias. "I know Damon, and if he is not here yet, he is on his way. Perhaps he ran into trouble on his journey. But I know he will be here."

At sunset, the guards led Pythias to the chopping block.

"What do you have to say now about your so-called friend, Pythias?"

"I trust him still," said Pythias as he set his head on the chopping block. "If Damon isn't here, he is dead already. For only death would keep him from this appointment.

As the executioner raised his ax, he heard a shout.

"WAIT!" called Damon as he entered the courtyard, gasping for breath. "I . . . am . . . here . . . my . . . . friend. I . . . am . . . here . . . my . . . king."

As Amarantos watched the two friends embrace, his heart warmed.

"Damon and Pythias, I have two questions for you," said King Amarantos.

"Yes, my king," they both replied.

"Pythias, how did you know that Damon would return?"

"He is my friend, my king. And friends keep their promises above all else."

The king looked at the ground.

"What is your other question, my king?" asked Damon.

"How can I earn your friendship?" said the king.

"That is easy, my king," said Pythias. "Do as we do. Help other people, keep your promises, and you will always be our friend."

And from that day on, the Kingdom of Sicily was a very different place.

Discuss

1. This is a story about friendship and trust. Can friendship exist without trust? Can trust exist without friendship?

2. Why did Damon trust that his friend would return?

3. Can you think of a time when you had to trust a friend or a group of friends? What happened?

Sources

Bateman, Teresa. *Damon, Pythias, and the Test of Friendship.* Park Ridge, IL: Albert Whitman & Co., 2009. 32pp. $16.99. ISBN 0807514454.

Gruenberg, Sidonie. *More Favorite Stories Old and New.* New York: Doubleday & Co., 1948. 512pp.

Pearmain, Elisa Davy. *Once Upon a Time: Storytelling to Teach Character and Prevent Bullying.* Greensboro, NC: Character Development Group, 2006. 377pp. $32.95pa. ISBN 1-892056-44-5pa.

Anansi's Dinner Guest (Ghana)

Skills: Assertive Communication, Problem Solving

Glossary:

Anansi (ah-NON-see) the Spider. *noun.* A lazy character who likes to play tricks on other animals.

Yam (YEAM) *noun.* Orange, starchy vegetable like the sweet potato many people eat on Thanksgiving.

Anansi the Spider loved to eat, and he loved to cook. One day he had spent the whole day cooking sweet yams for dinner. When he was just about to sit down to eat, there was a knock at his door. It was Turtle. Now Anansi knew that it would be rude to just close the door in Turtle's face, and he knew it was the custom to offer a guest some food. But Anansi didn't want to share his tasty yams with Turtle. So Anansi came up with a plan.

"Turtle, come right in," said Anansi. "I was just sitting down for dinner. After you wash your feet at the river, you are welcome to join me."

Turtle said, "Okay," and set off down the hill to the river. He carefully washed his feet and then walked up the hill for dinner, but since he walked on all four feet, his feet got dirty again.

Anansi looked at Turtle's feet with a smile. "Turtle, you need to wash your feet before you sit down to eat."

"I did wash my feet, but they got dirty on your trail back up from the river," protested Turtle.

"It's not my fault that you can't stay clean," said Anansi. "Go try again."

As Turtle turned to leave, he noticed that Anansi had already gobbled up half of the yams.

Turtle hurried down to the river and washed his feet again. This time he tried hopping up the hill on one foot, but he tripped and fell. All four of his feet got dirty again. When he walked into the house, he saw Anansi finishing the last of the yams.

"I am sorry, friend Turtle. But it seems there is no dinner left. If only you had been quicker about washing your feet."

At first, Turtle looked angry. But then his face softened to a smile.

"It is no problem at all, friend Anansi. In fact, to show you that there are no hard feelings, I would like to invite you to a feast at my house tomorrow night."

"Really?" said Anansi, surprised at his good luck.

"Yes, really. I live just under the river, where it makes a huge bend. My house is at the bottom of the river bed."

The next evening, Anansi walked to Turtle's house. He could smell the tasty vegetables that Turtle was preparing. He jumped into the water, but his body was so light that he couldn't dive deep enough to reach Turtle's house. Then he came up with an idea. Anansi went home and got a coat. He filled the coat's pockets with pebbles and then jumped into the water. The weight of the pebbles helped Anansi dive deep enough to reach Turtle's front door.

"Anansi, it is so good to see you!" said Turtle. "Welcome to my home. Let me take your coat for you."

"No thanks," said Anansi. "I'm feeling a little cold right now."

They walked over to Turtle's table. It was stacked high with apples, oranges, carrots, and sweet potatoes. Anansi licked his lips.

"Now Anansi, it is rude to eat a meal with your coat on. You don't want to be rude, do you?" said Turtle.

Reluctantly, Anansi took off his coat, and "Whoosh" he floated right to the surface of the river. Floating there, he watched as Turtle ate all that wonderful food all by himself.

Discuss

1. Why do you suppose Anansi acted the way that he did in this story? Would you have acted the same way? Why or why not?

2. Do you think that Turtle acted correctly? Would you have acted differently? Why or why not?

3. If Turtle had talked with Anansi about how he felt about Anansi's dinner trick, do you think that Anansi would have changed his behavior? Why or why not?

Sources

Courlander, Harold, and George Herzog. *The Cow-Tail Switch and Other West African Stories.* New York: Henry Holt & Co., 1947. 143pp.

DeSpain, Pleasant. *Thirty-Three Multicultural Tales to Tell.* Little Rock, AR: August House, 1993. 127pp. $15.00pa. ISBN 0-87483-266-7pa.

Gruenberg, Sidonie M. *More Favorite Stories Old and New for Boys and Girls.* Garden City, NY: Doubleday, 1948. 399pp.

Four Blind Men and the Elephant (India)

Skills: Assertive Communication, Teamwork

Long ago, four blind scholars heard that there was an elephant outside their village. Now you and I might know what an elephant is by looking at it, but these scholars had to touch things to learn about them. Since they had never touched an elephant before, the scholars asked their servant to lead them to the creature. They found it tied to a tree at the edge of town, eating its dinner.

The first scholar stepped forward and touched the elephant's trunk.

"Ahh, an elephant is like a powerful snake that can bend and twist in any direction," he said.

The second scholar walked forward and touched the elephant's ear.

"No, you are wrong; an elephant is like a great leaf that flutters back and forth in the wind."

The third scholar touched the elephant's leg and said, "You are both wrong. An elephant is like a tree trunk, thick and powerful."

The fourth scholar reached out and touched the elephant's tail.

"You men are crazy. Don't you know that an elephant is like a rope?"

The scholars argued and argued and argued until sunset, when the elephant driver took the elephant down the road. And some people say that those four scholars are arguing still.

Discuss

1. In this story, four different men described an elephant in four different ways. Who was right?

2. Is it possible for them to all be right and still not have the "whole picture" of what an elephant is? Why or why not?

3. It didn't occur to the scholars to work together to come up with the "big picture" of what makes an elephant. How could the servant have helped make this happen? For a group to work together as a team, it often needs a "leader" and it needs to have "followers." What does a leader need to do? What do followers need to do? Who could have been a leader in this story?

Sources

Leach, Maria. *Noodles, Nitwits and Numskulls.* Cleveland, OH: World, 1961. 96pp.

Pearmain, Elisa Davy. *Once Upon a Time: Storytelling to Teach Character and Prevent Bullying.* Greensboro, NC: Character Development Group, 2006. 377pp. $32.95pa. ISBN 1-892056-44-5pa.

Quigley, Lillian. *The Blind Men and the Elephant: An Old Tale from the Land of India.* New York: Scribner's, 1959. ISBN 0684127822.

From *Story Solutions: Using Tales to Build Character and Teach Bully Prevention, Drug Prevention, and Conflict Resolution* by Kevin Strauss. Santa Barbara, CA: Libraries Unlimited. Copyright © 2011.

The Parable of the Stomach (Aesop)

Skills: Teamwork, Assertive Communication, Problem Solving

Long ago, all the parts of a body got to talking about how hard their lives were. Each of them had a worse story than the last one.

The Eyes said, "All I do all day is look for things to eat, and what do I get for that? Nothing."

The Hands said, "You think you have it hard? I have to lift food to the mouth all day long, and do the hard work to make money for the food."

The Legs said, "You think that's hard? I have to walk mile after mile to work and to find and gather food. What's more, once I get to the food, I have to carry it back home. I'm always on the job."

The Mouth said, "I have to chew at the meals and that takes work, especially with muscles as small as mine. You may feed me, but I enjoy the food for only a moment and then it slides down my throat to the Stomach. That is who really profits from all of our labor."

Then Eyes said, "I've had enough of this. It is time that we teach that lazy Stomach what it means to pull his weight around here. I say we all go on strike and don't feed him any more food."

All the parts cheered, that is except Stomach, who stayed quiet. For the first few days, everything went fine. But then as time went on, Stomach started to growl. The other body parts just ignored it. Then the Eyes started to get blurry. The Hands started to shake. The Legs felt weak, and the Mouth was dry and sore.

It was then that the parts realized all of the things that Stomach did for them. Even though they couldn't see it happening, Stomach kept them strong.

"Maybe we should feed Stomach," suggested Hands.

Everyone else agreed, and after that, Eyes stayed clear, Hands and Legs stayed strong, Mouth could chew, and Stomach kept doing whatever it is that Stomach does to keep that whole body working right.

Discuss

1. This is a story about cooperation. What lesson do you hear in this story?

2. Why do you think the other body parts didn't see the value of the Stomach? What changed by the end of the story.

Sources

Handford, S. A. *Aesop's Fables.* New York: Puffin, 1994. 212pp. $4.99pa. ISBN 0-14-130929-6pa.

Jacobs, Joseph, ed. *The Fables of Aesop.* Mineola, NY: Dover Publications, 2002. 196pp. $2.50pa. ISBN 0-486-41859-6pa.

Zipes, Jack. *Aesop's Fables.* New York: Signet Classic, 1992. 288pp. $4.95pa. ISBN 0-451-52565-5pa.

The Heaviest Burden (Adapted from Indonesia)

Skills: Teamwork, Self-Control

Long ago there was a huge apple tree growing at the edge of a forest. The tree was tall and proud of its branches, and it carried large, round, red apples. One night, a whisper rose from the roots. It was the sound of complaining.

"We roots do all of the hard work around here!" said the Roots. "We're tired of it. We spend every day sucking up water and keeping you all rooted. We have to hold up the trunk and the branches and the leaves and all of the fruit. All the weight makes us sink into the ground, and we never get to feel the breeze or see the bright sun. We work day and night so the rest of you parts can take it easy. Look at the trunk. It has an easy life, just resting in the air and being lazy. Why can't we do that?"

"Easy? Is that what you think our work is?" said the Trunk. "I work harder than anyone else. I hold the whole tree together. If I were to fall, it would be the end of you all. I have to stand against the storm winds. I have to pass water up and food down my body. And suffering? I know all about suffering. Animals scratch my bark. People break my branches for firewood. It's not me who has an easy life; it is the leaves. Look at them, dancing in the sun. I wish I could be like them."

"That's garbage!" hissed the Leaves. "Our lives aren't easy. All day long we make sugar out of sun, soil, water, and air. Day and night we shade the rest of you from the hot sun and protect you from the hard rain. The wind tears us from the branches and blows us here and there. The bugs eat us and people burn us. Oh if only we were like the fruit. Fruit just hangs there and takes its ease in the sun."

"That's a lie!" growled the Fruit. "You airhead leaves know nothing! We do more than all the rest of you combined. Sure we grow fat, but it is for a good reason. We have to sacrifice ourselves for the rest of the tree. We are the reason that people don't chop down the tree for firewood. Do you think we like being eaten by deer and by bugs and by people? It is the seeds that have the easiest time of all. The seeds just wait inside me all summer long. They wait until they fall to the ground to sleep and grow. That is the job that I want."

"Shhh" whispered the Seeds, lying at the feet of the tree. "We should not argue, my friends. We each have a job to do, and each of us needs the others. United we stand. When it is my time, I have work to do as well. I crack open and grow a new root and new sprout. Some day, my new tree might be as big as you are now. Some day, some day."

Just then, a woman arrived to pick apples and the tree fell silent. Did the leaves and trunk and roots agree with the seed? What do you think?

 From *Story Solutions: Using Tales to Build Character and Teach Bully Prevention, Drug Prevention, and Conflict Resolution* by Kevin Strauss. Santa Barbara, CA: Libraries Unlimited. Copyright © 2011.

Discuss

1. What would have happened in this story if the parts of the tree kept arguing?

2. Who do you think has the best claim for working hard? Is that the right question to ask?

3. Coaches often say, "There is no 'I' in the word 'team'." What do they mean by that?

Sources

Brand, Jill. *The Green Umbrella: Stories, Songs, Poems and Starting Points for Environmental Assemblies.* London: A & C Black, 1991. 106pp. $17.95pa. ISBN 0-7136-3390-5pa.

Sechrist, Elizabeth Hough. *Once in the First Times: Folktales from the Philippines.* Philadelphia: Macrae Smith Company, 1949. 215pp.

Strauss, Kevin. *Tales with Tails: Storytelling the Wonders of the Natural World.* Westport, CT: Libraries Unlimited, 2006. 231pp. $35.00pa. ISBN 1-59158-269-5pa.

The Difference Between Heaven and Hell
(Adapted Jewish Tale)

Skills: Teamwork, Problem Solving

Long ago, a man named Jacob who had lived a particularly good life was growing old. One fall day he shared his meal with an old beggar whom he had met on the road. When they had finished their meal, the beggar looked at Jacob and smiled.

"You see Jacob, I am no beggar at all. I am an angel, and because of your generosity, I will grant you a wish."

"Well, Angel, I would like to see what I could expect in the afterlife."

"It's not a usual request, but you shall have it," said the Angel.

The Angel reached out and grabbed Jacob's arm. There was a flash and in a moment, they were standing in a green, grassy field on a pleasant summer day. In the middle of the field was a huge table laden with sausages and cake and pancakes and strawberries and oranges.

"This must be heaven," said Jacob.

"Don't judge so fast," said the Angel.

Jacob could see people walking toward the table. They wore strange white shirts that had long metal sleeves with no bend at the elbow.

It didn't take long for Jacob to realize that with no bend in the elbows, the people couldn't bend their arms to feed themselves. It was then that Jacob realized that the people's faces were gaunt and thin. They wore frowns and just stared at the sumptuous food on the table.

"This must be hell," said Jacob.

The Angel smiled and touched Jacob's arm. There was another flash. Suddenly they were standing in a green, grassy field on a pleasant summer day. In the middle of the field was a huge table laden with sausages and cake and pancakes and strawberries and oranges. Once again Jacob watched people with white shirts and metal sleeves walking to the table. But these people looked completely different. They had rosy round cheeks. They were smiling and laughing and talking together. When they reached the table, they sat down. And then each person turned to his or her neighbor, picked up some food and fed that neighbor. Everyone had plenty to eat.

The Angel turned to Jacob.

"Now that you have seen what you can expect in the afterlife, I will let you choose. Where would you like to go when you die?"

Jacob thought about what he had seen. Then his mouth broke into a wide grin.

"I want to go to hell . . . and teach those people how to feed each other."

Discuss

1. Why do you think Jacob made the choice he did at the end of the story?

2. Think of two ways you could apply the lessons of this story to your life. What would you do?

Sources

Outcalt, Todd. *Candles in the Dark: A Treasury of the World's Most Inspiring Parables.* Hoboken, NJ: John Wiley & Sons, 2002. 237pp. $15.95pa. ISBN 0-471-43594-5pa.

Pearmain, Elisa, ed. *Doorways to the Soul: 52 Wisdom Tales from Around the World.* Cleveland, OH: Pilgrim Press, 1998. 138pp. $13.00pa. ISBN 1556357400pa.

Stavish, Corinne, ed. *Seeds from Our Past: Planting for the Future.* Washington, DC: B'nai B'rith Center for Jewish Identity, 1997. 96pp. $10pa. ISBN 0-910250-31-6pa.

It's in Your Hands (Jewish)

Skills: Assertive Communication, Problem Solving

Long ago in a forest at the edge of a small village, there lived a hermit. Most people avoided the hermit. They thought he was strange. After all, who lives in the woods? Who lives on his own without family or friends? But people told stories about the hermit. Some said that he understood the speech of animals. Others said he could just look at the sky and tell how long it would be before it rained.

Way back then, children were sometimes naughty, as they are today. There was one group of children who always liked tricking adults. One day, the older children gathered together.

"I've got a plan! I've got a great plan to fool that silly old hermit," said a boy named Abel. "First, we'll catch a bluebird. Then we'll go up to that hermit's hut. I'll put the bird behind my back, and we'll ask that hermit what kind of bird it is. He can't possibly know what kind of bird it is. But if he does, then we'll ask him a second question that he can't possibly answer.

"We'll ask him, 'Is the bird alive or is it dead?' If he says the bird is dead, I will just open my hand and let the bird fly into the air. If he says that the bird is alive, I will clench my fingers and crush the bird and then hold it out for him to see. No matter how he answers, he'll be wrong!"

The older children thought this was a good idea. The younger children weren't sure, but they went along with the older ones and ran to catch a bird in the forest. That night, they crept out of their houses and walked into the woods. The children, even the older ones, felt a little frightened, but it was exciting, too. They were going to trick that stupid old hermit!

They saw a small light in the window of the hermit's hut as they walked up the path. They were almost close enough to knock on the door when the door opened. There stood the hermit.

"Welcome children, I have been waiting for you. I understand that you have two questions for me."

"How did he know we were coming? How did he know we had questions?" whispered the children.

"Sh, sh, sh," said Abel. "Well, old man, you think you're pretty smart, and we do have questions for you. You see, I have a bird behind my back, and if you're so smart, tell me what kind of bird it is."

The hermit looked at the children and stroked his white beard.

"Well, child, I believe that you have a bluebird behind your back."

"How did he know that? How did he know that?" whispered the children.

"Sh, sh, sh," said Abel.

"Well, I guess you know some things, old man. But answer me this. Is the bird alive, or is it dead?"

The old hermit looked into the wide eyes of each of the children. Then, very slowly he told him, "The answer to that question is in your hands."

Discussion

1. Sometimes when we hear news reports, we might get lulled into thinking that we don't have much control over our lives. While it is true that we can't control everything in our lives, we can control some things. Make a list of things that you can control in your life, either through you own actions or by asking someone else for help.

2. Did the hermit answer the children's question? Why or why not?

3. If you were the child holding the bird in this story, what would you do? Why?

Sources

MacDonald, Margaret Read. *Earth Care: World Folktales to Talk About.* North Haven, CT: Linnet Books, 1999. 162pp. $17.50pa. ISBN 0-208-02426-3pa.

Porcina, John. *Spinning Tales, Weaving Hope: Stories, Storytelling, and Activities for Peace, Justice and the Environment.* Philadelphia: New Society Publishers, 1992. 296pp. $24.95pa. ISBN 0865714479pa.

Strauss, Kevin. *Tales with Tails: Storytelling the Wonders of the Natural World.* Westport, CT: Libraries Unlimited, 2006. 231pp. $35.00pa. ISBN 1591582695pa.

How Rattlesnake Got Her Venom and Her Rattles (Adapted African American Tale)

Skills: Problem Solving, Self-Control, Assertive Communication

Long ago, when the animals were first made, Maker made every creature and gave it a job to do. Deer was supposed to eat the bushes and trees, so they didn't get too tall. Wolf was supposed to chase and eat the Deer, so they didn't eat all the plants. Mouse was supposed to eat seeds and chew on the bones left over from the dead animals, and Snake was supposed to eat the Mice, so they didn't eat too many seeds.

But Snake had a problem. Since she didn't have any legs, she couldn't move all that fast. And since she was so low to the ground, sometimes animals trampled right over her without a second thought. She didn't think most of them were doing it on purpose, but she couldn't be sure sometimes. She did know that her brown and green scales made her hard to see on the ground. That was handy when Broadwing Hawk was in the neighborhood, looking for a meal, but annoying when a herd of deer came tramping by.

One day, after being trampled half to death by Black Bear, Snake decided that she needed to do something about it.

"I'll go find Maker," she said. "He made us, he should be able to help solve our problems, and if he doesn't, we snakes might just go on strike and stop doing our job in the world."

Snake had heard that Maker lived on a high mountain in the west. So she crawled on her belly, day after day, until she got to the top of that mountain. There she found Maker sitting on a chair and admiring his work.

"Welcome Snake, what brings you to these parts?" said Maker.

"Well, to tell you the truth, I come here with a problem," said Snake. "You see, I can't move all that fast, and from time to time, I get trampled by the other animals. I have tried talking with them, and some of them, especially the smaller ones like Rabbit and Raccoon, have promised to be more careful, but the bigger ones like Bear and Deer don't really seem ready to be neighborly. They act like they are way too busy to bother with the likes of a lowly snake."

"That might have been a design flaw," said Maker.

"A what?"

"A design flaw," said Maker. "You see, I made all animals, including people, a bit selfish. I figured that was a good way to make sure they survived. But I might have overdone it in a few cases. You know, too much of a good thing, is not a good thing . . . ."

Maker thought for a few moments.

"Well, no use crying over spilled milk. Let's give them a reason to be a little more careful around snakes."

With that, Maker reached up into the sky and came down with two sharp fangs and a jar of clear liquid.

"Open wide," said Maker.

And he put the fangs into Snake's mouth and gave her a drink of that liquid.

"Now, if anyone bothers you, you can bite them, and the venom in your fangs will give them a good reason to avoid you. You shouldn't have any problems with those bigger animals after this."

Snake thanked Maker and set off back to her forest.

Now after all of those years of getting stepped on by the other animals, Snake was looking for a little payback, and she had a way to collect. She would lie down in the middle of the path, and when an animal came by, even if it didn't step on her, she would bite it on the ankle, and more often than not, give it a dose of venom. Pretty soon, forest animals were dropping like leaves in October, and everyone was afraid of Snake because she had power.

Pretty soon all the animals had a meeting, but they didn't invite Snake. Rabbit led the meeting.

"We've got to do something about that Snake," said Rabbit. "I've been to fifteen funerals this week, and it's only Tuesday. What's more, Snake isn't killing for food, like most animals do, she's just killing and leaving them there, lying on the ground."

"Yeah," said Frog. "Snake already killed four uncles, two brothers, and a second cousin. We can't leave the pond to catch bugs with that Snake around."

So the animals talked and talked about what they should do. Some wanted to talk to Snake, others wanted to just get together and finish her off. But a few of the more sensible ones had a different idea.

"How about we talk to Maker?" said Owl. "He's the one who gave Snake those fangs and venom in the first place."

You know how it is when you're on a committee. If you make a suggestion, then you become the one to carry it out. So Owl had to fly up and talk with Maker on the mountaintop. It didn't take long for Owl to get there.

Maker saw him coming.

"How's it going there, Owl?" said Maker. "How are those 'night vision' eyes working for you?"

"Oh, the eyes, they're doing great, Maker. I can find a mouse in the starlight. Couldn't ask for anything better," said Owl.

"So what brings you up here?" said Maker.

"Well, Maker, it's Snake," said Owl. "With those fangs and poison you gave her, we animals are dropping like ripe fruit. If this keeps up, soon there won't be many of us left, and I know that wasn't your plan. Do you think you could take away the venom?"

"Now I can do a lot of things," said Maker. "But I'm not sure I just want to take away Snake's venom until I look into this matter a little further. Tell Snake to come back up here right away."

Owl flew off and told the birds about Maker's message, since birds are one of the few animals that can get close to Snake without getting bitten. A few weeks later, the slow-moving snake reached the mountaintop.

"Snake, it appears that you and I need to talk about that venom I gave you," said Maker.

"What about it? It works great. I haven't been stepped on in weeks," said Snake.

"That's just it, Snake; from what I hear, you're using it for insurance instead of protection," said Maker. "I didn't mean for you to kill every animal in the forest just to keep them from stepping on you. They have jobs to do, too, and with you killing them left and right, they can't get much done."

"I'm sorry, Maker, but I guess I'm a little gun-shy after getting stepped on all those years," said Snake. "Me being so low to the ground means that it's hard to tell who is my friend and who might be an enemy, so I just bite whomever comes by."

"Well, maybe this was a little bit my fault, as well. Making you all camouflaged certainly doesn't help things," said Maker.

He thought for a minute and then reached into his pocket.

"Here Snake, take these rattles and put them on the end of your tail," said Maker. "If you hear someone coming, just shake your rattles. That will be a warning. If the animal is smart, it will go the other way. But if it isn't, then it probably deserves to get bitten."

That's why, to this day, we call those snakes "rattlesnakes." They still have their venom, and they still shake their tails to warn us when they are near.

Discuss

1. Snake tried to solve one problem but caused another. Was Snake's solution an example of an aggressive, assertive, or passive response to a problem? What might have been a more effective approach?

2. Sometimes it seems easy to use aggression to solve a problem. What are the disadvantages of using aggression to solve a problem? Is aggression a long-term or a short-term solution to a problem?

Sources

Hurston, Zora Neale. *Mules and Men.* New York: HarperCollins, 1990. 291pp. $13.95pa. ISBN 0-25320-208-6pa.

Lester, Julius. *Black Folktales.* New York: Grove Press, 1969. 110pp. $9.95pa. ISBN 0-8021-3242-1pa.

Strauss, Kevin. *Tales with Tails: Storytelling the Wonders of the Natural World.* Westport, CT: Libraries Unlimited, 2006. 231pp. $35.00pa. ISBN 1-59158-269-5pa.

Chapter 10

Conflict Resolution Activities

Resolving conflicts is a little like juggling and chewing gum at the same time. Children and teens (and adults for that matter) need to be aware of their own emotions and work to control them. Then they need to listen to the other person in the conflict and work with that person to come up with solutions that could resolve the conflict. The activities in this chapter help children and adults learn the building block conflict resolution skills of self-control, teamwork, problem solving, and assertive communication.

Activity 10-1: Empathy Role-play

Objective: Children and teens will learn how to develop the skill to listen empathetically to another person and try to imagine what the other person is thinking and feeling.

Skills: Assertive Communication, Teamwork

Grade Level: 4–8

Materials: "Sample Conflicts Handout" for each pair of students, paper, pencils

Background

Developing empathy, the ability to imagine and care about what another person is thinking and feeling, is a critical skill for resolving conflicts. In this activity, students role-play conflict situations, so they can begin to understand both sides.

Activity

1. Choose a conflict from the handout. Choose one person to be Person A and another to be Person B. Act out the role-play.
2. After going through the conflict, participants will write down what they think their character is thinking and feeling. Then they will write down what they think the other person is thinking and feeling.
3. Have each pair of children or teens get together with another pair. Ask them to describe their conflict and then describe how they thought the characters would think and feel in that situation.
4. Have students answer the following questions:

    Did you and your partner come up with the same list of thoughts and feelings for each character?

    Was it easier to come up with thoughts and feelings for your character or for the other character? Why?
5. Choose another conflict and have students do the activity over again. Like any skill, this gets easier the more you do it.

Evaluation

Have students turn in their emotional descriptions and write a one-page reflection paper on what they learned about the hard work of understanding other people's feelings.

Sample Conflicts

Conflict 1. Person A bumps into Person B as they are walking down the hall. Person A trips and falls. He gets up angry and is sure that Person B tripped him on purpose. Person B didn't mean to trip Person A. Person B feels sorry for what happened, but she becomes defensive and doesn't want to apologize.

Conflict 2. Person A gets into line and then Person B cuts in line ahead of her. Person A isn't sure how to respond, but she is glaring at Person B and she's getting angrier and angrier. Soon her anger boils over.

Conflict 3. Person A reaches for a marker at the art room table, but Person B grabs the marker and holds it in his right hand while writing with another marker in his left hand.

Conflict 4. During a playful shoving match at the lunch table, Person A hits Person B with a frosted piece of cake. Person B is not happy. Both have to decide what to do next.

Conflict 5. Student A learns that Student B is spreading mean rumors about her.

Activity 10-2: Four Steps to Resolving a Conflict

Objective: Students will learn four steps that anyone can use to resolve a conflict.

Skills: Teamwork, Problem Solving

Grade Level: 4–8

Materials: "The Four Steps to Resolving a Conflict" (p. 203) and "Sample Conflicts" (p. 201) handouts for each pair of children or teens in the group, paper, pencils

Background

Resolving conflicts is a skill just like riding a bike or driving a car. To really learn a skill, you need to try it out and practice until it becomes easy. This activity helps children practice the "Four Steps to Resolving a Conflict."

Activity

1. Have children choose a partner, or assign partners. Have pairs choose a conflict from the handout and act it out. One person will be Person A and the other person will be Person B.
2. Have children act out the role-play but this time, rather than stopping with the conflict, practice using "The Four Steps to Resolving a Conflict."
3. After going through the conflict, participants will write down the steps that their characters took to try to resolve it.
4. Have students get together with another pair and describe their conflict and how each student tried to resolved it.
5. Have students choose another conflict and do the activity all over again. Like any skill, this gets easier the more you do it.

Evaluation

Have students write a one-page review paper about how it felt to use "The Four Steps to Resolving a Conflict " and how they might use these steps in their lives.

The Four Steps to Resolving a Conflict

1. Cool down. Take five deep breaths. Control your emotions, especially any anger or fear you might be feeling.

2. Talk to the other person in the conflict and use "I" messages to explain your thoughts and feelings.

3. Look the other person in the eyes and use "active listening" to hear his or her side of the story.

4. Brainstorm at least five conflict solutions and use the one that seems the "most fair."

Activity 10-3: Crossing the Delaware

Objective: Children will develop teamwork skills by solving a group challenge.

Skills: Problem Solving, Teamwork

Grade Level: 6–8

Materials: three grocery-sized paper bags for each team, large activity space (gym, empty cafeteria, etc.)

Activity

In this activity, participants must work together to get everyone across a simulated river in the middle of winter.

1. Either move the chairs or desks to the walls to create a large open space or move to an auditorium or gymnasium. Divide the group into smaller groups of five. Give each group three standard-sized paper grocery bags. Have students gather along one wall. Tell them that they are the survivors of a winter plane crash. They must cross a frozen river to reach the safety of a nearby town. Their goal is to get their entire group across safely. The only tools they have to cross the frozen river, without falling through the thin ice, are three pieces of aluminum scavenged from the airplane (the paper bags). Each piece of aluminum, and the ice it covers, will support the weight of two people. But if anyone's foot touches the floor before he or she can touch the opposite wall, that person breaks through the ice, and the whole group has to start over again.

2. When one group finishes, they can help other groups cross. There is no rule against groups teaming up to solve this problem, but let them figure this out on their own. There is no "prize" for the team that gets across first.

3. For older students who might figure out how to use fifteen paper bags to build a bridge across the ice, compliment them for their creativity and then challenge them to do the activity again without help from other groups.

4. After completing this exercise, sit down with students and discuss the following questions:

   How did your group get across the frozen river?

   What was the most effective way to cross the frozen river? Why? (There are several good solutions.)

   What skills did your group need to solve this problem?
   (leadership, communication, problem solving, and teamwork)

   If someone from your group fell through the ice, did you blame that person ("He's so clumsy!") or did you blame your plan ("I guess that didn't work.")? Which approach fosters teamwork and cooperation? (It's always better to attack the problem than to attack and complain about people, since everyone makes mistakes sometimes.)

   Apply what you learned here to another school or community setting. How can you use these teamwork skills somewhere else?

Evaluation

Have students write a one-page description of what happened while they were "Crossing the Delaware."

Activity 10-4: Emotion Charades

Objective: Children and teens will learn how to read body language by playing a body language simulation game.

Skills: Assertive Communication, Problem Solving, Teamwork

Grade Level: 4–8

Materials: two sets of "Feeling Cards" (p. 206)

Activity

Understanding body language can help you to understand and develop empathy for other people. In this activity, participants use charades to communicate emotions.

1. Divide the group into two teams. Have each team huddle in opposite corners of the room. Print off two copies of the "Feeling Cards" (following) on thick paper and put a stack of cards in front of each team. When you say "go," one person from each team runs up, grabs a card, and then acts out the emotion. When someone on a team guesses the emotion, he or she takes the card back to the team and tags the next person in line. That person goes up, grabs a card, and acts out that emotion. The cardholder can't use words or verbal sounds. He or she can't write things down. There may be more than one of each kind of emotion in the stack, especially for sixth to eighth graders.

2. When one group goes through all of their cards, they join the other team to help them finish up.

3. After completing this exercise, sit down with students and discuss the following questions:

   Which emotions were the easiest to express with body language? Why?

   Which emotions were the most difficult to express with body language? Why?

   Do you think it is easy to hide your emotions, or do they always "show up" in the end, no matter what you do?

Evaluation

Model five different emotions for students and ask them to write down which emotion you are modeling. Discuss how misreading someone's emotions can lead to problems.

Feeling Cards

Anger	**Fear**
Disgust	**Shy**
Sad	**Worried**
Happy	**Excited**
Silly	**Bored**
Confused	**Proud**
Surprised	**Afraid**
Annoyed	**Elated**

Activity 10-5: How Not to Listen

Objective: Students will learn assertive communication skills by modeling both effective and ineffective communication skills.

Skills: Assertive Communication, Self-Control

Grade Level: 4–8

Materials: none

Activity

In this activity, participants model effective and ineffective listening techniques and they see how those techniques make them feel.

1. Divide the group into teams of two. Have participants decide who in each team will be Person A and who will be Person B.

2. Person A starts by talking about a favorite hobby or activity. Person B models ineffective listening techniques like looking at the floor, crossing his or her arms, turning sideways to the speaker, interrupting, moving around in his or her chair, tapping his or her fingers, looking around the room.

3. Then Person B talks about a favorite hobby or activity while Person A uses ineffective listening techniques.

4. Have both people write down as much as they can remember from the conversations. Have them write down how it felt to be the speaker and how it felt to be the listener.

5. Person A starts by talking about a favorite hobby or activity (something different from earlier in the activity). Person B models effective listening techniques like maintaining eye contact, smiling, nodding, leaning toward the speaker, asking questions about the topic, and focusing on the speaker.

6. Then Person B talks while Person A uses effective listening techniques like maintaining eye contact, smiling, nodding, leaning toward the speaker, asking questions about the topic, and focusing on the speaker.

7. Have both people write down as much as they can remember from this second set of conversations. Have them write down how it felt to be the speaker and how it felt to be the listener.

8. Have each pair join another pair to discuss their findings. What happened? What surprised them?

9. After completing this exercise, sit down with students and discuss the following questions:

   How did it feel when you weren't being listened to?

   How did it feel to be listened to?

   Which set of listening techniques helped you remember more of what you heard?

   Which ineffective listening techniques do you most often see from your friends and classmates?

   Which ineffective listening techniques do you most often use yourself?

Evaluation

Have students model first ineffective and then effective listening skills while the teacher or a guest speaker (principal, school counselor) talks with them. Then have students write a half-page reflection paper on the experience.

Activity 10-6: The Story of the Amazing Me!

Objective: Children and teens learn reflective listening skills and discover how to learn more about a classmate.

Skills: Assertive Communication, Teamwork

Grade Level: 4–6

Materials: "Sample Story Questions" handouts for each pair, paper, pencils

Activity

The more we learn about a person, the more likely we are to get along with that person. In this reflective listening activity, students practice listening to answers and then repeating the words and the emotions they hear from the speaker. Reflective listening is an important communication skill that provides the information people need to work together and solve conflicts.

1. Divide the group into teams of two. Have children decide who in each group will be Person A and who will be Person B.

2. Person A acts as the Questioner/Listener, while Person B acts as the Speaker. After asking a question and using effective listening skills to focus on the answer, Person A will
   summarize Person B's answer in one sentence and
   describe the emotions that Person B was expressing on the topic.
   Person B always has the option of asking for another question, if he or she isn't comfortable answering a chosen question.

3. After answering three questions, Person A writes down as much as he or she can remember about the conversation. Then the participants switch roles.

4. After completing this exercise, sit down with participants and discuss the following questions:

   How did it feel to have to listen to and summarize someone else's words?

   How did it feel when someone else summarized what you said and described your feelings?

   If someone used these techniques with you when you were feeling angry or upset, do you think these techniques would help you feel more angry or upset or more calm? Why?

Evaluation

Have each participant write a one-page "story" about his or her partner in this activity. Have the "subject" of the story review the story and suggest changes and improvements to the story's author.

If you have time, have each participant introduce his or her partner by telling that partner's story to the rest of the class. This last part of the activity can go a long way toward helping participants learn about and understand one another. As my friend, storyteller Dan Keding (www.dankeding.com), always reminds us, "You can't hate someone once you have heard his story."

Sample Story Questions

1. If you could meet any one person in the world, from any period of time, who would it be, and why?

2. If you won the lottery and had a million dollars to spend on your favorite hobby or activity, how would you spend the money?

3. What is the best movie you've ever seen, and why?

4. Describe a time you got really angry. What happened?

5. Describe a time when you were very happy. What happened?

6. If you could travel anywhere in the world, where would you go, and what would you do there?

7. Tell me about a time when you learned an important lesson.

Activity 10-7: Four Ways to Face a Problem

Objective: Participants will learn four approaches to handling a crisis: anger, fear, escapism, and problem solving.

Skills: Problem Solving

Grade Level: 4–8

Materials: "Four Ways Story" handout for each participant, paper, pencils

Background

There are many ways that a person can face a problem. In this activity, students hear or read a story and then decide how effective each person's problem-solving strategy was.

Activity

1. Have participants read or listen to the "Four Ways" story.

2. As a group, answer the following questions:

   • Which approach is most likely to help the friends get into their movie,

   • Sammy's fear, Wilma's anger, Aaron's escapism, or Betty's planning? Why?

   • In what ways could the other friends use their emotions to help solve this problem?

   (For example, Sammy's fear could help the group anticipate, discuss, and deal with upcoming angers. Wilma's anger, if properly funneled, could inspire friends to work harder to solve the problem. Archie's escapism could help the group calm down and relax, so they don't get so wound up when parts of the plan fail.)

3. Have participants write an ending for this story explaining what happened to each friend, based on his or her initial reactions to this problem.

4. To help her solve this problem, Betty followed the Stop, Think, Observe, Plan process (S.T.O.P.). This is a good process to use for problem solving, because it can prevent or preempt emotions that encourage us to get angry, be scared, or give up on life.

5. Based on their initial actions, who do you think would be the most likely to get a boost in self-esteem from what happened in this story? Why?

Evaluation

Have participants write a one-page ending for the above story or a one-page reflection paper on which approach would have the greatest likelihood of success, defined as "finding a way for the friends to have a fun day."

Four Ways Story

One Saturday, four friends decided to go to the movies, so they rode their bikes to the movie theater. But when they got there, they learned that the movie they wanted to see, *Captain Nitro's Super-Powered Adventure,* had sold out.

"Oh no!" cried Sammy. "I told my mom that we were going to see this movie. If she finds out that we were late, then I'm in BIG trouble! She won't let me got anywhere with you guys after this."

He sat down on the curb and sulked.

Wilma scowled at her friends. "This was all your fault, Sammy! If you didn't waste so much time getting ready, we would have been here early enough to get tickets!"

Aaron looked at his friends and shrugged his shoulders.

"Oh well, I didn't really want to see that movie anyway. While you guys figure out what to do, I'm going to play with my video game."

He took out a pocket video game and started playing with it.

Only Betty looked at the ticket seller and asked, "When's the next show."

When she heard it wasn't for three hours, she sat down on the curb to think up a plan.

Additional Readings

Fiction (Grades 4–8)

Cofer, Judith Ortiz. *The Meaning of Consuelo*. Boston: Beacon Press, 2004. 194pp. $15.00pa. ISBN 978-0807083871pa.

> Life is conflict for teenage Consuelo, who has to balance her parents' competing values and figure out how to help a younger sister who seems more and more troubled. What's more, the bookish Consuelo has to find out how to make her way in a Puerto Rico that is changing more and more every day.

Kimmel, Elizabeth Cody. *Unhappy Medium*. New York: Little, Brown, 2009. 277pp. $10.99. ISBN 978-0316066877.

> Kat talks to dead people. So when she joins a friend on a trip to a musicians' conference, she figures she can relax. But the dead don't take a vacation. Soon Kat is trying to free the spirit of a deceased medium, and her friend Jac needs help with a big conflict in the material world as well.

Krisher, Trudy. *Uncommon Faith*. New York: Holiday House, 2003. 263pp. $17.95. ISBN 978-0823417919.

> Millbrook, Massachusetts, seems like an ordinary town in 1837. But it holds some secrets. Ten townspeople describe their lives there and how some people are willing to take chances to help others. One of them, a teenager named Faith, gets into conflicts when she stands up for what she thinks is right. Women just didn't do that back then.

Marchetta, Melina. *Saving Francesca*. New York: Knopf Books for Young Readers, 2006. 256pp. $8.95pa. ISBN 978-0375829833pa.

> Being the first at anything is hard. That's what Francesca finds out when she is one of the first girls in a formerly all-boy Catholic school. But that's not the worst of it. She comes home every night to a depressed mother. What's more, there are all those teenage relationship issues to figure out.

Moriarty, Jaclyn. *The Year of Secret Assignments*. New York: Scholastic Paperbacks, 2005. 352pp. $8.99pa. ISBN 978-0439498821pa.

> No one thought they would like the assignment. But they still had to do it. Three "upper crust" girls have to be pen pals with three boys from the rival "lowlife" public school. What starts out as a way for students at feuding schools to learn about each other quickly turns into another source of conflict, as Matthew threatens his pen pal, Cassie. But Emily and Lydia aren't going to let anyone hurt their friend. Soon both sides are in the spying and revenge business.

Schmidt, Gary D. *Lizzie Bright and the Buckminster Boy*. New York: Laurel-Leaf Books, 2008. 240pp. $6.99pa. ISBN 978-0375841699 pa.

> Just forty-five years after the end of slavery, a small town in Maine still prefers to see white people in town and wants those other people to keep to themselves. But loner Turner, the son of the new minister, strikes up a friendship with African American Lizzie Bright, who lives on a nearby island with her family. The problem is that city elders want Lizzie and her people to move away so their town can become a tourist destination.

Tracy, Kristen. *Camille McPhee Fell Under the Bus*. New York: Delacorte Press, 2009. 293pp. $16.99pa. ISBN 9780385906333pa.

> Camille McPhee has a lot on her plate for a ten-year-old. She has to control her low blood sugar, figure out how to deal with her overbearing parents, and learn how to cope when her best friend moves away. That's a big list for fourth grade, but Camille faces it all, one step at a time.

Nonfiction (Grades 4–8)

Drew, Naomi. *The Kid's Guide to Working Out Conflicts: How to Keep Cool, Stay Safe, and Get Along.* Minneapolis, MN: Free Spirit Publishing, 2004. 146pp. $13.95pa. ISBN 1-57542-150-Xpa.

There are several books that teach kids how to work out conflicts, but this book uses survey data and teens' own words to talk about conflicts and how to resolve them. It also provides easy, step-by-step instructions for how to avoid or get out of situations most likely to escalate teenage conflicts.

Hayhurst, Chris. *Stay Cool: A Guy's Guide to Handling Conflict.* New York: Rosen Publishing, 2000. 48pp. $27.95. ISBN 0-8239-3159-5.

While everyone has conflicts, a dispute between boys can quickly result in a fistfight. That's why this guide helps boys (and girls, for that matter) understand what conflicts are, why they happen, and some effective ways to resolve them.

Judson, Karen. *Resolving Conflicts: How to Get Along When You Don't Get Along.* Berkeley Heights, NJ: Enslow Publishers, 2005. 112pp. $31.93. ISBN 0-7600-2359-1.

Conflicts may be inevitable, but solutions aren't. Judson walks readers through the steps to understand the wide range of conflicts that people have and the various ways we can resolve them.

Rue, Nancy N. *Peer Mediation.* New York: Rosen Publishing, 1997. 64pp. ISBN 0-8239-2435-1.

Peer mediation, or having a fellow classmate help two people solve a conflict, can be a very effective solution to many teenage conflicts in school. This guide teaches teens what mediation is, how it can help them resolve problems, and how to get involved in peer mediation programs.

References

Drew, Naomi. 2004. *The Kid's Guide to Working Out Conflicts: How to Keep Cool, Stay Safe, and Get Along.* Minneapolis, MN: Free Spirit Publishing. 146pp. $13.95pa. ISBN 1-57542-150-Xpa.

Judson, Karen. 2005. *Resolving Conflicts: How to Get Along When You Don't Get Along.* Berkeley Heights, NJ: Enslow Publishers. 112pp. $31.93. ISBN 0-7600-2359-1.

Reprint Permissions

Kevin Strauss and Libraries Unlimited gratefully acknowledge the following publishers for permission to reprint the material in this book.

Introduction:

"How To Use This Book," "Six Skills That Help Us Solve Problems," and portions of "The Effects of Storytelling" adapted from *Building Heroes/Blocking Bullies: The Teacher and Parent Guide to Simple, Repeatable, Assertive Techniques That Anyone Can Use to Stay Safe and Stop Bullies*. Kevin Strauss. © 2010 by Kevin Strauss. Reproduced with permission of Trumpeter Press, Eden Prairie, MN (http://www.trumpeterpress.com).

"The Power of Story," "Definitions," "Why Tell Stories," and portions of "The Effects of Storytelling" are adapted and reprinted sections of pages 3–8 in *Tales with Tails: Storytelling the Wonders of the Natural World*. Kevin Strauss. © 2006 by Kevin Strauss. Reproduced with permission of ABC-CLIO, LLC.

Chapter 1:

Portions of Chapter 1 are adapted and reprinted sections of pages 3–8 in *Tales with Tails: Storytelling the Wonders of the Natural World*. Kevin Strauss. © 2006 by Kevin Strauss. Reproduced with permission of ABC-CLIO, LLC.

Chapter 2:

"Blocking and Preventing Bullying Behavior" adapted and reprinted from *Building Heroes/Blocking Bullies: The Teacher and Parent Guide to Simple, Repeatable, Assertive Techniques That Anyone Can Use to Stay Safe and Stop Bullies*. Kevin Strauss. © 2010 by Kevin Strauss. Reproduced with permission of Trumpeter Press, Eden Prairie, MN. (http://www.trumpeterpress.com)

Chapter 3:

"Three Goats and a Troll," "The Three Clever Pigs," "The Monster in the Cave," "The Danger of Fear," "The King and His Falcon," "The Doorways of Success and Failure," "How Beetle Won A Colorful Coat," "The Fox With Hundreds Of Tricks, Cat with One," "The Samurai and the Island," "It's Not Our Problem," "The Moon Goddess," "How Guinea Fowl Got Spots on Her Wings," "The Man on the Moon," "The Cat Monk," "Three Butterfly Friends," "The Strength of a Bundle of Sticks," "The Lion and the Mouse," "The Grasshoppers and the Monkeys," "Three Bulls and the Lion," "A Trumpeter Taken Prisoner," and "The Company You Keep" have been reprinted from *Building Heroes/Blocking Bullies: The Teacher and Parent Guide to Simple, Repeatable, Assertive Techniques That Anyone Can Use to Stay Safe and Stop Bullies*. Kevin Strauss. © 2010 by Kevin Strauss. Reproduced with permission of Trumpeter Press, Eden Prairie, MN (http://www.trumpeterpress.com).

"Putting Feathers Back in the Pillow" reprinted from page 198 in *Tales with Tails: Storytelling the Wonders of the Natural World*. Kevin Strauss. © 2006 by Kevin Strauss. Reproduced with permission of ABC-CLIO, LLC.

Chapter 4:

Activities 4-1 through 4-12 have been reprinted from *Building Heroes/Blocking Bullies: The Teacher and Parent Guide to Simple, Repeatable, Assertive Techniques That Anyone Can Use to Stay Safe and Stop Bullies*. Kevin Strauss. © 2010 by Kevin Strauss. Reproduced with permission of Trumpeter Press, Eden Prairie, MN (http://www.trumpeterpress.com).

Chapter 6:

"The Peddler of Swaffham," "King Midas and the Gift of the Golden Touch," "The Wild Boar and the Fox," "Grasping at the Moon," "The City Mouse and the Country Mouse," "Pandora's Box," "The Farmer and the Snake," "Elders Feed the People," and "Good News, Bad News" have been reprinted from *The Reading Ranger's Guide to 55 Fabulous Five-Minute Folktales That Everyone Should Read and Hear*. Kevin Strauss. © 2010 by Kevin Strauss. Reproduced with permission of Trumpeter Press, Eden Prairie, MN (http://www.trumpeterpress.com).

"The Goose That Laid the Golden Eggs" reprinted from page 200 in *Tales with Tails: Storytelling the Wonders of the Natural World*. Kevin Strauss. © 2006 by Kevin Strauss. Reproduced with permission of ABC-CLIO, LLC.

"The Man, the Boy, and Their Donkey" reprinted from page 30 in *Tales with Tails: Storytelling the Wonders of the Natural World*. Kevin Strauss. © 2006 by Kevin Strauss. Reproduced with permission of ABC-CLIO, LLC.

"Why Bear Has a Stumpy Tail" reprinted from pages 71–72 in *Tales with Tails: Storytelling the Wonders of the Natural World*. Kevin Strauss. © 2006 by Kevin Strauss. Reproduced with permission of ABC-CLIO, LLC.

"The Boy and the Jar of Raisens," "The Lotus-Eaters," "Never Enough," "The Money Fish," "The Three Impossible Gifts," "Cat and Parrot," and "Fox and Crow" have been reprinted from *Building Heroes/Blocking Bullies: The Teacher and Parent Guide to Simple, Repeatable, Assertive Techniques That Anyone Can Use to Stay Safe and Stop Bullies*. Kevin Strauss. © 2010 by Kevin Strauss. Reproduced with permission of Trumpeter Press, Eden Prairie, MN (http://www.trumpeterpress.com).

Chapter 7:

Activities from 7-2 through 7-6 have been reprinted from *Building Heroes/Blocking Bullies: The Teacher and Parent Guide to Simple, Repeatable, Assertive Techniques That Anyone Can Use to Stay Safe and Stop Bullies*. Kevin Strauss. © 2010 by Kevin Strauss. Reproduced with permission of Trumpeter Press, Eden Prairie, MN (http://www.trumpeterpress.com).

Chapter 9:

"Ant and Magpie" has been reprinted from *Building Heroes/Blocking Bullies: The Teacher and Parent Guide to Simple, Repeatable, Assertive Techniques That Anyone Can Use to Stay Safe and Stop Bullies*. Kevin Strauss. © 2010 by Kevin Strauss. Reproduced with permission of Trumpeter Press, Eden Prairie, MN (http://www.trumpeterpress.com).

"Just Desserts," "The Enormous Carrot," "The 'Missing' Ax and the 'Guilty' Boy," "The Blind Hunter's Catch," "The Third Friend," "Anansi's Dinner Guest," and "Four Blind Men and the Elephant" have been reprinted from *The Reading Ranger's Guide to 55 Five-Minute Fabulous Folktales That Everyone Should Read and Hear*. Kevin Strauss. © 2010 by Kevin Strauss. Reproduced with permission of Trumpeter Press, Eden Prairie, MN (http://www.trumpeterpress.com).

"The Parable of the Stomach" reprinted from pages 195–196 in *Tales with Tails: Storytelling the Wonders of the Natural World*. Kevin Strauss. © 2006 by Kevin Strauss. Reproduced with permission of ABC-CLIO, LLC.

"The Heaviest Burden" reprinted from page 205 in *Tales with Tails: Storytelling the Wonders of the Natural World*. Kevin Strauss. © 2006 by Kevin Strauss. Reproduced with permission of ABC-CLIO, LLC.

"The Difference Between Heaven and Hell" reprinted from page 207 in *Tales with Tails: Storytelling the Wonders of the Natural World*. Kevin Strauss. © 2006 by Kevin Strauss. Reproduced with permission of ABC-CLIO, LLC.

"It's In Your Hands" reprinted from page 206 in *Tales with Tails: Storytelling the Wonders of the Natural World*. Kevin Strauss. © 2006 by Kevin Strauss. Reproduced with permission of ABC-CLIO, LLC.

"How Rattlesnake Got Her Poison and Her Rattles" reprinted from pages 130–133 in *Tales with Tails: Storytelling the Wonders of the Natural World*. Kevin Strauss. © 2006 by Kevin Strauss. Reproduced with permission of ABC-CLIO, LLC.

Chapter 10:

Activities 10-6 and 10-7 have been reprinted from *Building Heroes/Blocking Bullies: The Teacher and Parent Guide to Simple, Repeatable, Assertive Techniques That Anyone Can Use to Stay Safe and Stop Bullies*. Kevin Strauss. © 2010 by Kevin Strauss. Reproduced with permission of Trumpeter Press, Eden Prairie, MN (http://www.trumpeterpress.com).

Subject and Story Index

Skills Index

Assertive Communication

People with this skill can verbally describe how they think and feel in a respectful manner. They can also actively listen to, understand, and respect the thoughts and feelings of others.

Goal Setting

People with this skill demonstrate the abilities to decide what is important to them, set priorities, plan for the future, and create a process for following those plans. Children who can set goals for the future and imagine themselves achieving their goals are usually too busy to "waste time" with mood-altering chemicals (or television and video games, for that matter).

Kindness

People with this skill demonstrate the interest and ability to care about others and to treat others with respect, friendship, and helpfulness. Children who care about others tend to have a lot of friends and have more support from family and friends to help them resolve problems.

Problem Solving

People with this skill demonstrate the ability to think carefully about a difficult situation and use a step-by-step approach to resolve that situation. They also have the ability to come up with several possible solutions for a problem and to determine and implement the best solution.

Self-Control

People with this skill demonstrate the ability to control their thoughts, words, emotions, and actions so that they do not harm others or themselves. Children who have a positive sense of self and good control of their emotions are more likely to be able to control their bored, fearful, or aggressive impulses. They can also better use their rational minds to come up with short-term and long-term solutions to problems.

Teamwork

People with this skill demonstrate the ability to cooperate with a group of people to determine and accomplish a common goal. Children who have the ability to work together to find common goals and develop "win-win" solutions to conflicts will have a much easier time resolving problems than those who lack this skill.

About the Author

Photograph by Steve Foss

    KEVIN STRAUSS, MS Ed., is an award-winning author, speaker, and motivational storyteller based in Minnesota. He presents innovative bullying prevention, drug prevention, conflict resolution, and self-esteem programs at schools, libraries, and community events across the country.

    This is Strauss's second Libraries Unlimited book and fourth published book. Other titles include *Tales with Tails: Storytelling the Wonders of the Natural World* (Libraries Unlimited, 2006), winner of the Storytelling World Award, and *Loon and Moon: And Other Animal Stories* (Raven Productions, 2005). He is the storytelling star of two recordings, including *The Mountain Wolf's Gift: Wolf Tales from Around the World* (Naturestory Productions, 2003) and *U Tell a Tale* (National Institute on Media and the Family, 2007), and winner of a Parents' Choice Award and a National Parenting Publications Gold Award (NAPPA).

    You can learn more about Strauss's other publications and his programs online at www.naturestory.com as well as his bullying prevention site at www.bullyblocker.com.